McGRAW-HILL'S
OUR NATION, OUR WORLD

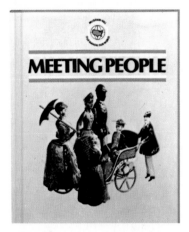

MEETING PEOPLE

School, Self, Families,
Neighborhood, and
Our Country

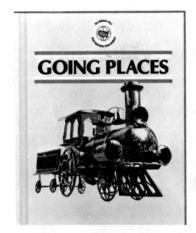

GOING PLACES

People in Groups, Filling
Needs in Communities
and on Farms

COMMUNITIES

Geography and History of
Cities in the United
States, Canada, and Mexico

EARTH'S REGIONS

Geography and Ways of
Living on Five Continents,
Studying the 50 States

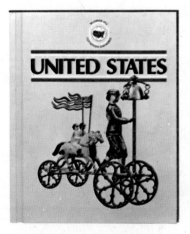

UNITED STATES

Chronological History
of the United States,
North America Today

THE WORLD

World History, Ancient
Civilizations, Important
Nations Today

CONSULTANTS

BONNIE AMASON
A.M. Davis Elementary School
Richmond, Virginia

DR. L. JO ANNE BUGGEY
Educational Consultant
Minneapolis, Minnesota

MILDRED CROWELL
Jamestown Academy
Williamsburg, Virginia

CORA DVERSDALL
Parkview Elementary School
Oklahoma City, Oklahoma

DON FELICE
Falling Creek Middle School
Richmond, Virginia

JUDY A. FISHER
Dennis Elementary School
Oklahoma City, Oklahoma

CAROLYN FITZGERALD
Powhatan Middle School
Powhatan, Virginia

SANDY HANNINGTON
Central Elementary School
Yukon, Oklahoma

CAROLYN HERBST
Eli Whitney Vocational High School
Brooklyn, New York

DR. RONALD J. HERMANSEN
Staff Assistant, Social Studies
Granite School District
Salt Lake City, Utah

DR. LEONORE HOFFMANN
City University of New York
Former Director, Federal Projects
Modern Language Association

SISTER M. JEANNETTE, I.H.M.
Archdiocese of Philadelphia
Philadelphia, Pennsylvania

ELAINE S. JONES
Woodinville, Washington

SISTER SHARON KERRIGAN
Diocese of Joliet
Joliet, Illinois

HERELYNN KIDD
Shedeck Elementary School
Yukon, Oklahoma

MARY S. McDADE
St. Joseph's School
Petersburg, Virginia

JEAN McGRADY
Western Oaks Elementary School
Bethany, Oklahoma

SISTER GLENN ANNE McPHEE
Archdiocese of Los Angeles
Los Angeles, California

ELAINE MAGNUSON
Canyon Creek Elementary School
Bothell, Washington

SHERRILL MILLER
Seattle, Washington

FRED PEFFER
Central Elementary School
Yukon, Oklahoma

SUZANNE PHELPS
Traub Elementary School
Midwest City, Oklahoma

BETSY PIERCE
Hamilton-Holmes Elementary School
King William, Virginia

SUSIE REYNOLDS
Overholser Elementary School
Bethany, Oklahoma

JOANNE ROBERTSON
Redmond, Washington

SISTER ANN SCHAFER
St. Luke's School
Seattle, Washington

KENNETH SUNDIN
Hollywood Hill Elementary School
Woodinville, Washington

JANE THOMAS
Robious Middle School
Midlothian, Virginia

NORA WASHINGTON
Byrd Primary School
Hadensville, Virginia

RONALD GRIGSBY KIRCHEM
Editorial Consultant and Contributing Writer

Editor in Chief:	Leonard Martelli
Senior Editor:	Alma Graham
Editing and Styling:	Linda Richmond
Photo Editing Supervision:	Rosemary O'Connell
Production Supervision:	Salvador Gonzales, Judith Tisdale
Assistant Editors:	James Allan Bartz, Ronald J. Bogus
Photo Editor:	Alan Forman
Design by:	Function Thru Form Inc.
Cover Design by:	Blaise Zito Associates
Cover Photography by:	Bill Holland
Photo Credit:	From the Collection of The Perelman Antique Toy Museum

EARTH'S REGIONS

BY Leonard Martelli, Alma Graham, Cleo Cherryholmes, Gary Manson, Anna Ochoa

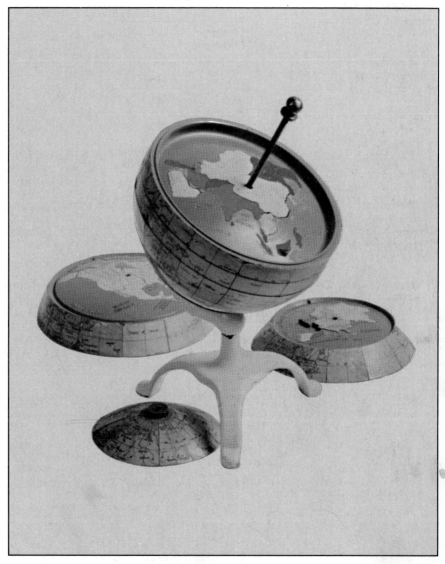

Webster Division, McGraw-Hill Book Company

New York   St. Louis   San Francisco   Auckland   Bogotá   Düsseldorf
Johannesburg   London   Madrid   Mexico   Montreal   New Delhi
Panama   Paris   São Paulo   Singapore   Sydney   Tokyo   Toronto

3

LIST OF MAPS AND CHARTS

ISBN 0-07-039944-1

1985 printing

5 6 7 8 9 10 KGP KGP 91 90 89 88 87 86 85 84

CONTENTS

1777

1795

1818

1861

1912

1959

LEARNING ABOUT
OUR EARTH

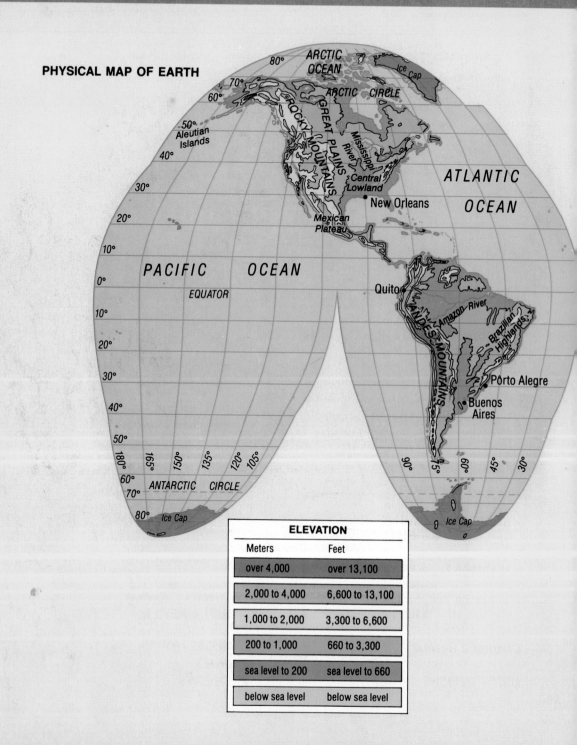

PHYSICAL MAP OF EARTH

ARCTIC OCEAN

80°
70°
60°
50°
40°
30°
20°
10°
0°
10°
20°
30°
40°
50°
60°
70°
80°

Ice Cap

ARCTIC CIRCLE

ROCKY MOUNTAINS
GREAT PLAINS
Mississippi River
Central Lowland
New Orleans
Mexican Plateau

Aleutian Islands

ATLANTIC OCEAN

PACIFIC OCEAN

EQUATOR

Quito
ANDES MOUNTAINS
Amazon River
Brazilian Highlands
Pôrto Alegre
Buenos Aires

180°
165°
150°
135°
120°
105°
90°
75°
60°
45°
30°

ANTARCTIC CIRCLE

Ice Cap
Ice Cap

ELEVATION	
Meters	Feet
over 4,000	over 13,100
2,000 to 4,000	6,600 to 13,100
1,000 to 2,000	3,300 to 6,600
200 to 1,000	660 to 3,300
sea level to 200	sea level to 660
below sea level	below sea level

ARCTIC OCEAN 80° 70° 60° BERING SEA 50°

ARCTIC CIRCLE

Moscow URAL MOUNTAINS 40°

London EUROPEAN PLAIN ALPS

Plateau of Asia Minor Plateau of Tibet Hwang Ho Tokyo 30°

Mediterranean Sea HIMALAYAS 20°

SAHARA Cairo Alexandria Ganges River Yangtze PACIFIC 10°

Nile River Deccan Plateau Dacca OCEAN

Congo River EQUATOR 0°

PRIME MERIDIAN 10°

INDIAN OCEAN 20°

Western Plateau Great Plains Eastern Highlands 30°

ATLANTIC OCEAN 40°

50°

15° 0° 15° 30° 45° 60° 75° 90° 105° 120° 135° 150° 165° 180° 60° 70°

ANTARCTIC CIRCLE 80°

Ice Cap Ice Cap

Kilometers 0   5000
SCALE
Miles 0   4000

9

ATLAS

POLITICAL MAP OF EARTH

1 Belize
2 Jamaica
3 Dominican Republic
4 Trinidad and Tobago
5 Antigua and Barbuda
6 Austria
7 Czechoslovakia
8 Hungary
9 Albania
10 Denmark
11 West Germany
12 East Germany
13 Netherlands
14 Belgium
15 Switzerland
16 Benin
17 Central African Republic
18 São Tomé and Príncipe
19 Djibouti
20 Equatorial Guinea
21 Gambia
22 Ghana
23 Guinea
24 Guinea-Bissau
25 Seychelles
26 Cyprus
27 Lebanon
28 Kuwait
29 Qatar
30 United Arab Emirates

31 Tuvalu
32 Nauru
33 Solomon Islands
34 Kiribati

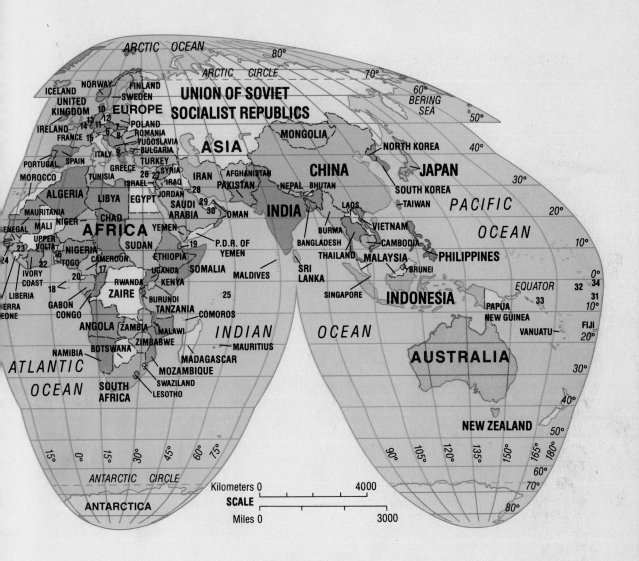

ARCTIC OCEAN 80°
ARCTIC CIRCLE 70°
60°
BERING SEA 50°

ICELAND NORWAY FINLAND
UNITED SWEDEN UNION OF SOVIET
KINGDOM 10 EUROPE SOCIALIST REPUBLICS
IRELAND 14 11 7 POLAND ASIA MONGOLIA NORTH KOREA 40°
FRANCE 15 5 8 ROMANIA
ITALY 9 YUGOSLAVIA CHINA JAPAN
BULGARIA 30°
PORTUGAL SPAIN TURKEY SOUTH KOREA
GREECE 26 27 SYRIA IRAN AFGHANISTAN TAIWAN
MOROCCO TUNISIA ISRAEL IRAQ PAKISTAN NEPAL BHUTAN PACIFIC 20°
ALGERIA LIBYA EGYPT JORDAN 28 INDIA LAOS OCEAN
MAURITANIA CHAD SAUDI 29 OMAN BURMA VIETNAM 10°
SENEGAL MALI NIGER ARABIA 30 BANGLADESH CAMBODIA PHILIPPINES
UPPER AFRICA YEMEN THAILAND MALAYSIA 0°
23 VOLTA SUDAN 19 P.D.R. OF BRUNEI EQUATOR 34
24 NIGERIA YEMEN SRI SINGAPORE 32 31
IVORY TOGO ETHIOPIA SOMALIA MALDIVES LANKA 33 10°
COAST 20 17 CAMEROON UGANDA INDONESIA PAPUA
LIBERIA 18 RWANDA KENYA 25 NEW GUINEA FIJI
SIERRA GABON ZAIRE BURUNDI VANUATU 20°
LEONE CONGO TANZANIA COMOROS
ANGOLA ZAMBIA INDIAN OCEAN AUSTRALIA
NAMIBIA MALAWI MAURITIUS 30°
ATLANTIC BOTSWANA ZIMBABWE
MADAGASCAR
OCEAN MOZAMBIQUE 40°
SOUTH SWAZILAND NEW ZEALAND 50°
AFRICA LESOTHO

15° 0° 15° 30° 45° 60° 75° 90° 105° 120° 135° 150° 165° 180° 60°
70°
ANTARCTIC CIRCLE 80°
ANTARCTICA

Kilometers 0   4000
SCALE
Miles 0   3000

11

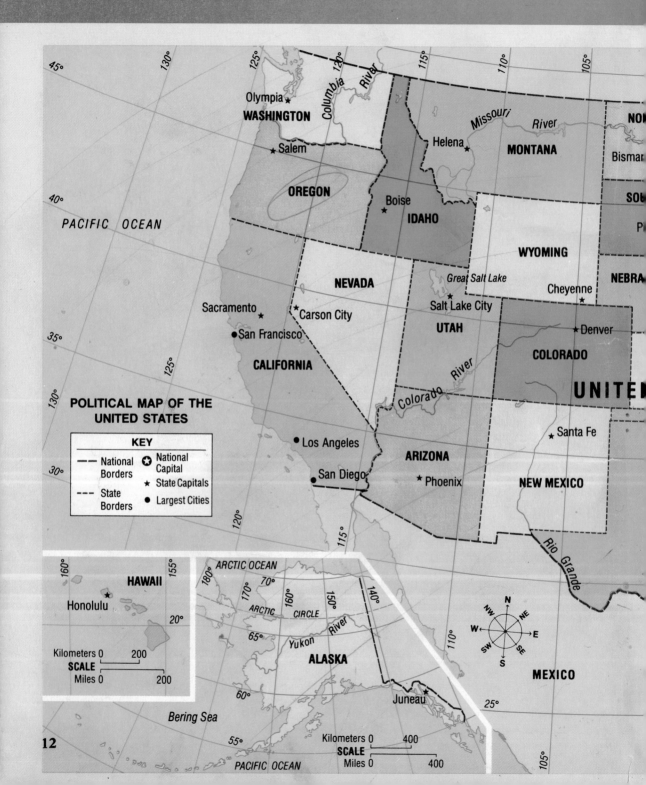

POLITICAL MAP OF THE
UNITED STATES

KEY

— — National Borders	✪ National Capital
- - - State Borders	★ State Capitals
	● Largest Cities

45°
130°
125°
120°
115°
110°
105°

Olympia ★
WASHINGTON

Columbia River

Missouri River

Helena ★
MONTANA

NOR

Bismar

★ Salem

40°
OREGON

PACIFIC OCEAN

Boise ★
IDAHO

WYOMING

SOU

Pi

NEBRA

Great Salt Lake

Cheyenne ★

Salt Lake City ★

Sacramento ★
35°

Carson City ★

NEVADA

UTAH

★ Denver

● San Francisco

CALIFORNIA

Colorado River

COLORADO

130°
125°

UNITE

★ Santa Fe

30°

● Los Angeles

ARIZONA

NEW MEXICO

San Diego ●

★ Phoenix

120°

115°

Rio Grande

HAWAII

160°
155°

Honolulu

20°

Kilometers 0 — 200
SCALE
Miles 0 — 200

160°
180°
170°
150°
140°

ARCTIC OCEAN

70°

ARCTIC CIRCLE

65°

Yukon River

ALASKA

110°

N
NW — NE
W ✦ E
SW — SE
S

MEXICO

60°

Juneau ★

25°

Bering Sea

105°

55°

Kilometers 0 — 400
SCALE
Miles 0 — 400

PACIFIC OCEAN

CANADA

Lake Superior

MINNESOTA

WISCONSIN

──MICHIGAN──

KOTA

KOTA

St. Paul ★

Mississippi River

Lake Huron

Lake Michigan

Lake Ontario

Niagara Falls

Lake Erie

St. Lawrence River

VERMONT

MAINE

★ Augusta

Montpelier ★

NEW HAMPSHIRE

★ Concord

★ Boston

Albany ★

NEW YORK

Hartford ★ ★ Providence

RHODE ISLAND

MASSACHUSETTS

CONNECTICUT

45°

40°

Madison ★

Detroit

Lansing ★

● Chicago

IOWA

Des Moines ★

Lincoln ★

ILLINOIS

Springfield ★

INDIANA

Indianapolis ★

OHIO

Columbus ★

Philadelphia ●

PENNSYLVANIA

Harrisburg ★

Baltimore ●

Annapolis ★

Washington, DC

WEST VIRGINIA

Charleston ★

Richmond ★

VIRGINIA

New York City

NEW JERSEY

Trenton ★

MARYLAND

★ Dover

DELAWARE

Topeka ★

KANSAS

MISSOURI

Jefferson City ★

Ohio River

Frankfort ★

KENTUCKY

Raleigh ★

NORTH CAROLINA

35°

STATES

OKLAHOMA

Oklahoma City ★

ARKANSAS

Little Rock ★

Nashville ★

TENNESSEE

Memphis ●

Columbia ★

SOUTH CAROLINA

70°

Dallas ●

TEXAS

LOUISIANA

MISSISSIPPI

Jackson ★

ALABAMA

Montgomery ★

Atlanta ★

GEORGIA

ATLANTIC OCEAN

30°

Austin ★

Houston ●

San Antonio ●

Baton Rouge ★

★ Tallahassee

FLORIDA

25°

Gulf of Mexico

Kilometers 0   500

SCALE

Miles 0   500

13

SUN

MERCURY

VENUS

EARTH

MARS

JUPITER

CHAPTER 1
EARTH AND MAPS

Lesson 1: Planet Earth

FIND THE WORDS

star	sun	planet
moon	solar system	

Earth is our home. It is the home of all human beings. It has air we can breathe. It has water for us to drink. It has plants and animals that we can eat. It has solid ground to stand on. Earth is not too hot or too cold for us. It has everything we need to live.

We are on Earth. But we can see things that are not on Earth. Early in the morning, we can see the sun come up. All day, the sun seems to move across the sky. Late in the day, we can see the sun go down. But the sun is not really moving around us. We are the ones who are moving. Every morning, we turn toward the sun. Every night, we turn away from it. Every year, we go around it. Earth is our spaceship. All of us in

14

SATURN

URANUS NEPTUNE PLUTO

the ship are riding around the sun.

At night, we can often see the moon and stars. From Earth, stars look like little points of light. But stars are really very big. They look small because they are so far away. From Earth, stars may seem cold. But stars are really very hot. A **star** is a great mass of burning gas. It gives off light and heat. Our **sun** is a star. And all the other stars in the sky are also suns.

Our sun is much closer to Earth than the other stars are. That is why it looks so much bigger and brighter than they do. The heat of the sun keeps Earth warm. Suppose Earth were farther away from the sun. It would be much colder here. Suppose Earth were closer to the sun. It would be much hotter all year long.

The sun is a star. Earth is a planet. A **planet** is a world that moves around a star. Nine planets move around our sun. The planets get their light and heat from the sun. A planet that is close to the sun is hot. A planet that is far from the sun is cold.

Look at the picture on pages 14 and 15. Which two planets are closest to the sun? Which two planets are farthest away? The picture shows how big the planets are, compared with the sun.

Earth is the third planet from the sun. It is a small, warm planet. Jupiter and Saturn are giant planets compared to Earth. They are also much colder.

Some of the planets have moons. A **moon** goes around a planet just as a planet goes around a star. Earth has only one moon. Some planets have more. Mercury and Venus do not have any moons.

The sun, planets, and moons make up our **solar system.** *Solar* (SOH lur) means "of the sun." A *system* is a group of parts that work together as a whole. The solar system is the sun and its family of planets and moons. We do not know if any other stars have solar systems. But there are billions of stars. Some of these stars might have planets moving around them. Do you suppose they do?

REVIEW

WATCH YOUR WORDS

1. Earth is a____.
   star   moon   planet
2. A____gives off light and heat.
   planet   star   moon
3. A____moves around a star.
   solar   planet   sun
4. ____means "of the sun."
   System   Lunar   Solar
5. A____moves around a planet.
   star   sun   moon

CHECK YOUR FACTS
Look at the Picture

6. How many planets are in the solar system?

7. Which planet is closest to the sun?
8. What two planets are closest to Earth?

Look at the Lesson

9. What makes Earth a good planet to live on? Name three things. Can you name more?
10. A planet that is far away from the sun is (hot/cold).

THINK ABOUT IT

Do you think there could be life on other worlds? What would a new world have to be like for us to live there?

Lesson 2: Time and the Seasons

FIND THE WORDS

revolve   orbit
axis   North Pole
South Pole   rotate
tilted   season

The Moving Earth

Have you ever heard someone say, "Time flies"? Time doesn't fly. We do. Time tells us how long the trip takes. Our spaceship Earth moves in two ways. It rides around the sun. And it spins in a circle. A year is the time it takes Earth to go around the sun. A day is the time it takes Earth to spin around in a circle.

We say that Earth **revolves** (ri VOLVZ) around the sun. That means Earth moves in a special path. You know that an airplane has a flight path to follow. Earth's flight path around the sun is called an **orbit** (OR bit). Earth takes 365 days to revolve around the sun. That is why our year is 365 days long.

Earth moves in its orbit around the sun the way a toy train moves around a track. But Earth also moves in another way. As it goes around the sun, Earth spins like a top. Like a top, Earth spins around an axis (AK sis).

Take a little, round cherry to-mato. Stick a toothpick through

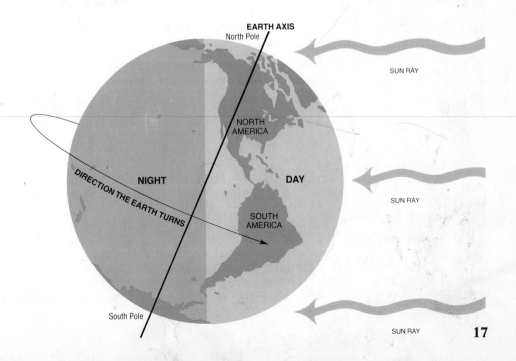

EARTH AXIS
North Pole

SUN RAY

NORTH AMERICA

NIGHT

DIRECTION THE EARTH TURNS

DAY

SOUTH AMERICA

SUN RAY

South Pole

SUN RAY

the middle, from top to bottom. Then hold the toothpick still. Turn the tomato from left to right. The tomato turns around the toothpick the way Earth turns around its axis.

Earth's **axis** is an imaginary line through the center of Earth. It goes from the North Pole to the South Pole. The **North Pole** is as far north as you can go on Earth. The **South Pole** is as far south as you can go.

To spin around an axis is to **rotate.** Earth takes 24 hours to spin around once on its axis. That is why our day is 24 hours long. *Day* also means the part of the 24 hours when we have sunlight.

You turned the tomato from left to right. Earth turns on its axis from west to east. In the morning, we see the sun come up in the east. That means our part of Earth is turning toward the sun. In the evening, we see the sun go down in the west. That means our part of Earth is turning away from the sun. The sun seems to move because Earth is rotating.

As Earth spins on its axis, only one side faces the sun at a time. The side facing the sun has day. The side turned away from the sun has night. When morning comes to New York, it is still dark in California. When it is late afternoon in California, it is already night in New York.

The Sun and the Seasons

Day and night are not always the same length. The reason for that is Earth's axis. Our axis is not straight up and down. It is **tilted.** That means it slants, or leans. The Earth itself is tilted. Look at your classroom globe. The North Pole is not at the very top. The globe is tilted, just like the Earth.

Earth has four **seasons.** They are spring, summer, fall, and winter. In many parts of Earth, the weather changes with the seasons. That happens because the axis of Earth is tilted. It also happens because Earth moves around the sun.

Look at the picture on the next page. On June 22, the North Pole is tilted toward the sun. The northern half of Earth gets a lot of light and heat. Day is longer than night. The weather is warm or hot. It is summer in the United States.

On June 22, the South Pole is tilted away from the sun. The southern half of Earth gets less of the sun's light and heat. Night is longer than day. The weather is cool or cold. It is winter in Argentina.

Now look at December 22 in the picture. Since June, Earth has revolved halfway around the sun. So the North Pole is tilted away from the sun. It is winter in the

THE SEASONS

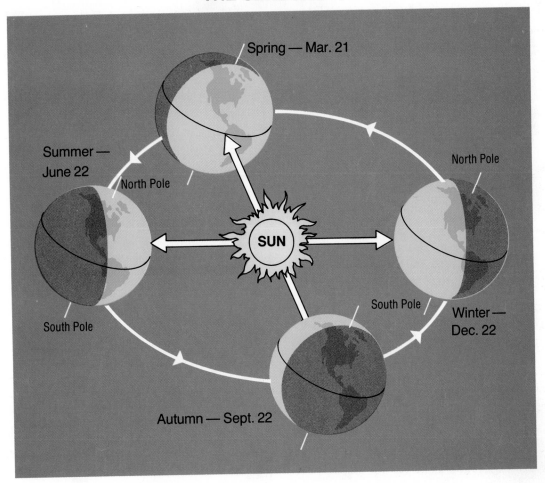

Spring — Mar. 21

Summer — June 22

North Pole

South Pole

SUN

North Pole

South Pole

Winter — Dec. 22

Autumn — Sept. 22

United States. But the South Pole is tilted toward the sun. People in Australia may be swimming at the beach. But it may be snowing in St. Louis, Missouri.

The middle part of Earth is never tilted away from the sun. The rays of the sun always come straight down on it. The middle part of Earth gets a lot of light and heat all year. Suppose you lived in Rio de Janeiro (REE oh di juh NAIR oh), Brazil. The weather would be warm in spring, summer, fall, and winter.

Near the North Pole, the sun's rays hit Earth at a slant. This makes the weather cold all year. But summer at the North Pole is very different from winter. In the summer, it is light all day and all night. In the winter, it is dark all night and all day. This is true at the South Pole, too. But the South Pole's summer comes in December instead of June.

Now, let's leave the North Pole. Let's travel part way toward the middle of Earth. Suppose you lived in Richmond, Virginia. The weather there changes from season to season. It gets cool in the fall.

Near the North Pole in summer, the sun shines even at midnight. This happens because the North Pole is tilted toward the sun.

It is cold in the winter. It gets warm in the spring. It is hot in the summer.

REVIEW

WATCH YOUR WORDS

1. Earth____around the sun.
   rotates revolves tilts

2. Earth's flight path around the sun is its____.
   axis season orbit

3. To spin around an axis is to____.
   revolve tilt rotate

4. An imaginary line from the North Pole to the South Pole is Earth's ____ .
   tilt axis season

5. Something that slants is____.
   rotated seasoned tilted.

CHECK YOUR FACTS

6. Which way does Earth turn on its axis?

7. How long does it take Earth to rotate once?

8. How long does it take Earth to revolve around the sun?

9. What is strange about summer at the North Pole?

10. In the United States, why is June warmer than December?

THINK ABOUT IT

Suppose Earth were not tilted on its axis. How would life be different? Name three ways.

Lesson 3: Earth and the Globe

FIND THE WORDS

**globe   continent   ocean
equator   hemisphere**

It would be fun to travel around the Earth. We could drive across the United States, from California to Virginia. We could fly across the Atlantic Ocean to Portugal and Spain. We could travel through Greece and Turkey all the way to the Soviet Union. From there, we could keep heading east to China and Japan. At last, we could sail across the Pacific Ocean. It would bring us back to California. We would have circled the Earth. And there would still be many more places to see!

Few people can travel all over the Earth. Most of us learn about our world in other ways. One way to learn about Earth is to use a globe.

A **globe** is a model of Earth. It is round like Earth. But it is much, much smaller. A globe can tell you many things about Earth. Globes use different colors to help you tell land from water. Earth has seven large masses of land, called **continents** (KON tuh nunts). North America and South America are two continents. They are linked by a narrow strip of land.

Europe and Asia look like one continent on a globe. Actually, they are separated by mountains. The other continents are Africa, Australia, and Antarctica (ANT AHRK tuh kuh). Find the seven continents on a globe.

A globe also shows where the four **oceans** are. Oceans are the largest bodies of water on Earth. Seven-tenths of the whole surface of Earth is covered by water. The United States lies between the Atlantic Ocean and the Pacific Ocean. The Indian Ocean lies between Africa and Australia. The Arctic Ocean is at the top of the globe.

A globe is round like Earth. Its shape makes it the best model of Earth.

NORTH POLE

ARCTIC OCEAN

UNION OF SOVIET SOCIALIST REPUBLICS

EUROPE

SPAIN

TURKEY

ASIA

PORTUGAL GREECE

CHINA

JAPAN

EGYPT

INDIA

PACIFIC OCEAN

UPPER VOLTA

AFRICA

EQUATOR

ATLANTIC OCEAN

INDIAN OCEAN

AUSTRALIA

SOUTH AFRICA

ANTARCTICA

SOUTH POLE

EASTERN HEMISPHERE

WESTERN HEMISPHERE

ARCTIC OCEAN

NORTH POLE

ALASKA (U.S.)

CANADA

UNITED STATES

VIRGINIA

CALIFORNIA

NORTH AMERICA

ATLANTIC OCEAN

HAWAII (U.S.)

MEXICO

EQUATOR

SOUTH AMERICA

PACIFIC OCEAN

BOLIVIA

BRAZIL

NEW ZEALAND

Earth can be divided into Eastern and Western Hemispheres. It can also be divided into Northern and Southern Hemispheres.

ANTARCTICA

SOUTH POLE

The North Pole is in the Arctic Ocean. You know that Earth's axis runs from the North Pole to the South Pole. Another important line on the globe is the **equator** (i KWAY tur). Like the axis, the equator is an imaginary line. It is halfway between the North Pole and the South Pole. The equator circles Earth around the middle, like an invisible belt. It divides Earth into two equal parts.

Pretend that the globe is a ball of clay. The ball has a line around its middle. Suppose you cut the ball in two along the line. Each half of the ball is called a **hemisphere** (HEM uh SFIR). *Hemi-* means "half" and *sphere* means "ball."

Half of the globe is above the equator. The North Pole is in that half. So the top half of the globe is called the *Northern Hemisphere*. The United States is in the Northern Hemisphere.

Half of the globe is below the equator. The South Pole is in that half. So the bottom half of the globe is called the *Southern Hemisphere*. Argentina is in the Southern Hemisphere.

You can cut the globe in half another way. You can divide the western half from the eastern half. North America and South America are in the western half. This half of the globe is called the *Western Hemisphere*. Europe, Asia, Africa, and Australia are in the eastern

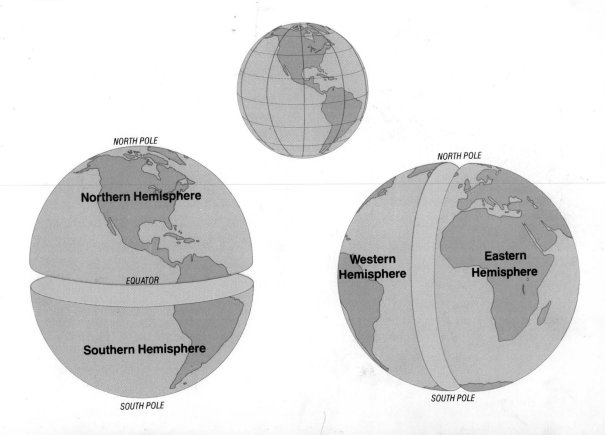

NORTH POLE

Northern Hemisphere

EQUATOR

Southern Hemisphere

SOUTH POLE

NORTH POLE

Western Hemisphere

Eastern Hemisphere

SOUTH POLE

In North America, people can see penguins only in a zoo. Penguins live near the South Pole. Many of them live in Antarctica.

Penguins are birds, but they cannot fly. They are fine swimmers, though. On land, they waddle about on two feet. To go faster, they slide over the ice on their bellies.

half. That half of the globe is called the *Eastern Hemisphere*. One continent is in the Western Hemisphere and the Eastern Hemisphere. It is Antarctica. What other hemisphere is Antarctica in?

Dividing the globe into hemispheres helps us find places on Earth. Look at the globes on page 22. Find Mexico and Bolivia. Find South Africa and India. Each nation is in two hemispheres.

REVIEW

WATCH YOUR WORDS

1. A round model of Earth is a____.
   circle map globe
2. North America is one of seven ____ .
   oceans continents hemispheres
3. The Atlantic and the Pacific are ____ .
   oceans hemispheres continents
4. The ____ is an imaginary line around the middle of Earth.
   axis globe equator
5. Half of a globe is a(n)____.
   hemisphere continent ocean

CHECK YOUR FACTS
Look at the Globe

6. Find the state of Alaska. What two hemispheres is it in?

7. Find the continent of Australia. What two hemispheres is it in?

Look at the Lesson

8. What is the equator? What is the Northern Hemisphere?
9. What continents are in the Western Hemisphere?
10. What continents are in the Eastern Hemisphere?

THINK ABOUT IT

Long ago, people thought the Earth was flat. Can you prove that Earth is round? How?

Lesson 4: Maps of Earth

FIND THE WORDS

map   key   symbol   nation
boundary   natural boundary
political boundary

Globes are round like Earth. This makes a globe the best model of our round planet. But we can also learn a lot about our world from maps. A **map** is a flat drawing of places on Earth. One map may show the whole Earth. Another map may show a single continent. A third map may show only a few city blocks. But all maps are useful. They help us find where places are. People have used maps for a long time. The oldest map in the world is almost 5000 years old!

It is hard to show the round Earth on a flat map. All the parts won't fit. So a mapmaker has to change their shape. Look at the drawing on this page. It shows what happens when you peel off the surface of a globe. It is like peeling an orange. The peel can be flattened out. But it no longer looks like the orange.

Look at this flat map. Then look at the map of the world at the front of the book. The person who drew that map took a lot of the water out. This changed the size and shape of the oceans. But it made the shape of the land areas more nearly right.

Now look at the map on page 26. There, the mapmaker added land and water to the map. Look at the continents on the two maps. Then look at a globe. Which map looks most like the globe?

When you look at maps, remember this: The shape of the land is not always exactly right.

Suppose you flattened out a globe. This is how it would look. Mapmakers sometimes add land and water to fill in the gaps.

25

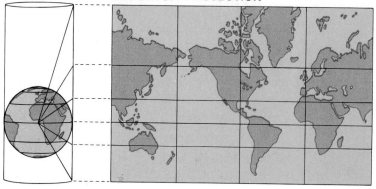

MERCATOR PROJECTION

The mapmaker added land and water to this map. The areas near the poles seem much larger than they really are.

But maps are handy. It is easy to carry them around.

Most maps have a **key.** A key can tell you what the colors on the map mean. It can show you what the symbols (SIM bulz) on the map stand for. **A symbol** is a mark or picture used in place of words. Look at the map on pages 12 and 13. Find the key. Look at the symbols in the key. Then find each symbol on the map.

Maps of Earth do not show only continents and oceans. They can also show nations. A **nation** is a land where people live under one government. The continent of North America has three large nations. They are Canada, the United States, and Mexico.

The shape of a nation is outlined by boundaries. A **boundary** is a line that divides one place from another. Some boundaries

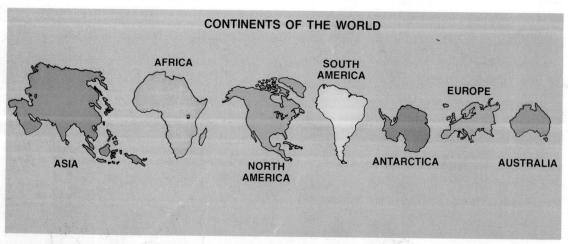

CONTINENTS OF THE WORLD

ASIA

AFRICA

NORTH AMERICA

SOUTH AMERICA

ANTARCTICA

EUROPE

AUSTRALIA

This chart shows the seven continents in order of size.

are natural boundaries. The Atlantic Ocean and Pacific Ocean are **natural boundaries** of the United States.

Other boundaries are called political (puh LIT uh kul) boundaries. **Political boundaries** divide one nation or state from another. The lines that separate Canada from the United States are political boundaries. Mexico is separated from Texas by a river, the Rio Grande. This is a natural boundary. But it is also a political boundary. It divides part of the United States from Mexico.

The map on pages 10 and 11 shows most of the nations in the world. Each nation on the map is a different color from the ones around it. The colors help you tell the nations apart. That is all the colors mean on this map. The map key tells you what the symbols mean. How does the map show boundaries between nations?

The map of nations tells us many things about the continents. Europe is a small continent. But it is divided into many nations. Africa has many nations, too. But North America has only three large nations. And Australia is a continent with only one nation— Australia! One continent has no nations at all. That is Antarctica. Almost all of Antarctica is covered by ice. Antarctica is popular with penguins. But would it be a good place for people?

REVIEW

WATCH YOUR WORDS

1. A flat drawing of places on Earth is a____.
   globe   map   boundary
2. A ____ shows what a map's symbols mean.
   globe   boundary   key
3. A line that divides one place from another is a____.
   boundary   symbol   nation
4. Canada is separated from the United States by a____boundary.
   natural   political
5. The United States is separated from Europe by a____boundary.
   political   natural

CHECK YOUR FACTS
Look at the Chart

6. Which two continents are the largest?
7. Which two continents are the smallest?

Look at the Lesson

8. The shape of land on a map of Earth (is/is not) exactly right.
9. What does a map key tell you?
10. What is a nation?
11. What are the three large nations of North America?
12. Which continent has no nations?

CHAPTER REVIEW

WATCH YOUR WORDS

1. Earth is a ___. It is part of the ___.
   star solar system planet moon

2. Earth takes 365 days to ___ around the sun.
   tilt revolve rotate

3. Earth rotates around an imaginary line, the ___.
   equator North Pole axis

4. A round model of Earth is a ___. Half of a ___ is a ___. (*Hint:* Use one word twice.)
   map hemisphere planet globe

5. A line that divides one nation from another is a ___.
   natural boundary hemisphere
   political boundary

CHECK YOUR FACTS

6. Why is Earth a good planet for people to live on?

7. Which way does Earth turn on its axis? How long does it take Earth to rotate once?

8. Why do we have summer in the United States in June instead of January?

9. What is a continent? How many continents are there on Earth? Can you name them?

10. What and where is the equator? What are the seasons like there? Why?

11. How far north can you go on Earth? How far south can you go?

12. On December 22, what season is it in Argentina? Why?

13. What is the difference between a map and a globe?

14. How many hemispheres are there?

15. Draw and label three symbols you find in a map key.

CLOSE THE MAP GAP

16. Draw a globe.
    a. Show where the North Pole, the South Pole, the axis, and the equator are.
    b. On your globe, show which way the Earth turns.
    c. Label the Northern Hemisphere and the Southern Hemisphere.

17. Draw the sun. Show where Earth is on June 22. Then show where Earth is on December 22. Put in Earth's axis, the poles, and the equator.

18. Draw an imaginary continent. Put oceans around it. Then divide it into three nations. You can name the nations anything you like. Include a map key.

THINK ABOUT IT

19. Suppose you were on a planet in another solar system. What would our sun look like from there?

20. The planet Venus rotates from east to west. Suppose you could see the sunrise on Venus. Where would you see it? Where would the sunset be?

21. Venus takes 225 days to revolve around the sun. How long is a year on Venus? Is a Venus year longer or shorter than an Earth year?

22. Why does a mapmaker change the shape of Earth's land and water?

23. When are a natural boundary and a political boundary the same?

CHAPTER 2

ALL ABOUT MAPS

Lesson 1: How Far? . . . Distance

Maps can show places of many different sizes. Some maps show the whole world. Other maps show a state or a city. Maps can show places no larger than your school. In fact, you could draw a map of your room.

Look at the maps of Chestnut County and one small section of that county. Each map covers the same amount of space on the page. But one map shows a much larger place than the other map. Which map shows the larger place? What do the symbols in the map key stand for?

Each map has a **scale.** You can use the scale to find how much land the map covers. Look at the map of Chestnut County on page 30. One centimeter stands for 100 kilometers (62 miles). The map of Chestnut County is 7 centimeters (about 3 inches) wide. So Chestnut County is 700 kilometers (430 miles) wide.

CHESTNUT COUNTY

KEY

- Towns ★ County Seat ✪ State Capital

1 centimeter = 100 kilometers

0   100   200   300   400

Plum Park
• Oaktown
•
Orangedale ✪

• Spruce City

★ Apple Junction

• Pine Springs   Cherry Point •

Willow Falls
•

Maple Ridge •

PART OF CHESTNUT COUNTY

KEY

- Towns ✪ State Capital

1 centimeter = 10 kilometers

0   10   20   30   40

• Oaktown

• Plum Park

Orangedale ✪

Now look at the map of Part of Chestnut County. This map is also about 7 centimeters across. But on it, 1 centimeter stands for 10 kilometers (6⅕ miles). So this section is really 10 times smaller than Chestnut County. It is 70 kilometers (about 43 miles) wide.

A map scale tells you something else, too. You can find how far one place on the map is from another place. How far one place is from another is the **distance** between the two. Look again at the map of Chestnut County. How far is it from Pine Springs to Willow Falls? On the map, those towns are 5 centimeters apart. Each centimeter stands for 100 kilometers. So, on Earth, those towns are 500 kilometers (310 miles) apart.

Find Plum Park on the map of the section of Chestnut County. Plum Park is 7 centimeters from Orangedale. On that map, each centimeter stands for 10 kilometers. How far is Plum Park from Orangedale? Which city is the state capital?

The Metric System

There are two major systems of measurement. One is the **customary system.** It uses inches, feet, yards, and miles to measure distances. The other is the **metric system** (MEH trik). It uses centimeters, meters, and kilometers to tell "how far." Most of the world uses the metric system. In this book, we use both systems.

We count by 10s. So does the metric system. The word *meter* means "measure." *Centi-* means 1/100. A cent is 1/100 of a dollar. A **centimeter** (SEN tuh MEE tur) is 1/100 of a meter. *Kilo-* means 1000.

A **kilometer** (KIL uh MEE tur *or* ki LOM uh tur) is 1000 meters.

Map scales in this book use centimeters and kilometers. They also show distances in miles.

> 1 centimeter = 2/5 inch
> 1 kilometer = 3/5 mile
> 5 centimeters = 2 inches
> 5 kilometers = 3 miles

Learn to "think metric." Then, you can figure out "how far" away a place is anywhere in the world.

REVIEW

WATCH YOUR WORDS

1. A ___ shows how much land a map covers.
   meter   centimeter   scale

2. The ___ system of measurement uses centimeters and kilometers.
   metric   solar   customary

3. A ___ is equal to 3/5 mile.
   meter   centimeter   kilometer

4. How far one place is from another is the ___ between them.
   time   rate   distance

5. A ___ is equal to 2/5 inch.
   meter   kilometer   centimeter

CHECK YOUR FACTS
Look at the Maps

6. How far is Plum Park from Apple Junction? How many centimeters? How many kilometers?

7. Is Cherry Point closer to Maple Ridge or to Pine Springs?

8. How far is Cherry Point from Willow Falls?

9. How far is Orangedale from Cherry Point?

10. How far is Plum Park from (a) Spruce City? (b) Oaktown?

TRY SOMETHING NEW

Figure out how tall you are in centimeters.

Lesson 2: Which Way? . . . Direction

FIND THE WORDS

cardinal directions   compass
intermediate directions

Maps tell us about distance. They help us answer the question "How far?" Maps also tell us about direction. They help us find out "Which way?"

There are four **cardinal directions** on Earth. The word *cardinal* means "most important." The four most important directions are north, south, east, and west. They are abbreviated N, S, E, W.

Look at the map of North America on page 33. *North* is printed at the top of the map. *South* is printed at the bottom. *East* is on the right. *West* is on the left.

But directions are more than words printed on a map. Directions apply to the planet Earth as well. *North* really means "toward the North Pole." *South* means "toward the South Pole."

Find Canada and Mexico on the map. Canada is closer to the North Pole than Mexico is. So Canada is north of Mexico. That means Mexico is south of Canada.

You know that Earth rotates from west to east. In the morning, we see the sun "rise" in the east. We are turning east, toward the sun. So east is "toward the sunrise." In the evening, we see the sun "set" in the west. We are turning away from the sun. So west is "toward the sunset." When you face toward the North Pole, the sunrise is on your right. The sunset is on your left. When we draw maps and globes, we usually face north. That means that north is usually at the top. So east is right, west is left, and south is at the bottom.

Find Cuba and Haiti (HAY tee) on the map. Which way would you travel to go from Cuba to Haiti? Would you travel east or west? Which way would you go to get from Haiti to Cuba?

Most maps do not print directions around the edges. Instead, some maps use a **compass.** A compass has arrows that point north, south, east, and west. On a compass, the cardinal directions are abbreviated: N, S, E, W. Some maps use only a single arrow, marked N, for north. If you know where north is, you can find south, east, and west.

NATIONS OF NORTH AMERICA

NORTH

80°   70°   60°

ARCTIC OCEAN

80°   70°

ASIA

Bering Sea

GREENLAND
(Denmark)

180°   70°   60°

ALASKA
(U.S.)

Yukon River

10°

20°

30°

170°

160°

Mackenzie River

40°

50°

50°

150°

Hudson Bay

WEST

CANADA

50°

40°

NORTH AMERICA

140°

Columbia River

Lake
Huron

St. Lawrence River

★ Ottawa

Missouri

Lake Superior   GREAT LAKES   Lake Ontario

Lake Michigan   Detroit   ● New York

River   Chicago   Lake   ● Philadelphia

EAST

Erie   ★ Washington, DC

St. Louis   Ohio River

30°

UNITED STATES

Colorado River

Mississippi

Memphis

ATLANTIC OCEAN

60°

30°

Los Angeles ●

Atlanta

Houston   New Orleans

PUERTO RICO
(U.S.)

Rio Grande

Gulf of Mexico

DOMINICAN
REPUBLIC

20°

PACIFIC OCEAN

20°

MEXICO

CUBA Havana
★

HAITI

Mexico City
★

JAMAICA

West Indies

10°

BELIZE

Caribbean Sea

HONDURAS

GUATEMALA

NICARAGUA

10°

EL SALVADOR

N
NW   NE

130°

W   E

COSTA RICA

SW   SE

PANAMA

Panama Canal

S

70°

0°

KEY
-- National Borders
★ National Capitals
● Cities

SOUTH

0°

120°   110°   100°   90°   80°

33

Intermediate Directions

The four cardinal directions help you find places on Earth. Try adding these directions together.

Look at the map of North America again. Mexico is south of Alaska. It is also east of Alaska. So we can say that Mexico is southeast of Alaska. Alaska is north and west of Mexico. So Alaska is northwest of Mexico.

Find Washington, DC, on the map. Mexico is south of Washington. It is west of Washington, too. So Mexico is southwest of Washington, DC. Washington is north and east of Mexico. So we can say that Washington, DC, is northeast of Mexico.

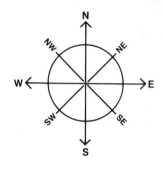

Northeast, northwest, southeast, and southwest are called the **intermediate directions.** These directions are often written NE, NW, SE, SW. Find them on the compass on this page.

Find the Bering Sea on the map of North America. It is in the far north. It is west of Alaska. Here, northwest North America almost touches Asia!

REVIEW

WATCH YOUR WORDS

1. North, south, east, and west are the ___.
   compass   cardinal directions
   metric system

2. Northeast and southwest are ___.
   cardinal directions   scales
   intermediate directions

3. A ___ on a map has arrows that point N, S, E, W.
   scale   key   compass

CHECK YOUR FACTS
Look at the Lesson

4. What does *north* really mean?

5. When you face north, where is south? Where is east? Where is west?

Look at the Maps (pages 33 and 30)

6. Mexico is ___ of Cuba. Cuba is ___ of Canada.
   north   south   east   west

7. Apple Junction is ___ of Pine Springs. Maple Ridge is ___ of Willow Falls.
   northeast   northwest   southeast   southwest

Lesson 3: Where and What? . . . Location

Maps tell you "which way" and "how far." They can also show you "where." Finding places on a map is easy if you use a grid. A map **grid** is made up of lines on the map. Some lines run north and south (up and down). Other lines run east and west (right and left). Together, the grid lines form squares all over the map.

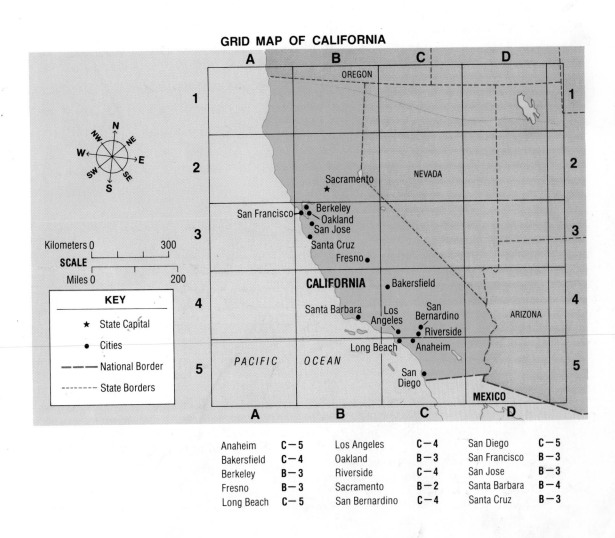

GRID MAP OF CALIFORNIA

Anaheim	C—5	Los Angeles	C—4	San Diego	C—5
Bakersfield	C—4	Oakland	B—3	San Francisco	B—3
Berkeley	B—3	Riverside	C—4	San Jose	B—3
Fresno	B—3	Sacramento	B—2	Santa Barbara	B—4
Long Beach	C—5	San Bernardino	C—4	Santa Cruz	B—3

On many maps, each square has a number and a letter. Look at the map on page 35. It shows some cities in California. Below the map is a list of those cities. Next to each place name are a letter and a number. The letter and the number are clues. They mark a square on the grid. The city is in that square.

Suppose you wanted to find Santa Barbara. Santa Barbara's place on the grid is B-4. Letters are at the top and bottom of the map. Find B. Numbers are at the sides of the map. Find 4. Santa Barbara is in square B-4.

You just used the grid to *find* "where." You can also use it to *tell* "where." Suppose you have a map with a grid but with no list of cities. You want to help a friend find San Diego (dee A goh). First, look at the square San Diego is in. Find the letter of the square. It is C. Find the number of the square. It is 5. You can say that San Diego is in square C-5. Then your friend will be able to find it.

Remember the map key? Look at the symbols in the key. Find those symbols on the map of California. What is the capital of the state of California?

REVIEW

WATCH YOUR WORDS

1. Lines on a map that form squares make up a ___.
   key   compass   grid
2. The symbol for a state capital on a map is in the ___.
   grid   key   cardinal directions
3. To measure distances on a map, you use the ___.
   compass   grid   scale

CHECK YOUR FACTS

Look at the Map

Cover up the list of cities. Then answer questions 4 and 5.

4. Find Los Angeles on the map. What square is it in?
5. Where in California are most of the cities? East or west?
6. Draw four symbols from the map key. Tell what they stand for.

Lesson 4: Latitude and Longitude

One special kind of grid can help you find any place on Earth. You can see this grid on your classroom globe. It is made up of two sets of lines.

Look at the globes below. The globe on the left has lines that run right and left. The globe in the middle has lines that run up and down. Now look at the globe on the right. When you put the lines together, they form a grid. This grid helps you find places.

The lines that go across the globe are called **lines of latitude** (LAT uh TOOD). The word *latitude* simply means "wideness." Lines of latitude run east and west.

The lines that go up and down are called **lines of longitude** (LON juh TOOD). The word *longitude* simply means "longness." Lines of longitude run north and south.

More about Latitude

Remember that the globe is round, like a circle. A circle is divided into 360 parts, or **degrees.** The distance from the North Pole to the South Pole is half a circle. Half a circle is 180 degrees.

Lines of latitude always start in the middle of the globe. The

Quito is the capital of Ecuador in South America. It lies on the equator. The land is very high, though. So the weather is not as hot as you might think.

The prime meridian of Earth passes through Greenwich, England. The old Royal Observatory building there has a split in it. This shows where longitude starts.

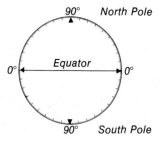

starting place is the equator. So the latitude of the equator is 0 degrees. It is 90 degrees from the equator to the North Pole. It is also 90 degrees from the equator to the South Pole.

We can say this another way. We measure distance from the equator in degrees of latitude. We write 90 degrees as 90°. The North Pole is 90° north of the equator. So the North Pole is at 90° north

latitude. The South Pole is 90° south of the equator. So the South Pole is at 90° south latitude.

Quito, Ecuador (KEE toh EK wuh DOR), is on the equator. So Quito is at 0° latitude. Every place between the equator and the poles has a number between 0 and 90°. New Orleans, in the United States, is at 30° north latitude.

Lines of latitude have another name. They are called **parallels.** When lines are parallel, they are an equal distance apart at every point. They never cross one another. Lines of latitude run in the same direction as the equator.

They are parallel to the equator. So we call them parallels.

More about Longitude

Lines of longitude run north and south. They go from the North Pole down to the South Pole. But there is no natural starting point for them. So scientists made up a starting point. They said that longitude would start in Greenwich, England. Greenwich (GREN ich) is near London. England's old Royal Observatory building is there.

Scientists also gave lines of longitude another name. They called them **meridians** (muh RID ee unz). The word *meridian* simply

means "midday." The line that passed through Greenwich was called the **prime meridian.** *Prime* means "first." So the longitude of Greenwich was set at 0°.

New Orleans, Louisiana, is 90 degrees west of Greenwich, England. So we say that New Orleans is at 90° west longitude. Dacca, Bangladesh, is 90 degrees east of Greenwich, England. So we say that Dacca is at 90° east longitude.

The farthest you can go from Greenwich is half a circle, or 180°. The line for 180° longitude goes through the Aleutian (uh LOO shun) Islands. They are part of Alaska. Can you find them on your globe? At the 180° line, east meets west.

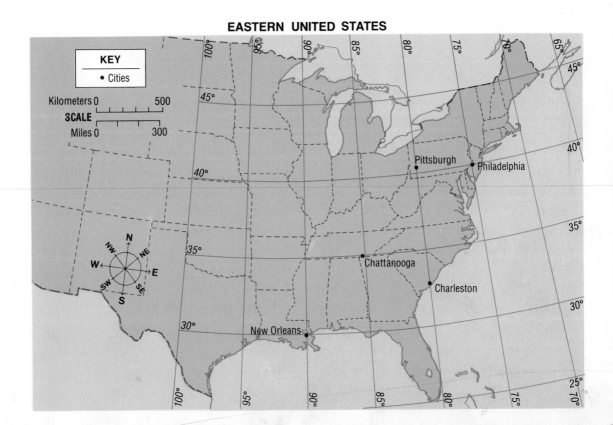

EASTERN UNITED STATES

Finding Places

Look at the map on page 39. It is a map showing part of the United States. The map has a grid. Lines of latitude run from east to west. They measure distance north and south of the equator. The degrees of the lines are marked on the sides of the map.

Lines of longitude run from north to south. They measure distance east and west of the prime meridian. The degrees of the lines are marked at the top and bottom of the map.

With latitude and longitude, you can find any place on Earth. Find New Orleans again. It is on the 30° line running east and west. It is north of the equator. So New Orleans is at 30° north latitude.

Now find the longitude of New Orleans. It is on the 90° line running north and south. It is west of the prime meridian. New Orleans is at 90° west longitude.

Now try finding places another way. Here are the clues: 40° north latitude, 75° west longitude. What is the city?

REVIEW

WATCH YOUR WORDS

1. Lines that run east and west on a globe are____.
   lines of longitude   lines of latitude   degrees

2. Greenwich, England, is the location of the____.
   lines of latitude   prime meridian   parallels

3. Lines that run north and south on a globe are____.
   lines of longitude   lines of latitude   parallels

4. A circle is divided into 360____.
   parallels   degrees   meridians

5. Lines of latitude are also called ____.
   meridians   parallels   degrees

CHECK YOUR FACTS

Look at the Lesson

6. What is the starting place for lines of latitude? Where do lines of longitude start?

7. How far north of the equator can you go?

8. How far west of the prime meridian can you go?

Look at the Map

9. Find Charleston, South Carolina, and Pittsburgh, Pennsylvania. What line of longitude are they on? Are they west or east of the prime meridian?

10. Find Chattanooga, Tennessee. What line of latitude is it on? Is it north or south of the equator? What line of longitude is it on? Is it west or east of the prime meridian? Now, state the location of Chattanooga.

Lesson 5: How High? . . . Elevation

FIND THE WORDS

meter
elevation   sea level
political map   physical map
physical-political map

Another question maps can answer about places is "How high?" To measure how tall a person is, you start at the floor. Then you measure to the top of the person's head. You can measure height in meters and centimeters. Or you can measure in feet and inches. Someone who is 3 feet, 3 inches tall is about 1 **meter** high.

1 meter = 3.28 feet
1 mile = 5280 feet = 1609 meters

The height of land is the land's **elevation** (EL uh VAY shun). To measure land's elevation, you start at **sea level**. Sea level is the surface of the ocean.

Suppose you are wading on a beach. The beach slopes up from the ocean. Where the beach meets the ocean is sea level. Now suppose there is no beach. A mountain goes all the way down to the sea. To measure the mountain, you start at sea level. Then you count the number of meters or feet from the ocean to the mountaintop. Now you know how high the mountain is. Its height above sea level is its elevation.

Suppose someone asks you, "What is the elevation of Sea Peak?" You could say, "Sea Peak is 4300 meters high." Or you could say, "Sea Peak is 14,100 feet above sea level." Both answers

FUN FACTS

Have you ever heard of Pikes Peak? It is a famous mountain in Colorado. Pikes Peak has exactly the same elevation as Sea Peak. It is 4300 meters (14,100 feet) above sea level. You can ride a train from the bottom of Pikes Peak to the top. But if you do, you will not go up 14,100 feet. You will go up only 7530 feet. How can that be so?

The reason is that the ground below Pikes Peak is high ground. It is 6570 feet above sea level. At the foot of the mountain, you are already over a mile high!

would be right. They are different ways of saying the same thing.

Now suppose you ask a map-maker, "What is the elevation of Sea Peak?" The mapmaker will make a map. The map won't *tell* you "4300 meters." But it can *show* you that Sea Peak is over 4000 meters high.

How can a flat map show where mountains are? How can it tell you whether land is high or low?

A map shows elevation in two ways. One way is to use different colors for different heights. Look at the drawing below. All land that is over 4000 meters high is colored brown. That is the highest land on the map. Mapmakers can use any colors they like to show the elevation of land. The key to an elevation map will say what the colors mean.

Many elevation maps show height by using colors. This one shows height by using lines and shading. Mountains look wrinkled on this map.

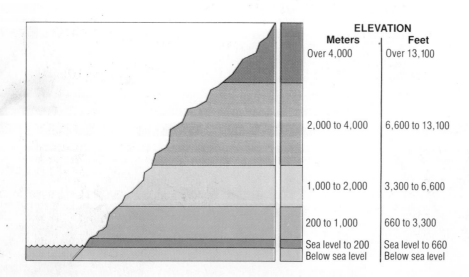

ELEVATION	
Meters	**Feet**
Over 4,000	Over 13,100
2,000 to 4,000	6,600 to 13,100
1,000 to 2,000	3,300 to 6,600
200 to 1,000	660 to 3,300
Sea level to 200	Sea level to 660
Below sea level	Below sea level

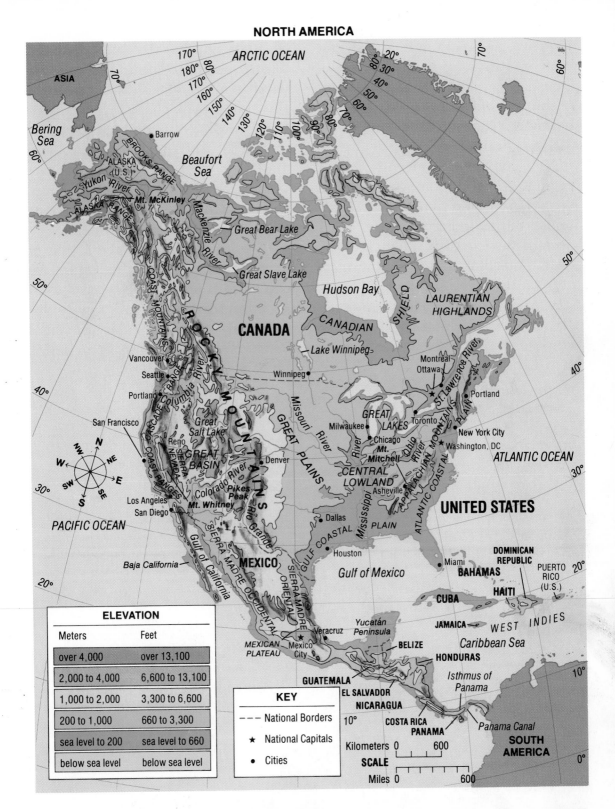

NORTH AMERICA

ARCTIC OCEAN

ASIA

Bering
Sea

Barrow

Beaufort
Sea

BROOKS RANGE

ALASKA
(U.S.)

Yukon River

ALASKA RANGE

Mt. McKinley

Mackenzie River

Great Bear Lake

Great Slave Lake

Hudson Bay

CANADIAN

SHIELD

LAURENTIAN
HIGHLANDS

CANADA

COAST MOUNTAINS

Vancouver

Seattle

Portland

Lake Winnipeg

Winnipeg

Montreal
Ottawa

St. Lawrence River

Portland

COLUMBIA RIVER

ROCKY MOUNTAINS

Columbia River

CASCADE RANGE

San Francisco

Reno

Great
Salt Lake

SIERRA NEVADA

GREAT
BASIN

COAST RANGES

Denver

Colorado River

Pikes
Peak

GREAT PLAINS

Missouri River

Platte River

GREAT
LAKES

Milwaukee

Chicago

Ohio River

Mt.
Mitchell

Toronto

New York City

Washington, DC

ATLANTIC OCEAN

APPALACHIAN MOUNTAINS

ATLANTIC COASTAL PLAIN

CENTRAL
LOWLAND

Asheville

Los Angeles

San Diego

Mt. Whitney

Rio Grande

Dallas

Mississippi River

PLAIN

UNITED STATES

PACIFIC OCEAN

Baja California

Gulf of California

SIERRA MADRE OCCIDENTAL

MEXICO

SIERRA MADRE ORIENTAL

GULF COASTAL

Houston

Miami

Gulf of Mexico

DOMINICAN
REPUBLIC

PUERTO
RICO
(U.S.)

BAHAMAS

CUBA

HAITI

JAMAICA

WEST INDIES

Caribbean Sea

MEXICAN
PLATEAU

Mexico
City

Veracruz

Yucatán
Peninsula

BELIZE

HONDURAS

GUATEMALA

EL SALVADOR

NICARAGUA

Isthmus of
Panama

COSTA RICA

PANAMA

Panama Canal

SOUTH
AMERICA

N
NW NE
W E
SW SE
S

ELEVATION

Meters	Feet
over 4,000	over 13,100
2,000 to 4,000	6,600 to 13,100
1,000 to 2,000	3,300 to 6,600
200 to 1,000	660 to 3,300
sea level to 200	sea level to 660
below sea level	below sea level

KEY

- - - National Borders

★ National Capitals

• Cities

SCALE

Kilometers 0 ___ 600

Miles 0 ___ 600

Mapmakers have another way to show elevation. An artist can show mountains by using lines and shading. Look at the drawing at the top of page 42. Areas with mountains look creased and wrinkled on the map.

Now look at the elevation map on page 43. How can you tell the elevation of Mexico City? First, look at the color of the land around Mexico City. Then look at what that color means in the map key. Is the land around Mexico City high or low? Next, look at Denver, Colorado. Do you know why Denver is called the "Mile-High City"?

Physical and Political Maps

In Chapter 1, you learned about political boundaries. You used a map that showed most of the nations of the world. A map that shows political boundaries is called a **political map.** A map showing the 50 states of the United States is a political map. So is a map showing the three large nations of North America.

A map that shows the shape of land is called a **physical map.** An elevation map is a physical map.

Sometimes a map shows both political boundaries and physical features. Such a map is called a **physical-political map.**

REVIEW

WATCH YOUR WORDS

1. You measure the height of a mountain by starting at ___.
   ground level   the prime meridian   sea level

2. The height of a mountain is its ___ .
   longitude   latitude   elevation

3. A map that shows the boundaries of the 50 states is a ___.
   physical map   political map   scale map

4. A map that shows the shape of land is a ___.
   political map   climate map   physical map

5. A map that shows elevation and political boundaries is a ___.
   political map   physical map   physical-political map

CHECK YOUR FACTS
Look at the Lesson

6. How does a flat map show elevation? Name two ways.

7. Why doesn't the railroad at Pikes Peak go up 14,100 feet?

Look at the Maps

8. What color is Miami, Florida, on the elevation map? What does this color stand for?

9. What color is Asheville, North Carolina, on the map? What does this color stand for?

10. Where are most of the mountains in North America?

CHAPTER REVIEW

WATCH YOUR WORDS

1. A ____ tells you how far one place on a map is from another.
   key   compass   scale

2. A ____ has arrows that point toward the ____ .
   scale   cardinal directions   key   compass

3. A pattern of squares on a map is a ____ .
   key   grid   scale

4. ____ , or ____ , measure distance north and south of the equator. ____ , or ____ , measure distance east and west of Greenwich, England.
   Lines of longitude   parallels
   meridians   Lines of latitude

5. The starting point for lines of latitude is the ____ . Lines of longitude start at the ____ .
   North Pole   prime meridian
   South Pole   equator

6. Latitude and longitude are measured in ____ .
   centimeters   meters   degrees.

7. A map showing the boundaries of the 50 states is a ____ .
   physical map   political map
   elevation map

8. A ____ map shows how high land is.
   political   climate   physical

9. The height of land is its ____ .
   sea level   elevation   longitude

10. Five ____ are equal to three miles.
    meters   centimeters   kilometers

CHECK YOUR FACTS

11. What are the two major systems of measurement?

12. List the cardinal directions and the intermediate directions.

13. Where is a place at 0° longitude? Where is a place at 0° latitude?

14. How do you measure the elevation of a mountain?

15. Which way do lines of latitude run on a map? Which way do lines of longitude run?

USE YOUR MAPS

16. Look at the distance map on page 30. How far is Pine Springs from Spruce City?

17. Look at the direction map on page 33. Fill in the cardinal directions:
    Ottawa is ____ of Washington, DC.
    The Columbia River is ____ of Ottawa.
    The Rio Grande is ____ of Canada.
    Puerto Rico is ____ of Mexico.

18. Look at the grid map on page 35. What square is Sacramento in? What square has the most cities?

19. Look at the elevation map on page 43. Is the highest land in the east or in the west?

20. Look at the latitude and longitude map on page 39. What is the latitude and longitude of Philadelphia?

THINK ABOUT IT

21. How can two maps the same size show places of different sizes?

22. How far west can you go on Earth?

23. Suppose you have two maps of California. One map tells you that Santa Cruz (KROOZ) is in square B-3. The other map shows Santa Cruz at 37° north latitude and 122° west longitude. Which map would a sailor use?

24. Why don't we just measure all mountains from the bottom to the top?

25. Suppose you were lost in the woods. How could you find east and west? How could you find north?

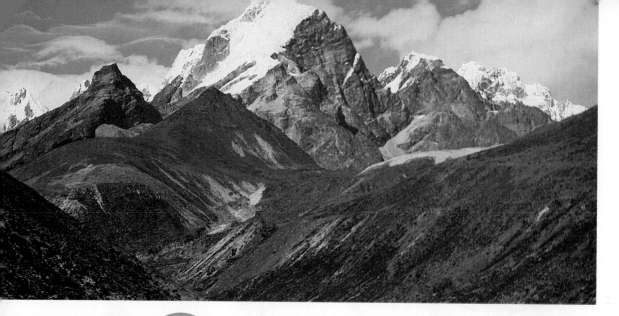

3 ALL ABOUT EARTH

Lesson 1: Landforms of Earth

FIND THE WORDS

landform   mountain   summit
mountain range   hill   valley
plateau   plain

No two people on Earth are exactly alike. No two places are exactly the same, either. Some places are hot, while others are cold. Some places have water, while others are dry. Some places have trees, while others have only sand. Even when places look alike, their plants and animals may be different.

The shape of the land also helps to make places different. The many shapes of land on Earth are called **landforms.** Earth has four main landforms. They are mountains, hills, plateaus, and plains.

The highest form of land on Earth is a **mountain.** It is much higher than the land around it. It goes up sharply and often has a jagged top. The bottom of a mountain is called the foot. The top is called the peak, or **summit.**

Mountains are usually found in groups. A group of mountains is called a **mountain range.** There are many different ranges in the Rocky Mountains. These mountains are in the western United States. Find the Rocky Mountains on the map on page 43. Then find the Appalachian Mountains in the eastern United States.

Now look at the map on pages 48 and 49. Where are the mountains in South America? Can you find the mountains that separate Europe and Asia?

A **hill** also rises higher than the land around it. But hills are not as high or as steep as mountains. A hill often has rounded sides and a rounded top. The low land between a group of hills or mountains is called a **valley.**

It is not easy to live in the hills or on a mountain. It is hard to travel up and down. It takes more time and work to get where you are going. It is also hard to build

A river carved the Grand Canyon out of a plateau. You can see the plateau at the back of the picture.

a road up a mountain. And it is hard to carry up the things you need to build a house.

Like a mountain, a **plateau** (pla TOH) rises above the land around it. But a plateau is usually flat on top. From the air, it looks like a table. So a plateau is sometimes called a *tableland*. Some plateaus are small. Others are very big. Look at the map of Earth on pages 48 and 49. Find the huge plateau in western China. It is in a region known as Tibet (ti BET). This plateau is the largest area of high land on Earth.

A **plain** is a big, open area of level land. Sometimes the land is as flat as a floor in every direction. Most times, the land is slightly "rolling." That doesn't mean the land moves. Rolling land has gentle little hills but no high ones. Usually, there are no big hills on the plains.

Hills are not as high or as steep as mountains. These hills are in Virginia.

PHYSICAL MAP OF EARTH

ARCTIC OCEAN

Ice Cap

ARCTIC CIRCLE

80°
70°
60°
50°
Aleutian
Islands
40°
30°
20°
10°
0°
10°
20°
30°
40°
50°

ROCKY MOUNTAINS

GREAT PLAINS

Mississippi River

Central Lowland

• New Orleans

Mexican Plateau

ATLANTIC OCEAN

PACIFIC OCEAN

EQUATOR

Quito •

ANDES MOUNTAINS

Amazon River

Brazilian Highlands

• Pôrto Alegre

• Buenos Aires

180° 165° 150° 135° 120° 105°

90° 75° 60° 45° 30°

60°
70°
ANTARCTIC CIRCLE

80° Ice Cap

Ice Cap

ELEVATION	
Meters	Feet
over 4,000	over 13,100
2,000 to 4,000	6,600 to 13,100
1,000 to 2,000	3,300 to 6,600
200 to 1,000	660 to 3,300
sea level to 200	sea level to 660
below sea level	below sea level

ARCTIC OCEAN

80°

ARCTIC CIRCLE

70°

60°
BERING
SEA

50°

Moscow

London

EUROPEAN PLAIN

URAL MOUNTAINS

ALPS

Plateau of
Asia Minor

Mediterranean Sea

Alexandria

Plateau of
Tibet

Hwang Ho

40°

Tokyo

30°

HIMALAYAS

SAHARA Cairo

Ganges River

Deccan
Plateau

Dacca

Yangtze

PACIFIC

20°

OCEAN

Nile River

Congo River

10°

0°

EQUATOR

10°

PRIME MERIDIAN

INDIAN   OCEAN

20°

Western
Plateau

Great
Plains

Eastern
Highlands

30°

ATLANTIC

40°

OCEAN

50°

15°   0°   15°   30°   45°   60°   75°

60°

ANTARCTIC   CIRCLE

90°   105°   120°   135°   150°   165°   180°

70°

80°

Ice Cap

Ice Cap

0

Kilometers 0   5000

SCALE

Miles 0   4000

Many crops are grown on the plains. Here, hay is being gathered in.

Often, plains are lowlands. But the land on top of a plateau can also be a plain. Look at the map on page 43. Find the Great Plains in the middle of the United States. Some places in the Great Plains are as high as mountains. For example, Dodge City, Kansas, is 761 meters (2496 feet) high.

There are many large plains on Earth. Look at the map on pages 48 and 49. Can you find the plain that goes across the middle of Europe? Try to find the plains on every continent.

Plains are the places on Earth where most people live. Land in the mountains is often rocky. But much of the land in the plains has rich soil. This land is good for growing food. It is also easier for people to farm flat land than hilly land. It is easier to build roads and houses where the land is level. And it is easier to travel from place to place.

What is the land like where you live? How high is it? What shape is it? What kind of land do you like best?

REVIEW

WATCH YOUR WORDS

1. A ___ is much higher than the land around it.
   hill   mountain   plain

2. A ___ is high and flat on top, like a table.
   plain   mountain   plateau

3. A ___ is flat or slightly rolling land.
   plain   mountain   hill

4. Plains, plateaus, hills, and mountains are different___.
   ranges   landforms   valleys

5. A group of mountains is a___.
   valley   landform   range

CHECK YOUR FACTS

6. What are the four main landforms of Earth?

7. How is a hill different from a mountain? Name two ways.

8. Why do many people live in the plains?

9. Why is it hard for people to live on a mountain?

10. The summit of a mountain (is/is not) much higher than the foot.

TRY SOMETHING NEW

Look up *plain* and *plateau* in a dictionary. Both words mean "flat." What languages do they come from?

Lesson 2: Weather and Climate

FIND THE WORDS

atmosphere   climate
tropical climate
mid-latitude climate
high-latitude climate
tropical rain forest
savanna   tundra
Arctic Circle   Antarctic Circle

"What is the weather going to be tomorrow?" That is something everyone wants to know. Will it be a fair day with sunny skies? We think of that as "good" weather. Will it be rainy or stormy? Then we say that "bad" weather is on the way. "Good" weather doesn't bother us. "Bad" weather can make us uncomfortable or spoil our plans. The weather report can tell us what the weather will be like. But what *is* the weather?

We live at the bottom of a thick layer of air. This air surrounds Earth. We call it Earth's **atmosphere** (AT muh SFIR). When we talk about the weather, we are really talking about the atmosphere.

What do you say when someone asks about tomorrow's weather? In summer, you might say, "It's going to be warm and rainy." In winter, you might say, "It's going to be cold, windy, and clear." In both cases, you are really talking about the atmosphere. How hot or cold is the air? How wet or dry is it? Is the air still or moving?

The climate is more than just the weather. People won't ask you what the climate will be tomorrow. But someone might ask what winters are like where you live. Suppose you live in northern Vermont. You might say, "We have cold winters and a lot of snow." Suppose you live in southern Florida. You might say, "We have mild winters. It doesn't get cold enough to snow."

The average weather over a long period of time is the **climate.** Knowing the climate won't tell you exactly what tomorrow's weather will be. But it will tell you what to expect from season to season. In winter, you won't expect snow in southern Florida. But you will expect snow in northern Vermont.

There are many different climates on Earth. Among them are hot climates and cold climates, wet climates and dry climates. We can divide Earth's climates into three groups. There are **tropical climates** near the equator. There are **mid-latitude climates** between the equator and the poles. There

ARCTIC CIRCLE

TROPIC OF CANCER

EQUATOR

CLIMATES OF EARTH

CLIMATES

Ice Cap: covered with permanent thick ice

Tundra: cold and dry all year

Continental: mild to hot wet summer, cold wet winter

Marine: mild wet summer, mild wet winter

Highlands: various local climates

Steppe: hot summer, hot to cold winter, variable rainfall

Desert: hot summer, hot to cold winter, dry all year

Humid Subtropical: hot wet summer, mild wet winter

Mediterranean: warm dry summer, mild wet winter

Tropical Grasslands: hot wet summer, hot dry winter

Rain Forest: hot and wet all year

ANTARCTIC CIRCLE

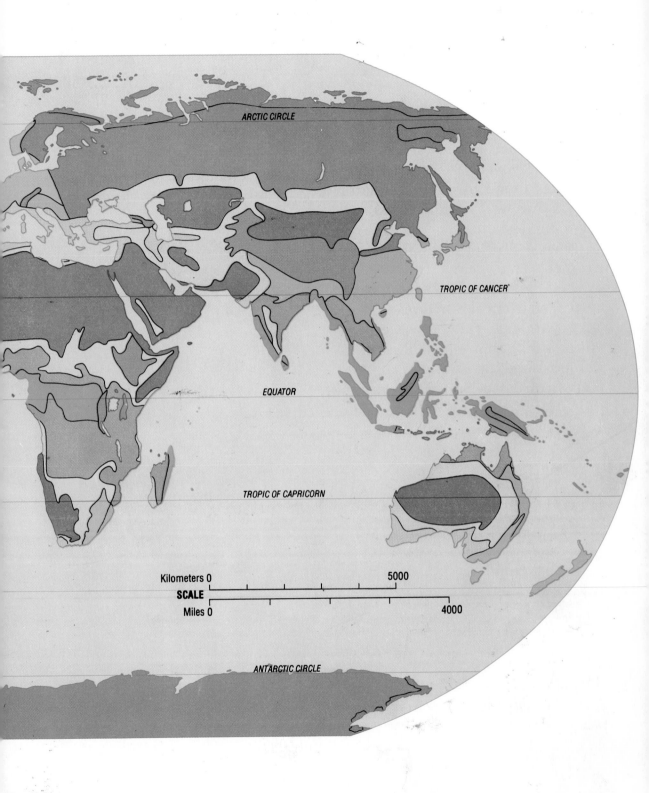

ARCTIC CIRCLE

TROPIC OF CANCER

EQUATOR

TROPIC OF CAPRICORN

Kilometers 0

SCALE

Miles 0

5000

4000

ANTARCTIC CIRCLE

53

are **high-latitude climates** near the poles. You will learn more about these climates as you read.

Tropical Climates

Near the equator, the weather is hot almost all year. The parts of Earth closest to the equator are called the *tropics* (TROP iks). So the climates found along the equator are known as tropical (TROP uh kul) climates.

A good deal of rain falls in the tropics. This heavy rain makes thick forests grow. These forests are called **tropical rain forests.** In an area with less rain, grass grows. An area like that is called a tropical grassland, or **savanna** (suh VAN uh). In areas where little or no rain falls, there are *deserts.* Few plants can grow in the desert.

Look at the climate map of Earth on pages 52 and 53. Find the tropical desert in northern Africa. Then find the tropical grasslands and rain forests.

Mid-latitude Climates

In mid-latitude climates, the weather changes a lot from season to season. Most of the United

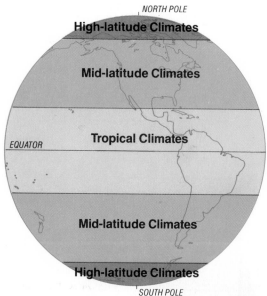

A tropical grassland is called a savanna.

States is located in this climate zone. Find your part of the United States on the climate map. There are seven kinds of mid-latitude climates on the map, including highlands and deserts. What climate area do you live in?

High-latitude Climates

High-latitude climates can be found near the North Pole and the South Pole. There, the weather is almost always cool or cold. The summers are short. The winters are very long.

The area of Earth closest to the North Pole is called the *Arctic*. In the Arctic, parts of the land and ocean are covered with ice and snow all year. Find the Arctic ice cap on the climate map.

South of the Arctic is an area called the **tundra** (TUN druh). Find the tundra on the climate map. The weather there is very cold. The land is almost bare. Some grass grows during the short, cool summer. Trees do not grow on the tundra. The ground is frozen most of the year.

Look at the globe on page 54. Find the line of latitude that is about 66° north of the equator. This is called the **Arctic Circle.** The Arctic and the tundra are north of the Arctic Circle.

Just south of the Arctic Circle is an area with a *subarctic climate*. This area has long, cold winters and short, cool summers. It is mostly covered with forests.

The area closest to the South Pole is called the *Antarctic*. Find the line of latitude that is about 66° south of the equator. This is called the **Antarctic Circle.**

Heavy rains fall in the tropics. The rains cause thick forests to grow. They are called tropical rain forests.

On the tundra, it is very cold. The ground is frozen most of the year.

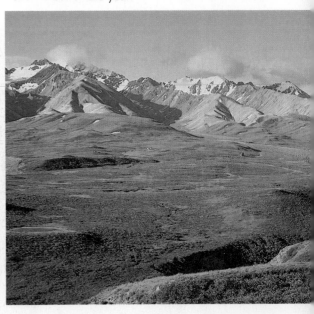

No matter what a climate area is like, the mountains are usually different. The higher you go above sea level, the thinner the air becomes. This thin air holds less heat and wetness than heavier air does. So, as you go up a mountain, the weather gets cooler and cooler. Did you ever drive to the top of a high mountain? You can go through subarctic and tundra regions when you do. Even in the tropics, the tops of high mountains are cold. Very high mountains in the tropics may be covered with snow all year round.

The Antarctic area includes the continent of Antarctica and the oceans around it. Antarctica is covered by thousands of feet of ice and snow. Penguins, whales, and fish live in the Antarctic. Some scientists live there, too. The weather is almost always cold.

People like to live in climates where they are comfortable. Because of this, most people live in certain parts of Earth. Few people live in the Arctic. Not many people live in the mountains or deserts. In fact, large areas of Earth have few people or none at all.

REVIEW

WATCH YOUR WORDS

1. Belém (buh LEM), Brazil, is near the equator. It has a___climate.
   mid-latitude   high-latitude
   tropical

2. Detroit, Michigan, is in the area between the equator and the North Pole. It has a___climate.
   tropical   mid-latitude
   high-latitude

3. Nome, Alaska, is just south of the Arctic Circle. It has a___climate.
   high-latitude   tropical
   mid-latitude

4. Another name for a tropical grassland is a___.
   rain forest   savanna   tundra

5. In the bare___, the ground is frozen most of the year.
   desert   savanna   tundra

CHECK YOUR FACTS

6. What is the difference between climate and weather?

7. What do we call the line of latitude 66° north of the equator? What do we call the line of latitude 66° south of the equator?

8. What is the climate like in the Arctic and the Antarctic?

9. What is a subarctic climate like?

THINK ABOUT IT

Look at the climate map. See if you can guess which parts of Earth have the most people.

Lesson 3: Resources of Earth

People can live on almost any part of Earth's land. But most people prefer places where the land and climate make living easier. People also like to live near the resources they need.

A **resource** is anything people use to help them live. Resources that are found on Earth are called **natural resources.** You use natural resources all the time. This book is made from resources. The paper and ink come from trees and other plants. The house you live in is made from resources. It may be built of wood, stone, clay, or metal. Your food and water are resources. The clothes you wear are made out of resources.

As you can see, there are many kinds of resources. But all natural resources can be put into one of two groups. One group is living resources. The other group is nonliving resources.

Living resources are plants, animals, birds, and fish. Some living resources grow by themselves. But often, people have to grow or raise these resources. Because the re-sources are alive, people can use some and grow more. But suppose people use all of a living resource. For example, suppose hunters kill all the seals in the sea. If we use up a resource, we run out of it.

Let's look for a minute at a few of our living resources.

Plants are very important to people. Plants such as cotton and flax are used to make cloth. We also get oils, dyes, rubber, and medicines from plants. From trees we get wood for houses and paper for books. We also get fruit. Apples, oranges, grapefruit, pears, and peaches grow on trees. Some other fruits grow on smaller plants.

We eat many other parts of plants besides their fruit. We eat seeds, such as peas, beans, and corn. We eat stems, such as celery. We eat leaves, such as lettuce. We eat roots, such as carrots and beets. We even eat flowers, such as broccoli and cauliflower!

Many of our most important foods come from grasses. Bread and spaghetti are made from wheat. Breakfast cereals are made from wheat, oats, and rice. Wheat, oats, and rice are all grasses with seeds we can eat. Most of the people on Earth eat one or more of these grass crops.

Cotton grows in the southern United States. We use the fluffy part of this plant to make cloth.

Some foods are made from grasses. Wheat is a grass with seeds we can eat. Wheat is used to make bread.

Most people also use animals, birds, and fish for food. From these animals we get meat, eggs, and milk. We also get leather for shoes and coats. We get wool for sweaters. We get feathers for pillows. We even get some medicines, such as cod-liver oil. And these are only a few of our living resources.

Nonliving resources are land, water, and minerals. Coal and oil are minerals. People burn coal and oil as fuel. Metals are also minerals. Iron, aluminum, and copper are metals. People use them to make tools, buildings, cars, and many other things. They use gold and silver for money and jewelry.

Two of our most important nonliving resources are land and water. People need good land to grow food. Nothing useful grows unless the soil is fertile (FUR tul). **Fertile soil** contains the minerals that plants need to be healthy. Sometimes the land needs extra minerals. Then people add them to the soil. These added minerals are called *fertilizer*.

But land is useless without water. Water is an important resource. People cannot live long without it. That is why few people live in deserts. There is no water in the desert, and few plants grow there.

People, animals, and plants drink water. But people use water in many other ways as well. We use water to wash, to cook, and to put out fires. People also use water for transportation. Sometimes, it is easier to travel over water than over land. So a river or seaport is a very valuable resource. What are some of the ways in which you use water?

Most nonliving resources cannot be replaced. When they are used up, there will be no more. When we use wood, we can plant more trees. But when we use fuel oil, we cannot replace it. When rain or snow falls, we get more water. But suppose it doesn't rain for a long time. Then we may not have as much water as we need. We may have a water shortage.

Many people are concerned about our resources. They say we must use resources carefully. They say we must not waste them. They believe we should learn to use them over and over again.

REVIEW

WATCH YOUR WORDS

1. Plants and animals are____.
   nonliving resources
   living resources

2. Land, water, and minerals are ____ .
   nonliving resources
   living resources

3. Plants grow well in____.
   mountains   deserts   fertile soil

CHECK YOUR FACTS

4. What is a resource?
5. Name three living resources.
6. Name three nonliving resources.
7. What parts of plants do we eat as food?
8. Why is water an important natural resource?

TRY SOMETHING NEW

Play "Twenty Questions" in a new way. Choose a place at home or at school. It can be indoors or outdoors. List the things you see there. Then say whether each thing is animal, vegetable, or mineral.

THINK ABOUT IT

Suppose your community did not have enough water. What would you do? Think of a plan. Then tell the class about it.

Lesson 4: People and Earth

FIND THE WORDS

population map   population
desert   oasis

"I can't find you. Where on Earth have you gone?" Have you ever heard anyone say that?

People have gone all over Earth. People could live almost anywhere on this planet of ours. But they don't. Most people live in only a few places. They live on only a small part of Earth's land.

Where on Earth are all the people? Look at the map below. It shows where most of the world's people live. This map is called a **population map.** The **population** (POP yuh LAY shun) of a place is the number of people who live there.

You can see that many people live in India and China. Many also live in the western part of Europe. And many live in the eastern part of North and South America. Why do people live crowded together

POPULATION OF EARTH

PEOPLE	
Per Square Kilometer	Per Square Mile
under 10	under 25
10 to 50	25 to 125
50 to 100	125 to 250
over 100	over 250

India is one of the most crowded nations on Earth.

SCALE
Kilometers 0   4000
Miles 0   3000

SIBERIA

URAL MTS.

ALPS

SAHARA

HIMALAYAS

Hwang Ho

Ganges River

Yangtze

Nile River

Congo River

61

The desert is very dry. Without water, few plants can grow there. The cactus grows in the desert, though. This plant can store water in its thick stems.

on Earth? Why don't they spread out more, instead? There are many reasons.

The lands around the poles are too cold for most people. Find the South Pole on the population map. No one lives on the continent of Antarctica. But a few scientists stay there to study the weather. Now find the North Pole and the Arctic Circle. Only a few people live in the Arctic. Those few who live there cannot farm and grow food. The ground is frozen. Instead, they must live by hunting and fishing. The animals and fish they catch are not enough to feed many people. So not many people live in the Arctic. In recent years, oil was found in the Arctic. Many workers went there to drill for it.

Food for them came from other lands.

Now find Africa on the population map. The largest desert in the world is in the north of Africa. It is the Sahara. A **desert** is a very dry place. Parts of it are often covered with sand. Few plants will grow there. Food grows only where there is water. So food does not grow in the desert.

A place in a desert where there is water is called an **oasis** (oh A sis). But an oasis can grow only a little food. This food is not enough to feed many people. So not many people live in the desert.

There is not much fertile land in the mountains, either. And the land in the mountains is not level. It is very hard to grow crops on hilly land. So not many people live in the mountains. Some people who do live there raise animals. They may keep sheep or goats. And mountain areas have other natural resources. Mountain people may work in mines to take minerals out of the Earth. Or they may cut down trees in the forests to get wood. These are some ways they can make a living.

Look at the population map again. Find the Ural Mountains between Europe and Asia. You can see that few people live in the mountains.

Next, find the Amazon River on the map. It is in South America. This river runs through the largest rain forest on Earth. Not many people live in the Amazon rain forest. Tropical rain forests are not good places for people. The heavy rains wash the minerals from the soil. So it is hard for people to grow food.

Now you can see why certain places cannot support many people. Some places are too cold. Some are too dry. Some are too wet. Some are too rocky and uneven.

Most people live where the land is level. They live where the climate is comfortable. They live where the soil is good for growing food. They live where there are natural resources for them to use.

Maps can tell you a lot about what places are like. They can also answer the question: "Where on Earth are all the people?"

REVIEW

WATCH YOUR WORDS

1. The people who live in a place are the_____.
   culture   population   resources

2. A place in a desert where there is water is a(n)_____.
   landform   rain forest   oasis

CHECK YOUR FACTS

3. How do people get their food in the Arctic?

4. What is the largest desert on Earth? Where is it?

5. What is the largest rain forest? Where is it?

6. Name three ways mountain people can make a living.

7. What kind of land is good for people to live on? Name three things this land should have.

TRY SOMETHING NEW

8. Compare the population map with the physical map. What landforms do most people live on?

9. Compare the population map with the climate map. What climate areas do most people live in?

Lesson 5: Ways of Living

FIND THE WORDS

culture   behavior   belief
language   artifact

People live in different places. They do things in different ways. But they are alike in at least one way. They all have the same basic needs.

All people need certain things to stay alive and well. They need air, water, and food. They need protection from the weather. They need to feel safe. And they need to feel good about themselves.

We do not think much about the air around our Earth. But we cannot live without it. We need air to breathe.

In cold lands, like the Arctic, people may build ice houses called igloos.

We also must have water to drink. People get water from rivers, lakes, and springs. In dry places, people dig deep holes in the ground to find water. In cold places, people melt ice. Sometimes, people build dams across rivers to hold back water. Or they dig ponds to catch water when it rains. In these ways, people can store water for future use.

People everywhere need food. All people eat plants. Most people also eat fish, birds, and certain other animals. But people prepare their food in many different ways.

People everywhere wear some form of clothes. In cold climates, people wear heavy clothes to keep warm. In hot climates, people wear less clothing. Clothes protect people from sun and cold, wind and rain.

People everywhere need places to live in. Some people build their homes of wood or stone. Others build homes of grass or clay. People may even build homes of ice and snow. Or they may live in caves or tents. People's homes may look very different. But they all serve the same purposes. A home protects people from the weather. It is a place where people can rest. Home is a place where people can feel safe.

People also need other people. People help each other. They protect each other. They share the work that has to be done. They have fun together. And they care about each other.

People everywhere live in groups. Most people live in families. A group of families may live together in a community. The community may be a village, a town, or a city.

To understand a group of people, we have to study their culture. **Culture** is the way of living shared by the people in a group. People in a culture share behavior, beliefs, language, and artifacts.

Behavior is anything people do. Smiling is a form of behavior. Shaking hands is behavior. Cooking is behavior.

People in the same culture behave like one another. Most of them do the same sorts of things. And they do things in the same ways. They prepare their food in much the same way. They raise their children in the same way. They act like one another when they work or play.

Sharing behavior does not mean that everyone acts exactly alike. People in a culture do not do exactly the same things. But they have the same ways of doing things. They are more alike than different.

A **belief** is anything people think

In warm lands, like Africa, people may live in grass huts.

is true or right. People in a culture believe certain things. They behave the way they do because of their beliefs.

People in a culture also share a **language.** The words in their language have special meanings for them. Other people cannot understand those meanings unless they learn the language. Some cultures have special words. The Innuit (IN yoo it), or Eskimos, have many different words for *snow*. Each word describes a different kind of snow. Other people on Earth live where it never snows. Some languages do not have even one word for *snow*.

People of different cultures make different artifacts. An **artifact** (AHR tuh FAKT) is any object that people make. A cup, a blanket,

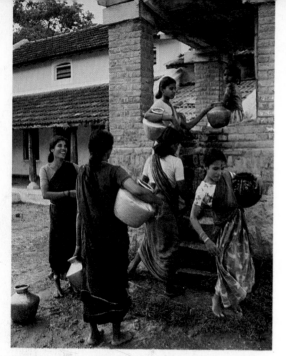
In dry lands, people dig holes in the ground to find water. They use jars or buckets to draw water out of these wells.

and a necklace are artifacts. A plow and a wagon are artifacts.

Artifacts tell us something about the people who made them. They show what the people of a culture can do. People who make blankets can weave. People who make wagons know how to use wheels.

In this book, you will be studying different places and people. You will learn about your own country and other continents. You will visit places with different landforms, climates, and resources. And you will see how people live in different regions of the Earth.

REVIEW

WATCH YOUR WORDS

1. A way of living that a group of people share is their____.
   behavior   belief   culture

2. ____are objects that people make.
   Artifacts   Beliefs   Languages

3. What people do is their____.
   belief   behavior   culture

4. ____ are things people think are true or right.
   Artifacts   Cultures   Beliefs

5. The words people speak make up their____.
   beliefs   language   culture

CHECK YOUR FACTS

6. Name five things that all people need.

7. Tell three ways by which people get water.

8. Why do people live together in groups?

9. Why do people have homes?

10. Here is a list of ten things. Which of them are artifacts? Which are natural resources?
    clothes   corn   dishes   gold
    coins   oil   ships   water
    weapons   wool

THINK ABOUT IT

Suppose you found a spear point and an arrowhead in a cave. What could you guess about the people who made them?

CHAPTER REVIEW

WATCH YOUR WORDS

1. A mountain, hill, plateau, or plain is a ___ .
   climate landform resource

2. Another name for a tableland is a ___ .
   mountain plain plateau

3. A flat or slightly rolling grassland is a ___ .
   plain plateau hill

4. A tropical grassland is a ___ .
   plateau savanna tundra

5. Treeless land where the ground is usually frozen is ___ .
   desert savanna tundra

6. Treeless land that is too dry for most plants is ___ .
   tundra desert savanna

7. A place at sea level close to the equator has a ___ climate.
   mid-latitude tropical high-latitude

8. Cotton, coal, oil, and rubber are ___ .
   artifacts resources minerals

9. People who share language, behavior, and beliefs make up a ___ .
   culture continent population

10. Jewelry, tools, pots, and arrows are ___ .
    natural resources artifacts
    nonliving resources

CHECK YOUR FACTS

11. What are the four main landforms of Earth?

12. How are the weather and the atmosphere alike? How do the weather and the climate differ?

13. What are the three main kinds of climates on Earth? Where do you find each kind?

14. Name four things that people in a culture share.

USE YOUR MAPS

15. Look at the physical map on pages 48 and 49. Find a mountain range in Europe. Find a plateau in Mexico. Find a river in South America.

16. Look at the climate map on pages 52 and 53. Where are the deserts in the United States? What part of the United States has a marine climate?

17. Look at the population map on pages 60 and 61. Which three continents have the most people?

18. Compare the physical map and the population map. On what kind of land do most people live? How high is that land?

19. Compare the climate map and the population map. In what climate areas do most people live?

THINK ABOUT IT

20. What kind of land do most people like best? Describe the landform, the climate, the soil, and the resources.

21. Think of all the ways we use water. Make a list of all the uses you can think of. Now, suppose there was a water shortage. List some ways we could save water.

22. What did you bring to school with you today? Look in your pocket, wallet, or purse. Look in your bookbag or notebook. Which of these things are artifacts? What resources were they made from? What do they tell about your culture?

23. Suppose you were all alone on an island. Suppose there were no other people to do things for you. What are some things you would have to do for yourself?

24. When would you be cold even if you were close to the equator?

UNIT REVIEW

WATCH YOUR WORDS

Use the words below to fill in the blanks. Use each term only once.

axis   globe
cardinal directions   grid
climate   key
compass   lines of latitude
continents   lines of longitude
elevation   map
equator   Northern Hemisphere

North Pole   revolves
oceans   rotates
physical maps   scale
planet   seasons
political boundaries   Southern Hemisphere
political maps   South Pole
prime meridian   tilt

Earth is a __2__ . Earth __3__ around its __4__ once every 24 hours. Every 365 days, Earth __4__ around the sun. The __5__ of Earth's axis causes the __6__ to change.

A round model of Earth is a __7__ .The __8__ is an imaginary line that circles Earth in the middle. It is midway between the __9__ and the __10__ . It divides Earth into the __11__ and the __12__ . The __13__ measure distance north and south of the equator.

The __14__ is an imaginary line that runs north and south through Greenwich, England. The __15__ measure distance east and west of Greenwich.

A flat drawing of Earth is a __16__ . A map __17__ tells what the symbols on the map mean. The map __18__ tells how much distance the map covers. The __19__ has arrows that point in the __20__ , which are north, south, east, and west. A map __21__ forms a pattern of squares on the map. Some maps show the __22__ between nations. These maps are called __23__ . Other maps show the height, or __24__ , of land. These maps are called __25__ . Earth has seven __26__ and four __27__ . Most people live in those parts of Earth where the __28__ makes them comfortable.

CHECK YOUR FACTS

1. What is the solar system?
2. What is Earth's orbit? Why is our year 365 days long?
3. What is Earth's axis?
4. Why is it summer in the Southern Hemisphere when it is winter in the Northern Hemisphere?
5. What is a globe? What is a map?
6. Name four things you can find on a map or globe.
7. What is the equator? What is the Arctic Circle? What is the Antarctic Circle?
8. What is a hemisphere?
9. Why is it hard to show the Earth on a flat map?

10. What is a key on a map? What is a map symbol?
11. What can you do with a map scale?
12. What are the cardinal directions?
13. What is a grid?
14. What are the lines of latitude and longitude? How can you use them?
15. What is the elevation of land?
16. What is a political map? What is a physical map?
17. Name three different ways that map-makers can use colors on maps.
18. Name the four main landforms of Earth.
19. Name the three main kinds of climates.
20. Name four living resources. Then name four nonliving resources.

CLOSE THE MAP GAP

Use the globe below to answer the following questions.

21. Identify the following if A is the North Pole.
   a. line *EF*   **b.** line *GH*
   c. line *AB*   **d.** line *CD*
   e. the area between *CD* and point *A*

22. Draw a globe.
   a. Label the North Pole, the South Pole, the equator, the Arctic Circle, and the Antarctic Circle.
   b. Give the latitude of each.
   c. Label the three main climate zones.
   d. Color the climate zone where you live.

USE YOUR MAPS

23. Look at the map on pages 10 and 11. List three nations in North America.

24. Look at the map on pages 12 and 13. Give the latitude and longitude of Denver, Colorado.

25. Look at the map on page 30. Measure the distance between Plum Park and Orangedale.

26. Look at the map on pages 48 and 49. What is the elevation of the Central Lowland? The Mexican Plateau?

27. Look at the map on pages 52 and 53. What climates can you find in North America? List them.

THINK ABOUT IT

28. Suppose Earth was not tilted on its axis. How would life be different on Earth?

29. You are at the North Pole. Your friend is at the South Pole. How far apart are you? Draw a globe with lines of latitude to show how far.

30. You are at 180° west longitude. Your friend is at 180° east longitude. How far apart are you? Draw a globe with lines of longitude to show how far.

31. Suppose all the land on Earth was a fertile plain. Suppose the climate everywhere was mild and pleasant. Suppose every place had plenty of living and nonliving resources. Would the population map change? How?

32. Where in the tropics would you find snow? Why?

TRY SOMETHING NEW

33. Get a map of your local community. Tell where you live by giving your latitude and longitude. Describe the climate.

PUT IT ALL TOGETHER

34. On a separate sheet of paper, draw an outline of an imaginary place. It could be a continent, a country, or an island. Then put these things on the map:
   a. a distance scale
   b. political boundaries
   c. cities
   d. a compass
   e. rivers and oceans
   f. labels for places on the map
   g. lines of latitude and longitude, with degrees to show where your place is located
   h. symbols that show where cities, roads, lakes, and mountains are

Make your map as fancy as you wish. You can use colors to show anything you like—elevation, climate zones, states, or countries. Use your map to show others what your place is like. Include a key that tells what the symbols and colors mean.

NORTH AMERICA AND
THE UNITED STATES

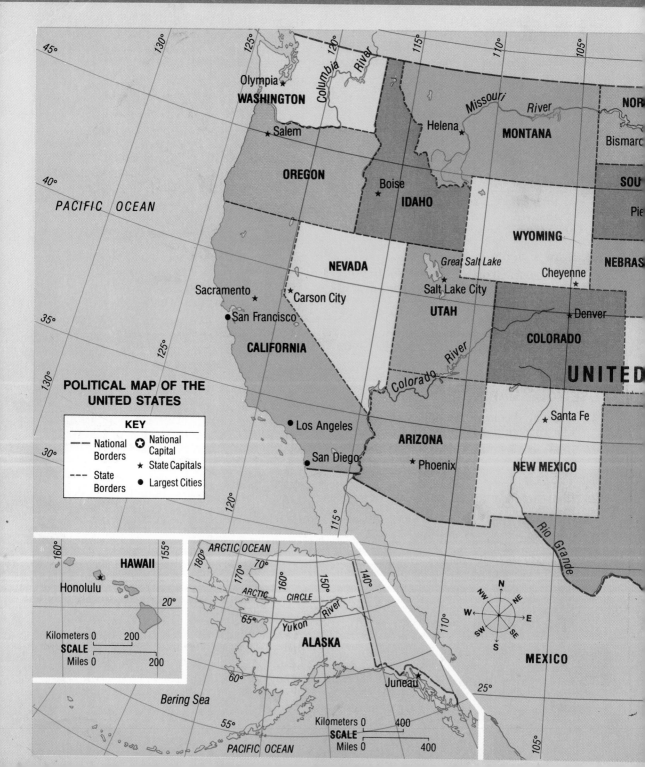

POLITICAL MAP OF THE
UNITED STATES

KEY

— — National Borders	✪ National Capital
	★ State Capitals
- - - State Borders	● Largest Cities

WASHINGTON
Olympia ★
Salem ★
OREGON

Columbia River

Helena ★
MONTANA
Missouri River
Boise ★
IDAHO

NOR
Bismarc

WYOMING
SOU
Pie

NEVADA
Great Salt Lake
Salt Lake City ★
UTAH
Cheyenne ★
NEBRAS

Sacramento ★
Carson City ★
San Francisco ●
CALIFORNIA

Denver ★
COLORADO

UNITED

Los Angeles ●
San Diego ●
ARIZONA
Phoenix ★
Santa Fe ★
NEW MEXICO

PACIFIC OCEAN
Colorado River
Rio Grande

45°
40°
35°
30°
130°
125°
120°
130°
125°
120°
115°
110°
105°

Hawaii inset

ARCTIC OCEAN
HAWAII
Honolulu ★

Kilometers 0   200
SCALE
Miles 0   200

20°
160°
155°

Alaska inset

ARCTIC OCEAN
70°
ARCTIC CIRCLE
65°
Yukon River
ALASKA
60°
Juneau ★
Bering Sea
55°
PACIFIC OCEAN

180°
170°
160°
150°
140°
110°

Kilometers 0   400
SCALE
Miles 0   400

MEXICO
25°
105°

N
NE
NW
W   E
SW   SE
S

CANADA

MINNESOTA

WISCONSIN

Lake Superior

MICHIGAN

Lake Huron

IOWA

St. Paul

Madison

Lansing

Chicago

Des Moines

ILLINOIS

INDIANA

Springfield

Indianapolis

Lincoln

Topeka

MISSOURI

STATES

Jefferson City

OKLAHOMA

Oklahoma City

ARKANSAS

Little Rock

Memphis

Dallas

TEXAS

Austin

Houston

San Antonio

LOUISIANA

Baton Rouge

MISSISSIPPI

Jackson

ALABAMA

Montgomery

Gulf of Mexico

OHIO

Columbus

WEST VIRGINIA

Charleston

KENTUCKY

Frankfort

Nashville

TENNESSEE

GEORGIA

Atlanta

Columbia

SOUTH CAROLINA

NORTH CAROLINA

Raleigh

VIRGINIA

Richmond

Mississippi River

Ohio River

Lake Michigan

Detroit

Lake Erie

Niagara Falls

Lake Ontario

NEW YORK

Albany

PENNSYLVANIA

Harrisburg

Baltimore

Annapolis

Washington, DC

MARYLAND

Dover

DELAWARE

Philadelphia

NEW JERSEY

Trenton

New York City

St. Lawrence River

VERMONT

Montpelier

MAINE

Augusta

NEW HAMPSHIRE

Concord

Boston

MASSACHUSETTS

Providence

Hartford

RHODE ISLAND

CONNECTICUT

Tallahassee

FLORIDA

ATLANTIC OCEAN

SCALE

Kilometers 0   500

Miles 0   500

CHAPTER 1 NORTH AMERICA AND ITS PEOPLE

Lesson 1: Land and Climate

FIND THE WORDS

gulf   coast   isthmus
canal   lock   sierra
foothills   prairie   lake

Most of the United States is on the continent of North America. North America is the third-largest continent on Earth. Only Asia and Africa are larger. Europe is much smaller than North America.

Look at North America on a globe. Part of the continent is north of the Arctic Circle. Some islands are less than 10° from the North Pole. Another part of the continent touches South America. The nation of Panama is less than 10° from the equator. So North America covers a lot of the Northern Hemisphere.

Now look at the physical map of North America on page 73. The

NORTH AMERICA

ARCTIC OCEAN

ASIA

Bering Sea

Barrow

Beaufort Sea

ALASKA (U.S.)

BROOKS RANGE

Yukon River

Mt. McKinley

ALASKA RANGE

Mackenzie River

Great Bear Lake

Great Slave Lake

Hudson Bay

CANADA

CANADIAN

SHIELD

LAURENTIAN HIGHLANDS

Lake Winnipeg

Vancouver

Seattle

Portland

San Francisco

COAST MOUNTAINS

Winnipeg

Columbia River

Fraser River

Montreal

Ottawa

Toronto

St. Lawrence River

Portland

GREAT LAKES

Milwaukee

Chicago

New York City

Washington, DC

ATLANTIC OCEAN

Reno

Great Salt Lake

Denver

Missouri River

GREAT PLAINS

Mt. Mitchell

Ohio River

APPALACHIAN MOUNTAINS

ATLANTIC COASTAL PLAIN

CASCADE RANGE

SIERRA NEVADA

COAST RANGES

GREAT BASIN

ROCKY MOUNTAINS

CENTRAL LOWLAND

Asheville

Colorado River

Pikes Peak

Los Angeles

San Diego

Mt. Whitney

UNITED STATES

Dallas

Mississippi River

PACIFIC OCEAN

Baja California

Gulf of California

Rio Grande

GULF COASTAL PLAIN

Houston

Miami

Gulf of Mexico

DOMINICAN REPUBLIC

BAHAMAS

PUERTO RICO (U.S.)

HAITI

CUBA

JAMAICA

WEST INDIES

MEXICO

SIERRA MADRE OCCIDENTAL

SIERRA MADRE ORIENTAL

Veracruz

Yucatán Peninsula

Caribbean Sea

BELIZE

HONDURAS

MEXICAN PLATEAU

Mexico City

GUATEMALA

EL SALVADOR

NICARAGUA

COSTA RICA

PANAMA

Isthmus of Panama

Panama Canal

SOUTH AMERICA

N NE E SE S SW W NW

ELEVATION

Meters	Feet
over 4,000	over 13,100
2,000 to 4,000	6,600 to 13,100
1,000 to 2,000	3,300 to 6,600
200 to 1,000	660 to 3,300
sea level to 200	sea level to 660
below sea level	below sea level

KEY
- - - National Borders
★ National Capitals
• Cities

SCALE

Kilometers 0 — 600

Miles 0 — 600

73

Pacific Ocean is on the west. The Atlantic Ocean is on the east. The Arctic Ocean is to the north. To the south are two smaller parts of the Atlantic Ocean. They are the Gulf of Mexico and the Caribbean (KAR uh BEE un) Sea. A **gulf** is part of an ocean with land curving around it.

The land next to an ocean is called a **coast.** Part of North America is near the Pacific Ocean. That part is called the Pacific Coast or the West Coast. Another part of the continent is near the Atlantic Ocean. That part is called the Atlantic Coast or the East Coast. The land around the Gulf of Mexico is called the Gulf Coast.

Find Panama again. There, a narrow strip of land links North America and South America. That narrow strip of land is called an **isthmus** (ISS muss). The Isthmus of Panama also divides the Pacific Ocean from the Caribbean Sea. In the early 1900s, the United States built the Panama Canal. A **canal** is a waterway that people build across the land. A ship canal connects one body of water with another. Now, ships can sail from the Atlantic to the Pacific. They pass through the Panama Canal.

FUN FACTS

Doors are not the only things with locks. Canals have locks, too. A **lock** is part of a canal with gates on either side. It works somewhat like an elevator. First, a ship enters a lock. Then the gates of the lock are closed. Suppose the ship is at sea level. Suppose the next part of the canal is a lake. This lake is above sea level. That means the water in the next part of the canal is higher. So more water is pumped into the lock. The water level in the lock gets higher. The ship rises with the water. Then the gates are opened. The ship can go into the next part of the canal.

Sometimes, the water in the next part of the canal is lower. Then water is drained out of the lock. The water level in the lock gets lower. The ship gets lower, too. Sometimes, a ship goes through two or three locks in a row. In the locks, it is raised or lowered. Then it can sail safely on its way.

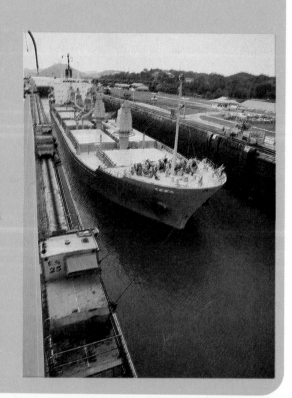

Landforms of North America

Do you remember the main landforms of Earth? They are mountains, hills, plateaus, and plains. North America has all these landforms.

Mountains run all the way down the western part of the continent. Find the Rocky Mountains on the map. They are also called the Rockies. This great mountain system stretches from Alaska to New Mexico. The Rockies are the longest, highest mountains in North America. They extend for more than 4800 kilometers (3000 miles). The highest mountain in North America is in the Rockies. It is Mount McKinley in Alaska. Mount McKinley is 6194 meters (20,320 feet) above sea level.

Now find the Appalachian (AP uh LAY chun) Mountains. The Appalachians are the major mountain system in the east. These mountains extend for more than 2570 kilometers (1600 miles). The highest mountain in the Appalachians is in North Carolina. It is Mount Mitchell. Mount Mitchell has an elevation of 2037 meters (6684 feet). Mount McKinley is three times higher than Mount Mitchell.

South of Alaska, the highest mountain in the United States is Mount Whitney. Mount Whitney is in California. It is in a mountain range called the Sierra (see EHR uh) Nevada. In Spanish, the word *sierra* means "a saw." Pointed mountain peaks look like the teeth of a saw. So a **sierra** is a range of steep mountains. Mount Whitney rises 4418 meters (14,494 feet) above sea level. It is more than twice as high as Mount Mitchell. The highest mountains in North America are in the west!

Near many mountain ranges are hills. Hills near the bottom of a mountain are called **foothills.** There are many hills and foothills in North America.

North America also has plateaus. Find Mexico City on the physical map on page 73. Mexico City is on the Mexican Plateau. Parts of this plateau are higher than Mount Mitchell. But the land on top of the plateau is flat. Mexico City is 2380 meters (7800 feet) above sea level!

North America has several large areas of plains. There are the Great Plains, the Central Lowland, and the coastal plains. The Great Plains are east of the Rocky Mountains. These plains are also a plateau. The western part of the Great Plains is the highest part. This part begins near the foothills of the Rockies. There, the land is 1830 meters (6000 feet) above sea level. Gradually, the Great Plains slope downward. The eastern part of the plains is much lower than the western part.

In the 1800s, American Indians hunted buffalo on the plains.

East of the Great Plains is the Central Lowland. The Central Lowland is very fertile. Many crops are grown there. Large parts of the Central Lowland and Great Plains were once prairies (PREHR eez). A **prairie** is a large area of flat or rolling grassland. It has fertile soil and few trees.

More plains are found along the Atlantic Coast and the Gulf Coast. These are called the coastal plains. In the west, there are coastal ranges of mountains.

Rivers and Lakes of North America

Rivers begin in high lands. They flow from higher lands to lower lands. Find the Mississippi River on the map on page 73. *Mississippi* is an American Indian word. It means "big river." The Mississippi begins in a lake in Minnesota. It flows south to the Gulf of Mexico. Many other rivers flow into the Mississippi.

Another big river in North America is the Missouri. It begins in the Rocky Mountains in western Montana. The Missouri River flows into the Mississippi River. Use your finger to trace the Missouri River on the map. Follow it from the Rocky Mountains to the Gulf of Mexico. Add on the part where the two rivers flow together. With the lower Mississippi added on, the Missouri is the longest river in North America.

The *Delta Queen* is a famous riverboat. It travels up and down the Mississippi River.

The second-longest river in North America flows north, not south. It is the Mackenzie River in Canada. The Mackenzie River begins at Great Slave Lake. It flows northwest into the Arctic Ocean. Another great river in North America is the Rio Grande (REE oh GRAND). *Rio Grande* means "big river" in Spanish. Part of the Rio Grande forms the border between Texas and Mexico. So it divides the United States and Mexico.

The Great Lakes are a famous feature of North America. These five lakes are between the United States and Canada. A **lake** is a body of water surrounded by land. Many lakes have fresh water. The Great Lakes do. They are the largest group of freshwater lakes in the world. Some lakes have salt water, though. Find the Great Salt Lake on the map. It is west of the Great Lakes. This lake is so salty that people float on the water.

Climates of North America

In the south, North America is close to the equator. In the north, it is close to the North Pole. So North America has many different kinds of climates. There are subarctic and tundra climates in the far north. There are tropical grasslands and rain forests in the far south. There are highlands in the west. There are deserts in the southwest. You can find North America's many climates on the map below.

CLIMATES OF NORTH AMERICA

KEY

– – – – National Borders

• Cities

CLIMATE KEY

Tundra: cold and dry all year

Continental: mild to hot wet summer, cold wet winter

Marine: mild wet summer, mild wet winter

Highlands: various local climates

Steppe (continental grasslands): hot summer, hot to cold winter, variable rainfall

Desert: hot summer, hot to cold winter, dry all year

Humid subtropical: hot wet summer, mild wet winter

Mediterranean: warm dry summer, mild wet winter

Tropical grasslands: hot wet summer, hot dry winter

Rain forest: hot and wet all year

Most of the people in North America live in mid-latitude climates. Look at the climate map on the facing page. Find the seven climates in the middle of the key. These are mid-latitude climates. Most of them have four seasons. Summer is warm or hot. Winter is cool or cold. During spring and fall, the weather changes. Many people enjoy the change of seasons. Others like climates where the weather is much the same all year. Whatever climate people like, they will probably find it in North America!

REVIEW

WATCH YOUR WORDS

1. The land next to an ocean is a ___.
   gulf   canal   coast
2. The part of North America near the Pacific Ocean is called the ___.
   East Coast   West Coast   Gulf Coast
3. A ___ may have fresh water or salt water.
   lake   sierra   gulf
4. A ___ is part of an ocean.
   canal   gulf   lake
5. A(n) ___ is a waterway built by people.
   gulf   isthmus   canal
6. A ship can be raised or lowered in a ___.
   lake   lock   gulf
7. A(n) ___ is a narrow strip of land.
   isthmus   prairie   lock
8. A(n) ___ is a range of high, steep mountains.
   prairie   isthmus   sierra
9. ___ are found near the bottom of mountains.
   Sierras   Foothills   Locks
10. ___ are fertile grasslands.
    Locks   Sierras   Prairies

CHECK YOUR FACTS

11. What continents are larger than North America?
12. List North America's three oceans.
13. Where is the Panama Canal? Why is it useful?
14. What are the longest, highest mountains in North America?
15. What is the major mountain system in eastern North America?
16. What is the highest single mountain in North America? Where is it found?
17. List three large areas of plains.
18. Name a river that flows south. Then name one that flows north.
19. What river divides Mexico and the United States?
20. Where are the Great Lakes?

THINK ABOUT IT

Look at the physical map and the climate map of North America. Suppose you could live anywhere on the continent. What place would you choose? What is the land like there? What is the climate like?

Lesson 2: Resources of North America

FIND THE WORDS

dairy   poultry   petroleum
conserve   conservation
preserve   pollution

North America is rich in natural resources. It has a great deal of fertile soil. Corn, wheat, and soybeans grow in most parts of the continent. Oats and barley grow in the west. Potatoes grow in the north. Cotton, rice, peanuts, and sugar cane grow in the south. There are many other crops, too.

North America also has good land for raising cattle and sheep. In the west, cattle are raised for their meat. Around the Great Lakes, they are raised for their milk. Cream, butter, cheese, and ice cream are made from milk. Milk and other foods made from it are called **dairy** products.

Plants and animals are living resources. Look at the map of North America's living resources on page 82. You can see that this continent produces a lot of food. Many different fruits and vegetables grow well in North America. Wheat is used to make bread and cereals. Cattle, hogs, and young sheep provide plenty of meat.

Chickens provide both meat and eggs. Chickens and turkeys are also called **poultry** (POHL tree). Along the coasts and rivers, people catch fish.

North America has resources to clothe its people, too. Cotton grows in the fields. Wool grows on animals. It is cut from sheep. The cotton and wool are used to make cloth and clothing.

North America also has extra resources to sell. Many people on other continents eat food that comes from North America.

North America also has many nonliving resources. The map of nonliving resources on page 83 shows a few of them. There are metals such as iron ore, copper, and lead. These metals are important in manufacturing. North America also has silver and gold. These metals have a high value all over the world.

Many other important minerals are found in North America. Coal and oil are used as fuels. Coal is also used with iron ore to make steel. Coal is like a black rock. Crude oil is a thick, dark liquid. Both coal and crude oil are found under the earth. Sometimes, crude oil is found beneath oceans and seas. Another name for crude oil is **petroleum** (puh TROH lee um). Other kinds of oil come from animals and plants. Whale oil was once used to make candles and fuel for lamps. Corn oil can be used for cooking.

Today, petroleum is one of the most important resources on Earth. It is burned to heat homes and to make electricity. It is also used to make gasoline. Most cars have gasoline engines. They cannot run without petroleum.

There is a lot of petroleum in Mexico. Mexico sells some of this petroleum to other nations. The United States has petroleum in Texas, Oklahoma, Louisiana, California, and Alaska. But the United States does not have enough petroleum to meet its needs. It has to buy the extra petroleum from other nations.

Conserving Resources

There is no limit to the things people want. But there is a limit

Some natural resources can be renewed. Young trees are planted to replace trees that were cut down.

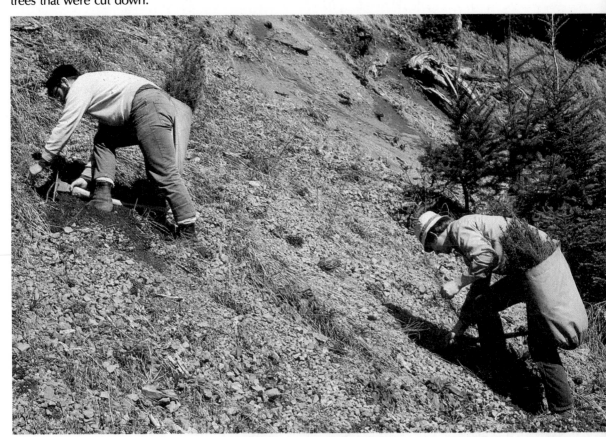

LIVING RESOURCES OF NORTH AMERICA

LIVING
RESOURCES

- Corn
- Cotton
- Beef Cattle
- Wood
- Barley
- Wheat
- Oats
- Dairy Cattle
- Fruit
- Potatoes
- Sheep
- Soybeans

Kilometers 0   1000
SCALE
Miles 0   500   1000

NONLIVING RESOURCES OF NORTH AMERICA

NONLIVING
RESOURCES

Petroleum

Iron Ore

Coal

Copper

Gold

Kilometers 0   1000
SCALE
Miles 0   500   1000

Elk are in danger of dying out. A game preserve in Grand Teton National Park protects them from hunters.

to the natural resources they have. Some resources can be used and then renewed. Flowing water can be used again and again. It can provide the power to make electricity. Sunlight renews itself every day. It can provide energy to heat homes and make wheels turn. Trees in a forest can be cut down for their wood. Then, more trees can be planted. But it takes many years for a tree to grow. So it is important not to cut too many trees too fast. That could destroy the forests.

Other resources can be used up. They cannot be renewed. They do not replace themselves. When they are used up, they disappear. Coal and petroleum are resources of this kind. It takes millions of years for these minerals to form in the earth! So it is important not to waste them.

To use resources carefully and wisely is to **conserve** them. Wise use of natural resources is called **conservation** (KON sur VAY shun). Resources such as water, forests, soil, and fuels can be conserved.

You conserve a resource when you use some and save some.

Another way to protect resources is to keep them as they are. People **preserve** resources by not letting them be destroyed. For example, some animals are in danger of dying out. Many of these animals are being preserved. No one is allowed to kill any of them. A game preserve is a place where wild animals are protected from hunters. Land in its natural state is preserved in national parks. But many people like to visit the parks. It is hard to protect the land completely. When people use the land, they often change it.

The continent of North America has a great wealth of resources. It has fertile soil, tall trees, and valuable minerals. It also has clean water and fresh air. But sometimes, people make the air and water dirty. Adding something harmful to air or water is called **pollution** (puh LOO shun). Breathing polluted air or drinking polluted water can make people sick.

Through conservation, we can use natural resources wisely. We can protect the air and water from pollution. We can preserve wild animals and natural land. That way, we can help save North America's resources for the future.

REVIEW

WATCH YOUR WORDS

1. Chickens and turkeys are called ____.
   dairy   poultry   cattle
2. Cheese, milk, and ice cream are ____ products.
   poultry   petroleum   dairy
3. Gasoline for cars is made from ____.
   petroleum   coal   copper
4. Wise use of resources is called ____.
   pollution   conservation   waste
5. Making the air dirty is called ____.
   conservation   preservation   pollution

CHECK YOUR FACTS

6. List five plants that grow in North America.
7. List three kinds of animals that are raised in North America.
8. How long does it take for coal and petroleum to form in the earth?
9. How do people conserve resources?
10. List two resources that are being preserved.

THINK ABOUT IT

Suppose North America used up all its coal and petroleum. What might happen then?

Lesson 3: Nations and People of North America

FIND THE WORDS

**province   territory   seaway
peninsula   pyramid**

Most of the world's continents have many nations. North America has only a few. Three large nations take up most of the continent. They are Canada, the United States, and Mexico. In this lesson, we will study Canada and Mexico. The next chapter will be about the United States.

Look at the political map of North America on page 87. Find Canada, the United States, and Mexico. Which of these nations is the largest? If you said the United States, you are wrong.

Canada

Canada is the largest nation in North America. In fact, Canada is the second-largest nation in the world. Only the Soviet Union has more land than Canada. But Canada does not have many people. Fewer than 25 million people live there. The United States has less land than Canada. But it has more than nine times as many people.

The nation of Canada has 10 provinces. A **province** in Canada is like a state in the United States of America. Canada also has two territories. A **territory** is part of a country that has not yet become a state or province. Find the 10 provinces on the map on page 88. Then find the Yukon Territory and the Northwest Territories. More than one-third of Canada's land is in those two territories. But very few people live there. Winters in those northern regions are very cold. Most of the people of Canada live in the southeast.

Citizens of Canada are called Canadians. Most Canadians live in the provinces of Ontario and Quebec (kwi BEK). Find these two provinces on the map. To the north, these provinces are divided by Hudson Bay. In the south, they border on the United States.

The Great Lakes form most of the southern boundary of Ontario. The United States and Canada share four of these five lakes. They also share the continent's most famous waterfall, Niagara Falls. Niagara Falls is between Lake Ontario and Lake Erie. One part of the falls is in New York. The other part is in Ontario. The capital of Canada is in Ontario. It is Ottawa. Find Ottawa on the map.

NATIONS OF NORTH AMERICA

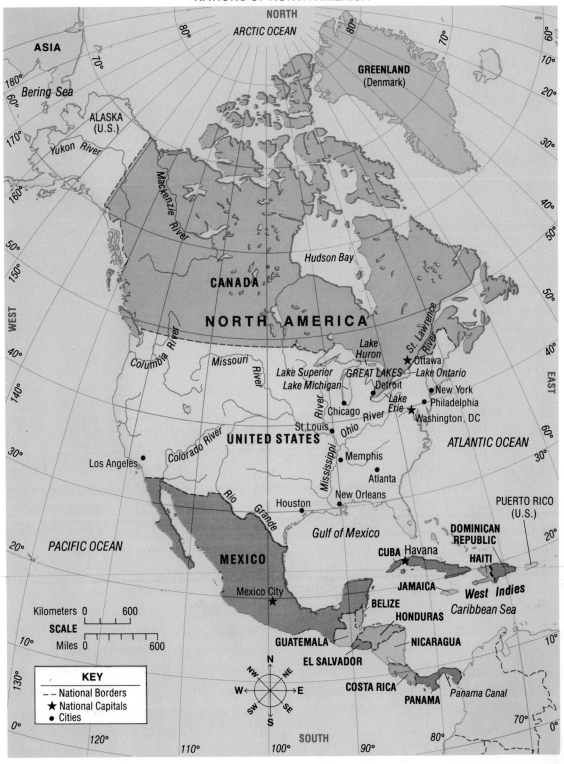

NORTH

ARCTIC OCEAN

80°   80°   70°

ASIA

GREENLAND
(Denmark)

Bering Sea

ALASKA
(U.S.)

Yukon River

Mackenzie River

Hudson Bay

CANADA

NORTH AMERICA

Columbia River

St. Lawrence River

Lake Huron

★ Ottawa   Lake Ontario

Missouri River

Lake Superior   GREAT LAKES

Lake Michigan   Detroit   ● New York

Lake Erie   ● Philadelphia

Chicago   ★ Washington, DC

St. Louis   Ohio River

UNITED STATES

ATLANTIC OCEAN

Colorado River   Mississippi River

Los Angeles ●   Memphis ●

Atlanta ●

Rio Grande   New Orleans

Houston ●   PUERTO RICO
(U.S.)

PACIFIC OCEAN   Gulf of Mexico

DOMINICAN
REPUBLIC

MEXICO   CUBA Havana ★   HAITI

JAMAICA   West Indies

Mexico City ★   BELIZE   Caribbean Sea

HONDURAS

GUATEMALA   NICARAGUA

EL SALVADOR

COSTA RICA

PANAMA   Panama Canal

Kilometers 0 — 600

SCALE

Miles 0 — 600

KEY

- - National Borders

★ National Capitals

● Cities

N
NW   NE
W   E
SW   SE
S

SOUTH

120°   110°   100°   90°   80°   70°   0°

87

The province of Quebec is east of Ontario. The St. Lawrence River flows through the southern part of this province. There is also a city named Quebec. It is on the St. Lawrence River. Find the city of Quebec on the map.

Do you remember what you learned about the Panama Canal? Canals have also been built between the United States and Canada. These canals link the St. Lawrence River and the Great Lakes. The canals are part of the St. Lawrence Seaway. This **seaway** is a water route to and from the ocean. Ships sail from the Atlantic Ocean through the river and canals to the lakes. That way, they

can reach the middle of the United States! These ships carry wheat, wood, coal, and iron ore from one place to another.

Canada has many other large rivers besides the St. Lawrence. It has thousands of islands. It has more lakes than any other nation on Earth! There are many other interesting facts about Canada. It is a nation of differences. In the far north, there is almost always ice and snow. In the south, there are great forests. In the west, there are huge cattle ranches. In the east, on Prince Edward Island, there are small farms. Canada's largest cities are in the south. Look at the map of Canada on

Ships use the St. Lawrence Seaway to travel between the Atlantic Ocean and the Great Lakes.

page 88. Find the cities of Montreal and Toronto. Then find Vancouver and Winnipeg.

One very important difference in Canada is language. Most Canadians speak English. But more than 7 million Canadians speak French. French is the language of the province of Quebec. The city of Montreal is in Quebec. There, French is spoken by almost everyone. Some people want Quebec to become a separate nation. Others want Quebec to remain a part of Canada. Many people in Canada speak both English and French. They like knowing two languages.

Did you know that some children in Maine go to French schools in Canada? Their families are French Canadians. These families moved south to the United States. But they still speak French as their native language. Every school day, the children cross the border into Canada. They go to a French school in the province of Quebec.

Canada has a wealth of natural resources. It also has many factories and manufactures many goods. Canada sells paper, wood, and minerals to the United States. The United States sells cars, clothes, machines, and other goods to Canada. These two giant nations depend on each other. They are good neighbors.

Mexico City is one of the largest cities on Earth. It lies on the Mexican Plateau.

Mexico

The United States has another good neighbor to the south. It is Mexico. Mexico is divided into 31 states and 1 federal district. The full name of the nation is the United Mexican States.

Citizens of Mexico are called Mexicans. Most Mexicans speak Spanish. More than 70 million people live in Mexico today. And the population is growing very fast. When you grow up, Mexico may have more than 125 million people!

Find Mexico on the physical map of North America on page 73. The Gulf of Mexico is on the east. The Pacific Ocean is on the west. Part of Mexico is directly south of California. This part is called Baja (BAH hah) California. The word *baja* means "low" in Spanish. On a map, Baja California looks like a long, narrow finger of land. There is water to the west and east of it. Land almost surrounded by water is called a **peninsula.** Mexico has another peninsula in the southeast. It curves upward like a hook. It is the Yucatán (YOO kuh TAN) Peninsula.

Like Canada, Mexico is a nation of great differences. Much of the north is desert. Much of the south is covered by tropical rain forests. In the east and west are mountains, the Sierra Madres (MAH drays). In the middle of Mexico is the Mexican Plateau. Most of Mexico's people live on the plateau. There, the climate is cool and dry. It is more comfortable than the desert and rain forests.

Mexico City is on the Mexican Plateau. It is the capital of Mexico. It is also one of the largest and highest cities on Earth! More than 9 million people live in Mexico City.

Not all Mexicans live in cities. Most live in villages and raise food on farms. Mexican farmers grow a lot of cotton, corn, and squash. They also raise cattle and grow coffee and sugar cane. Many Mexican farmers are poor. Their farms are small. Sometimes the soil is not very good. Often, these farmers use old-fashioned ways of farming.

Other farms in Mexico are large and modern. They have good soil. The owners of these farms use new and better ways of farming. They add minerals to the soil to make it richer. They use special seeds that grow large crops. They hire people to work in their fields. They use large farm machines. Money is needed to use these methods. Poor farmers cannot afford them. In Mexico, there is a great gap between the rich and the poor. They live very different lives.

Some Mexican families have moved north to the United States. These people are called Mexican-Americans. Their children often go to schools where two languages are used. The children speak Spanish as their native language. They are learning English in school.

Mexico buys many goods from other nations. It buys more than it sells. But this may change. In the 1970s, large amounts of petroleum

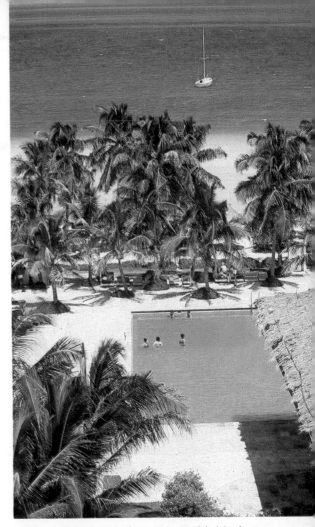

Many people from other nations visit Mexico. Cancun (kan KOON) is a vacation area on the Caribbean Sea.

were found in Mexico. Now, petroleum is Mexico's most important mineral resource. Mexico is selling petroleum to other nations. This resource promises a better future for the people of Mexico.

Central America

South of Mexico is a region called Central America. Central America is between North America and South America. It is part of the continent of North America. But in climate and culture, it is more like South America.

Look at the political map of North America on page 87. Central America has twice as many nations as the rest of North America! Guatemala (GWAH tuh MAH luh) and Honduras (hon DOO russ) are there. So are Nicaragua (NIK uh RAH gwah) and El Salvador. Costa Rica, Panama, and Belize (buh LEEZ) are in Central America, too. Find these nations on the map.

The West Indies

East of Central America are islands called the West Indies. Some of these islands are also nations. Cuba is the largest of these islands. It is a nation. East of Cuba on another island are two more nations. They are Haiti and the Dominican Republic. East of the Dominican Republic is Puerto Rico (PWEHR toh REE koh). Puerto Rico is part of the United States. Many people from Mexico, Central America, and the West Indies now live in the United States.

The Maya built great pyramids. They put temples on top.

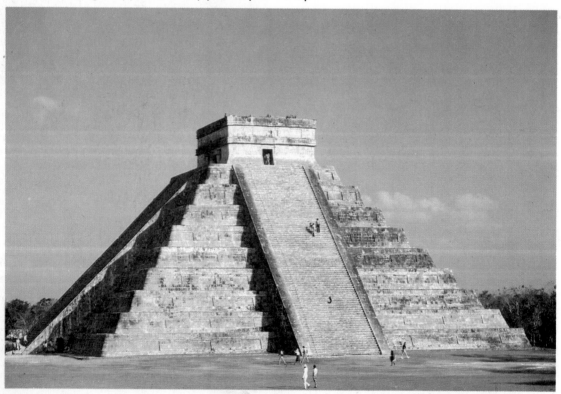

People of North America

We studied the nations of North America from north to south. We can study the people the same way. Experts think the first people came to North America thousands of years ago. At that time, part of the Bering Sea was land. People could walk across from Asia to North America!

The early people who came from Asia are now called American Indians. These people were the first Americans. Some of them stayed in Alaska and Canada. Others settled in the plains and woodlands of the United States. Still others went south to Mexico and Central America. There, they created great cultures long before people from Europe came.

One of the greatest cultures was that of the Maya (MAH yah). The Maya lived on the Yucatán Peninsula. There, they built great **pyramids** (PIR uh midz) with temples on top. A Mayan pyramid was not a tomb. It was a place of worship. The Mayan priests studied the movements of the moon and planets. They were expert at math. They made a calendar as good as the one we use today.

Later, the Aztecs came to power. They built Mexico City on two islands in the middle of a lake. In the lake, they built floating gardens. They grew vegetables and flowers there. Now the lake has been drained and filled in. But you can still visit floating gardens in Mexico City. And in parts of Mexico, you can climb pyramids.

Another group of people from Asia called themselves the Innuit (IN yoo it). *Innuit* means "the people." Others called these people Eskimos. *Eskimo* means "someone who eats raw fish." The Innuit stayed in the far north. They

This Innuit hunter uses a telescope to look for seals.

learned how to live in a cold climate. They fished for their food. They also hunted seals, whales, and deer. They used the animal skins to make clothes, tents, and canoes. They used whale oil for fuel. They kept strong dogs to pull their sleds across the snow. Sometimes, they even built houses out of blocks of ice. A house like this is called an igloo. Some of the Innuit still follow their old ways. Others have found new jobs. Some now work in mines or help drill for petroleum. The Innuit are still using the resources of their land.

In the 1500s, people from Europe began to come to North America. People from Spain came to Mexico and Central America. People from France and England settled in Canada. The English, French, and Spanish also settled in the United States. Since that time, people have come to North America from all over the Earth!

REVIEW

WATCH YOUR WORDS

1. Canada is divided into 10____.
   seaways territories provinces

2. Canada has two ____ in the far north.
   territories provinces states

3. The St. Lawrence River is part of a(n)____.
   peninsula seaway isthmus

4. Baja California is a____.
   seaway province peninsula

5. The Maya built____on the Yucatán Peninsula.
   canals pyramids seaways

CHECK YOUR FACTS

6. What is the largest nation in North America?

7. Do most Canadians live in the northwest or the southeast?

8. Where is the St. Lawrence Seaway? What is it?

9. Name two languages spoken in Canada.

10. What language do most Mexicans speak?

11. What is a peninsula?

12. Where do most Mexicans live? Why?

13. What is Mexico's most important mineral resource?

14. Where is Central America?

15. How did the Innuit use natural resources to live?

THINK ABOUT IT

Why do you think so many people settled in North America?

CHAPTER REVIEW

WATCH YOUR WORDS

1. A waterway was built across the ___ of Panama.
   Gulf   Isthmus   Peninsula

2. Ships can sail from one ocean to another through the Panama ___.
   Sierra   Peninsula   Canal

3. A(n) ___ is part of a canal.
   lock   isthmus   sierra

4. Canals are part of the St. Lawrence ___.
   Isthmus   Seaway   Lake

5. The ___ of Mexico is part of the Atlantic Ocean.
   Lake   Bay   Gulf

6. A ___ is land almost surrounded by water.
   pyramid   peninsula   sierra

7. The grasslands in the middle of North America were called ___.
   foothills   sierras   prairies

8. A(n) ___ is a range of mountains with pointed peaks.
   sierra   isthmus   pyramid

9. You can ___ a resource by using less of it.
   pollute   destroy   conserve

10. You can ___ a resource by keeping it from being destroyed.
    waste   preserve   pollute

CHECK YOUR FACTS

11. Name three of North America's coasts.

12. List three landforms found in North America. Give an example of each.

13. Where are North America's highest mountains?

14. Where are the Great Plains?

15. Name two of North America's longest rivers.

16. How are the Great Lakes like the Great Salt Lake? How do they differ?

17. Name four climates found in North America.

18. List four living resources and four nonliving resources of North America.

19. List two resources that can be renewed and two that cannot.

20. What are the three largest nations of North America?

CLOSE THE MAP GAP

21. Draw or trace an outline map of North America.

22. Label the Rocky Mountains and the Appalachian Mountains.

23. Label the Atlantic Ocean, the Pacific Ocean, the Arctic Ocean, the Bering Sea, the Caribbean Sea, the Gulf of Mexico, and Hudson Bay.

24. Color Canada red, the United States green, Mexico orange, and Central America yellow.

25. Label the capital cities of Canada, the United States, and Mexico.

THINK ABOUT IT

26. How would ships get from the Atlantic Ocean to the Pacific Ocean without the Panama Canal?

27. How are Canada and Mexico alike? How are they different? List as many answers as you can.

28. Suppose you had been one of the early peoples from Asia. Would you have stayed in Alaska or moved to Mexico? Tell why.

TRY SOMETHING NEW

29. Find out more about the Maya, the Aztecs, or the Innuit. Use your library. Then make a report to the class.

2 A NATION OF STATES

Lesson 1: The United States

FIND THE WORDS

colony   state   legislature
Congress   governor   capital
capitol   federal district
commonwealth   territory

The United States is a giant nation. It stretches across the center of North America, from coast to coast. It includes Alaska far in the north. It includes Hawaii far out in the Pacific Ocean. The United States ranks fourth among the world's nations in land. It also ranks fourth in numbers of people. Look at the chart on page 97. It shows which three nations have more land than the United States. It also shows which three nations have more people.

The United States may not be the largest nation in the world. But it is the world's most powerful nation. Size alone does not make a nation great. More important than size is good government.

From Colonies to States

Today, the United States includes 50 states. But the nation began as 13 colonies. A **colony** is an area of land that a foreign country rules. It is also the group of people who settle in such a place.

Great Britain started its first successful colony in North America in 1607. By 1776, there were 13 colonies along the East Coast.

Then, on July 4, 1776, these colonies changed the world. People from the 13 colonies signed the Declaration of Independence. In this paper, the colonies said they were free and independent states. A **state** has its own government. It is not ruled by another country.

The 13 states joined together to form the United States. They set up a new form of government. The states agreed that each state would send representatives to Congress. A group of representatives that meets to make laws is a **legislature** (LEJ iss LAY chur). **Congress** is the legislature of the United States.

The people of each state vote for President. They elect members of Congress. They also elect a governor and a state legislature. A **governor** is the chief leader of a state. In many ways, a governor is like the President.

Every state has a capital city. A **capital** is the city where the government of a state or a nation meets. A capital city is usually marked on a map with a star.

A **capitol** is a building where a legislature meets. In the capital city of your state, you can see the capitol building. The capital of the United States is Washington, DC. The Capitol is the building in Washington where Congress meets. Look at the picture of the Capitol on page 96.

FIVE LARGE NATIONS

Nation	Area		Number of people
	square miles	square kilometers	
SOVIET UNION	8,649,489	22,402,200	261,569,000
CANADA	3,851,787	9,976,128	23,499,000
CHINA	3,691,502	9,561,000	933,032,000
UNITED STATES	3,615,191	9,363,353	226,504,825
INDIA	1,261,810	3,268,090	638,388,000

Other Parts of the Whole

Some parts of the United States are not states. The nation also includes the District of Columbia and the Commonwealth of Puerto Rico. Several territories are also part of the United States.

The District of Columbia is between Maryland and Virginia. It is a **federal district.** That is an area where a national capital is located. The City of Washington is in the District of Columbia. So it is called Washington, DC. The city and the district are exactly the same size. That way, the national capital is not in any state.

The Commonwealth of Puerto Rico (PWEHR toh REE koh) is on islands south of Florida. A **commonwealth** is a place that is governed by its people. Some states are called commonwealths. Puerto Rico is not a state. But it is part of the United States.

A U.S. **territory** is an area governed by the United States. It is not a state, district, or commonwealth. However, 31 of the 50 states were once territories or parts of territories. The United States now has several island territories. Guam is an island territory in the Pacific Ocean.

REVIEW

WATCH YOUR WORDS

1. The city where a state government meets is the ___.
   capitol   Congress   capital
2. The building where a state legislature meets is the ___.
   capital   capitol   colony
3. A ___ is a group that meets to make laws.
   capitol   legislature   state
4. Puerto Rico is a ___.
   territory   state   commonwealth
5. Guam is a ___.
   state   territory   district
6. Washington, DC, is in a ___.
   federal district   state   colony

CHECK YOUR FACTS

7. What is the difference between a colony and a state?
8. How many states were there when the United States began?

USE YOUR CHART

9. What nations are larger than the United States in both land and people?
10. What nation has more land but fewer people? What nation has more people but less land?

THINK ABOUT IT

Why shouldn't the nation's capital be in one of the states?

Lesson 2: The New England States

Maine   New Hampshire   Vermont
Massachusetts   Rhode Island   Connecticut

FIND THE WORDS

bay   hardwood   softwood

Six states in the northeast are known as New England. They are Maine, New Hampshire, Vermont, Massachusetts, Rhode Island, and Connecticut. Look at the chart on this page. The six states in New England are small in area. Even so, several of these states have many people. Most of the people live in southern New England.

Many live along the Atlantic Coast.

The coast of New England is rocky and uneven. Find Cape Cod on the map on page 101. It is a hook of land that juts into the Atlantic Ocean. There, in a sheltered bay, the Pilgrims landed in 1620. **A bay** is a part of the ocean with land part way around it.

The Pilgrims had sailed from Plymouth, England, to Massachusetts. There, they started the first lasting colony north of Virginia.

THE NEW ENGLAND STATES

State name and nickname	Date state entered union	Area square miles	Area square kilometers	Number of people	State capital
Maine (Pine Tree State)	1820	33,215	86,027	1,124,660	Augusta
New Hampshire (Granite State)	1788	9,304	24,097	920,610	Concord
Vermont (Green Mountain State)	1791	9,609	24,887	511,456	Montpelier
Massachusetts (Bay State)	1788	8,257	21,386	5,737,037	Boston
Rhode Island (Ocean State)	1790	1,214	3,144	947,154	Providence
Connecticut (Constitution State)	1788	5,009	12,973	3,107,576	Hartford

Another group from England, the Puritans, came next. Soon, some settlers left Massachusetts to start other colonies. By 1790, four New England colonies were states of the United States.

Land and Climate

West of the coast, New England has many highlands and mountains. Several Appalachian Mountain ranges are in New England. In summer, visitors can hike in the Green Mountains of Vermont. They can listen to music in the Berkshire Hills of Massachusetts. They can also visit the White Mountains of New Hampshire. Some of the White Mountains are named for Presidents. The tallest is Mount Washington. There, visitors can ride in a train to the top of the mountain.

New England has a varied climate. In spring and fall, the air is crisp and cool. Winters are cold and snowy. Then, people from many Eastern states come to the mountains to ski. In summer, the weather gets warm or hot. Then, many people go swimming and boating at Cape Cod. New England is also famous for its forests. Fall brings a blaze of color to the

FUN FACTS

Many people think Captain John Smith named New England because the coast reminded him of England. Settlers often named their new homes for the places they had left.

What is a Yankee? A Yankee can be a Northerner in general or a New Englander in particular. In other nations, a Yankee can be any citizen of the United States.

Massachusetts was the place where the Pilgrims landed in 1620. The first Thanksgiving was celebrated there.

Maine once held its elections 2 months before the other states did. People believed other states would vote the way Maine had. They said, "As Maine goes, so goes the nation."

New Hampshire is always the first state to choose a candidate for President. Everyone running for President tries to get New Hampshire's votes.

Rhode Island is the smallest state. But it has more people than the largest state, Alaska! Rhode Island was founded by Roger Williams and Anne Hutchinson. Each of them went there to find religious freedom.

Connecticut was the first state to use modern methods of manufacturing. It was the home of Eli Whitney, a famous inventor.

Vermont is famous for its mountains, marble, and maple syrup. The Green Mountains gave the state its name. *Ver mont* means "green mountain" in French.

Sometimes, you could get blown away on top of Mount Washington in New Hampshire. This mountain had one of the highest surface winds ever recorded on Earth. On April 12, 1934, the wind blew there at 372 kilometers (231 miles) per hour!

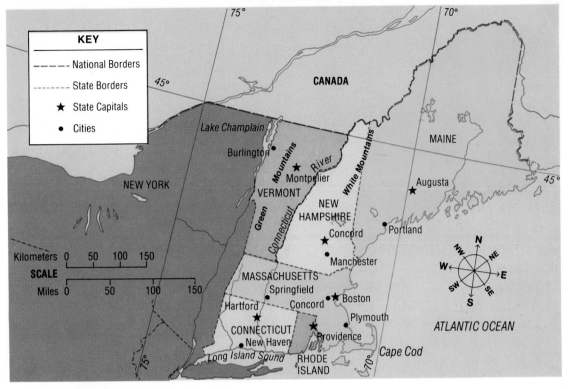

region. The leaves turn brilliant shades of red, yellow, and gold. Many visitors travel to New England to see the autumn leaves.

Resources

For New England, the Atlantic Ocean is a valuable resource. In the past, many of the people made a living by fishing. Some New Englanders hunted whales all over the world. Others caught fish such as cod and mackerel. New England is still famous for its fish and shellfish. Many people like to eat New England clam chowder.

Land in New England is not very good for farming. In most places, the soil is very thin. But New England is a good place for dairy farms. The cows can eat grass on the hillsides. The poor soil can be used to grow hay. People in the cities buy the milk products. Vermont is famous for its cheese.

Some parts of New England are known for special farm products. In Maine, farmers grow potatoes. In Vermont, people make maple syrup from the sap of sugar maple trees. Rhode Island is noted for its chickens, called Rhode Island Reds. In Massachusetts, farmers grow cranberries for cranberry sauce.

Visitors to Plymouth Plantation see what a Pilgrim village was like.

The thick forests of northern New England are another living resource. Some of the trees are cut down for their wood. Trees that lose their leaves, such as oaks and maples, are **hardwoods.** Hardwood goes to sawmills. It is cut into boards and used to build things. Trees with cones and needles, such as pines, are **softwoods.** Softwood can be ground up and used to make pulp. Then the wood pulp is used to make paper.

Manufacturing, Business, and Trade

Most people in New England make their living by manufacturing. Once, most factories in the United States were in New England. The mills of New England spun the nation's cotton and woolen cloth. Other New England factories made shoes and boots. New Englanders became famous as traders. Yankee merchants were known all over the world. The nation's fastest sailing ships were built in Mystic, Connecticut.

Today, New England still makes cloth and paper products. But now many cloth and clothing factories have moved to the Southern States. Some new factories have come to take their place. Now machines and plastics are made in New England. So are electrical products. Airplane engines, helicopters, and submarines are built in Connecticut.

Many New Englanders provide services to visitors. They run restaurants, gift shops, and hotels. New England is noted for its schools. It has famous colleges such as Harvard and Yale.

Places to Go

In December 1620, the Pilgrims anchored their ship, the *Mayflower*, near Plymouth Rock. Today, you can still see Plymouth Rock in Plymouth, Massachusetts. You can visit a ship built to look like the *Mayflower*. You can also visit a "living museum" nearby. It is called Plymouth Plantation. The people who work there dress like Pilgrims. You can see what life in a Pilgrim village was like.

Boston is the capital of Massachusetts. In Boston, you can walk along the Freedom Trail. You can see many places that have been important in American history.

REVIEW

WATCH YOUR WORDS

1. A ____ tree loses its leaves in the fall.
   softwood   hardwood   prairie

2. A ____ tree has needles and cones.
   prairie   hardwood   softwood

3. A(n) ____ is part of the ocean partly surrounded by land.
   peninsula   bay   island

CHECK YOUR FACTS

4. List the six states in New England.

5. Where and when did the Pilgrims land?

6. List four farm products of New England.

7. What are two ways in which wood is used?

8. List three modern products made in New England.

USE YOUR CHART

9. Four New England states were among the original 13 states. List them.

10. What was the last New England state to enter the Union?

11. Which New England state has the most land?

12. Which New England state has the most people?

13. Does the state with the least land have the fewest people?

USE YOUR MAP

14. Which New England state is not on the Atlantic Coast?

15. Name the river that forms the border between New Hampshire and Vermont.

CLOSE THE MAP GAP

16. Draw or trace an outline map of the United States. Draw the borders of the New England States. Label each state and its capital. Also label the Atlantic Ocean. Keep your map. Soon, you will have all 50 states on it.

THINK ABOUT IT

Suppose you could visit New England. In what season would you go? What things would you most like to see?

Lesson 3: The Middle Atlantic States

New York   New Jersey   Pennsylvania
Delaware   Maryland   West Virginia

FIND THE WORDS

harbor   natural gas   port

The Middle Atlantic States are south or west of the New England States. Six states and the District of Columbia are in this region. More than 40 million people live in the Middle Atlantic States. That is about 18 out of every 100 people in the United States.

People from northern Europe settled the Middle Atlantic States. Five of the Middle Atlantic States were among the original 13 states. In fact, Delaware was the first state to join the Union.

Land and Climate

Mountains stretch across much of New York, Pennsylvania, and West Virginia. You can see them on the map. Find the Adirondack

MIDDLE ATLANTIC STATES

KEY
— — — National Borders
⭐ National Capital
— — — State Borders
★ State Capitals
• Cities

CANADA
St. Lawrence River
Lake Champlain
ADIRONDACK MOUNTAINS
NEW YORK
VERMONT
Lake Ontario
Rochester
Niagara Falls
Buffalo Syracuse
Mohawk River
Albany
MASSACHUSETTS
Lake Erie
Allegheny River
Hudson River
CONNECTICUT
PENNSYLVANIA
Susquehanna River
Delaware River
Long Island Sound
Long Island
OHIO
Newark
New York City
Wheeling Pittsburgh Harrisburg
Trenton
Philadelphia Camden
Monongahela River
Baltimore
Wilmington
NEW JERSEY
Atlantic City
Potomac River
Dover
Ohio River
Delaware Bay
ATLANTIC OCEAN
WEST VIRGINIA
Charleston
Washington
DISTRICT OF COLUMBIA
Annapolis
DELAWARE
Kanawha R.
MARYLAND
KENTUCKY
APPALACHIAN MOUNTAINS
VIRGINIA
Chesapeake Bay

SCALE
Kilometers 0   100   200
Miles 0   100   200

80°   70°   40°

Mountains in New York. Then find the mountains in Pennsylvania, Maryland, and West Virginia. These ranges are part of the Appalachian Mountain chain.

Not many people live in the mountains. But millions of people live on the low plain along the coast. There, the land is flat and the climate is favorable. Look at the map again. Trace with your finger from New York City to Washington, DC. Few regions of Earth have as many people as this region. Some of the nation's largest cities are here. Find New York, Philadelphia, Baltimore, and Washington on the map. There are many more cities along the coast. The Middle Atlantic coast has good harbors for ships. **A harbor** is a protected place on a coast where ships can anchor. Other large cities are found near the Great Lakes and near important rivers.

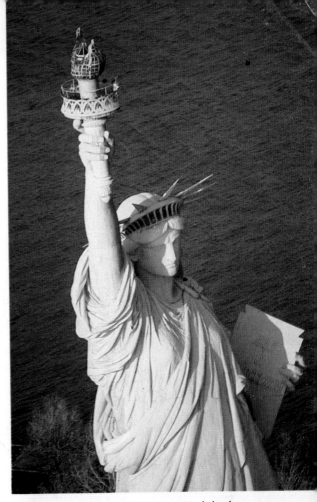

The Statue of Liberty is in New York harbor.

Resources

The Middle Atlantic States have farms as well as cities. There are large poultry farms in Maryland, Delaware, and New Jersey. They supply millions of chickens and eggs. All the Middle Atlantic States have vegetable farms. New York also has dairy farms. Still, the states of the Middle Atlantic region do not raise all the food they need. They buy a lot of their food from other regions.

Rivers, lakes, and the Atlantic Ocean are natural resources of this region. Pennsylvania and West Virginia have important mineral resources, too. West Virginia supplies much of the nation's coal and natural gas. **Natural gas** is a mixture of gases found in the ground. Like coal, it is used as a fuel. Coal and iron ore are found in Pennsylvania. They are used to make steel. There are many steel mills in Pennsylvania.

THE MIDDLE ATLANTIC STATES

State name and nickname	Date state entered union	Area square miles	Area square kilometers	Number of people	State capital
New York (Empire State)	1788	49,576	128,402	17,557,288	Albany
New Jersey (Garden State)	1787	7,836	20,295	7,364,158	Trenton
Pennsylvania (Keystone State)	1787	45,333	117,412	11,866,728	Harrisburg
Delaware (First State)	1787	2,057	5,328	595,225	Dover
Maryland (Old Line State)	1788	10,577	27,394	4,216,446	Annapolis
West Virginia (Mountain State)	1863	24,181	62,629	1,949,644	Charleston

FUN FACTS

The United States has had three capitals. All three have been in the Middle Atlantic region. New York City was the first capital of the United States. In 1789, George Washington was sworn in as President in New York. Philadelphia was the capital from 1790 until 1800. Then Washington, DC, became the capital in 1800.

Pennsylvania was founded by William Penn. The state name means "Penn's woods" in Latin.

New Jersey was the scene of 90 battles in the American Revolution. In one battle, Mary Ludwig Hays carried water to the soldiers. They called her Molly Pitcher. Another woman, Margaret Corbin, fought bravely in a battle in New York.

Delaware is the second-smallest state in the nation. It was named for Baron De la Warr. Until 1792, Delaware had a president, not a governor.

Maryland was a scene of battle in the War of 1812. There, the British attacked a fort in Baltimore. British ships fired bombs at the fort. But they could not get too close. The Americans had sunk ships to block the harbor. When the attack was over, the American flag was still flying. This inspired Francis Scott Key to write our national anthem, "The Star-Spangled Banner."

West Virginia wanted to stay in the Union during the Civil War. So it separated from Virginia and became the 35th state.

Manufacturing and Transportation

Many factories are found in the Middle Atlantic States. New York makes a variety of products, from clothing to cameras. New York, New Jersey, and Pennsylvania make machines and chemicals. West Virginia manufactures glass. Steel is made in Pennsylvania and West Virginia. These are only a few of the many products made in the Middle Atlantic States.

The Middle Atlantic States have many means of transportation. They have long highways, bridges, and tunnels. They have many railroads and airports. They have good river ports and sea-ports. A **port** is a town on the water where ships can load and unload. Cars, trucks, trains, planes, and ships move people and goods around.

Places to Go

New York is the largest city in the United States. In fact, it is one of the largest cities in the world. At New York, the Hudson River flows into the Atlantic Ocean. The harbor there is a fine place for ships to anchor. Ships and planes from all over the world come to New York. New York also has busy highways and railroads. It is a center of transportation.

Most of the nation's books and magazines are published in New York. Many television programs are made there. New York is world-famous for its Broadway plays. News and ideas from New York go all over the nation.

Every year, millions of people visit New York. They go to see the Statue of Liberty and the Empire State Building. They visit Wall Street, where traders buy and sell shares in the nation's businesses.

Independence Hall is in Philadelphia. The Declaration of Independence was signed there on July 4, 1776.

Philadelphia is another great city in this region. Independence Hall is in Philadelphia. In 1776, the Declaration of Independence was signed in Independence Hall. You can see the room where it was signed. Philadelphia is also the home of the Liberty Bell. The United States Mint was started in Philadelphia. The mint is the place which makes the nation's money. In Philadelphia, you can see how money is made. You can also visit the house where Betsy Ross lived. Some people believe she made the first American flag.

REVIEW

WATCH YOUR WORDS

1. A protected place on a coast where ships can anchor is a(n)____.
   isthmus   harbor   canal
2. A town on the water where ships can unload is a____.
   port   lock   seaway
3. ____ is a mixture of gases found in the ground.
   Coal   Iron ore   Natural gas

CHECK YOUR FACTS

4. List the six states of the Middle Atlantic region.
5. Which was the first state to join the Union?
6. List four large cities in the Middle Atlantic region.
7. Name a mineral resource that is found in both Pennsylvania and West Virginia.
8. Where was the Declaration of Independence signed?

USE YOUR CHART

9. Which Middle Atlantic state has the most people?
10. Which Middle Atlantic state entered the Union last?
11. Find a very small state with more than 5 million people

USE YOUR MAP

12. Which Middle Atlantic states are not on the Atlantic Coast?
13. What river forms the boundary between Pennsylvania and New Jersey?

CLOSE THE MAP GAP

14. Add the Middle Atlantic States to your map of the United States. Label each state and its capital. Also label Washington, DC, Lake Ontario, and the St. Lawrence River.

THINK ABOUT IT

15. What kinds of transportation does your state have?
16. Why did people build cities on seacoasts and by lakes and rivers?

Lesson 4: The Southern States

Virginia North Carolina South Carolina Georgia Florida Kentucky Tennessee Alabama Mississippi Arkansas Louisiana Oklahoma Texas

FIND THE WORDS

wilderness barge delta swamp refine

There are 13 states in the South. The Southern States cover almost a fourth of the land in the United States. They have more than a fourth of the people. About 67 million people live in the Southern States. That is 30 out of every 100 Americans.

Today, the South is growing faster than most other parts of the nation. Many people and businesses are moving to the Southern States. These states have a mild climate. All 13 states gained population from 1970 to 1980.

THE SOUTH

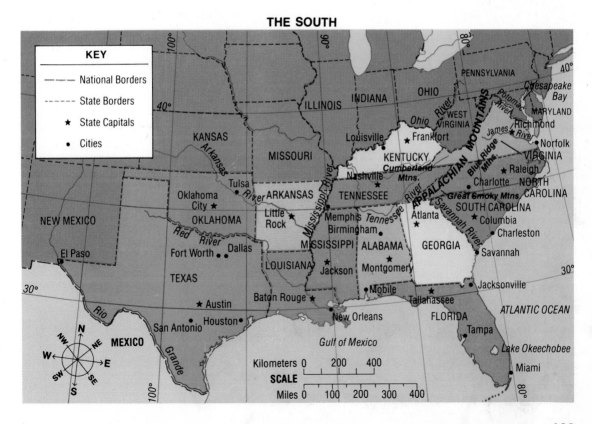

KEY

----- National Borders
- - - - State Borders
★ State Capitals
• Cities

PENNSYLVANIA
Chesapeake Bay
40°
MARYLAND
OHIO
INDIANA
WEST VIRGINIA
Richmond
ILLINOIS
Ohio River
James River
Norfolk
40°
Louisville
Frankfort
VIRGINIA
KANSAS
MISSOURI
KENTUCKY
Raleigh
Cumberland Mtns.
Nashville
Charlotte
NORTH CAROLINA
Tulsa
River
Arkansas
ARKANSAS
TENNESSEE
Great Smoky Mtns.
SOUTH CAROLINA
Oklahoma City ★
Little Rock ★
Memphis
Tennessee
Atlanta ★
Columbia
NEW MEXICO
OKLAHOMA
Birmingham
Charleston
Red River
Dallas
MISSISSIPPI
ALABAMA
GEORGIA
Savannah
El Paso
Fort Worth
LOUISIANA
Jackson
Montgomery
TEXAS
Mobile
Jacksonville
30°
Austin ★
Baton Rouge ★
Tallahassee
Rio Grande
San Antonio
Houston
New Orleans
FLORIDA
ATLANTIC OCEAN
30°
MEXICO
Gulf of Mexico
Tampa
Lake Okeechobee
Kilometers 0 200 400
Miami
SCALE
Miles 0 100 200 300 400
APPALACHIAN MOUNTAINS
Blue Ridge Mtns.
Potomac River
Mississippi River
Savannah River

N NE E SE S SW W NW

109

History

The South has always been a very important region. The history of the colonies and the nation began there. In 1565, the Spanish built a fort at St. Augustine, Florida. This was the first lasting European settlement in the United States. Later, in 1607, the first lasting English colony began in Jamestown, Virginia.

Virginia, North Carolina, South Carolina, and Georgia were among the original 13 states. All four of these states are on the East Coast. Next, settlers began to move west of the Appalachian Mountains. For a long time, these mountains had blocked the way west. Then, explorers found the Cumberland Gap. It was a natural opening between the mountains. American Indian trails led on into Kentucky. In 1775, Daniel Boone marked and connected these trails. Boone's big trail was called the Wilderness Road. **Wilderness** is wild land where no one lives. The Wilderness Road opened up this mountain region to settlers. Now people could go from Virginia into Kentucky and Tennessee.

Then, in 1803, the United States bought Louisiana from France. Louisiana was a huge region. It stretched from the Mississippi River to the Rocky Mountains. What is now the state of Louisiana was only a small part of it. The Louisiana Purchase doubled the size of the United States. Look at the map on the next page. You can see how much land was added in 1803.

The United States got Florida from Spain. Florida was a territory before it was a state. Texas was an independent nation. Until 1835, Texas was part of Mexico. Then the Texans fought for their independence. For 9 years, Texas was a nation. Then, in 1845, Texas became a state.

The last Southern state to enter the Union was Oklahoma. For many years, Oklahoma was an American Indian territory. In 1907, Oklahoma became a state.

Land and Climate

Most of the land in the Southern States is a low plain. The land is level along the Atlantic and Gulf coasts. In some places, the coastal plain goes inland for hundreds of miles. Many rivers flow through the plain. Much fertile soil is found there.

Appalachian Mountain ranges stretch across many states in the region. Have you heard of the beautiful Blue Ridge Mountains of Virginia? Actually, these mountains go all the way from Georgia to Pennsylvania. The Great Smoky Mountains stretch along the border between North Carolina and Tennessee. Forests grow there.

110

WHERE WE ARE IN TIME AND PLACE

STATES OF THE UNITED STATES

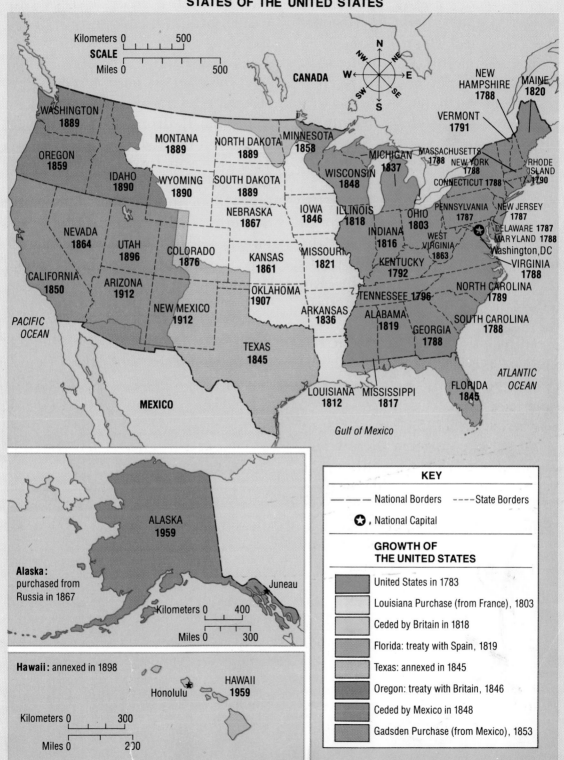

Kilometers 0 — 500
SCALE
Miles 0 — 500

N NW NE W E SW SE S

CANADA

NEW HAMPSHIRE 1788
MAINE 1820
VERMONT 1791

WASHINGTON 1889

MONTANA 1889
NORTH DAKOTA 1889
MINNESOTA 1858
MICHIGAN 1837
MASSACHUSETTS 1788
NEW YORK 1788
RHODE ISLAND 1790
CONNECTICUT 1788

OREGON 1859

IDAHO 1890
WYOMING 1890
SOUTH DAKOTA 1889
WISCONSIN 1848

NEBRASKA 1867
IOWA 1846
ILLINOIS 1818
OHIO 1803
PENNSYLVANIA 1787
NEW JERSEY 1787
DELAWARE 1787
MARYLAND 1788

NEVADA 1864
UTAH 1896
COLORADO 1876
KANSAS 1861
MISSOURI 1821
INDIANA 1816
WEST VIRGINIA 1863
Washington, DC
VIRGINIA 1788

CALIFORNIA 1850
ARIZONA 1912
KENTUCKY 1792
NORTH CAROLINA 1789

NEW MEXICO 1912
OKLAHOMA 1907
TENNESSEE 1796
SOUTH CAROLINA 1788

ARKANSAS 1836
ALABAMA 1819
GEORGIA 1788

TEXAS 1845

PACIFIC OCEAN

ATLANTIC OCEAN

MEXICO

LOUISIANA 1812
MISSISSIPPI 1817
FLORIDA 1845

Gulf of Mexico

ALASKA 1959

Alaska: purchased from Russia in 1867

Juneau

Kilometers 0 — 400
Miles 0 — 300

Hawaii: annexed in 1898

HAWAII 1959
Honolulu

Kilometers 0 — 300
Miles 0 — 200

KEY

— — — National Borders
- - - - State Borders
⭐ National Capital

GROWTH OF THE UNITED STATES

- United States in 1783
- Louisiana Purchase (from France), 1803
- Ceded by Britain in 1818
- Florida: treaty with Spain, 1819
- Texas: annexed in 1845
- Oregon: treaty with Britain, 1846
- Ceded by Mexico in 1848
- Gadsden Purchase (from Mexico), 1853

East of these mountain ranges is the Piedmont (PEED mont) Plateau. *Piedmont* means "at the foot of a mountain." Parts of Virginia, the Carolinas, Georgia, and Alabama are on this low plateau. It slopes gently downward from the mountains to the coast. Many rivers flow from the mountains through the Piedmont to the sea.

The Southern States have many important rivers. Look at the map on page 109. Find the James River where the colony of Jamestown was started. Find the Ohio River. It forms Kentucky's northern border. Find the Rio Grande. It forms the boundary between Texas and Mexico.

Now find the Mississippi River. This river is a "road" through the middle of the nation. Long, flat boats called **barges** carry goods up and down the river. Barges can travel by water from the Great Lakes to the Gulf of Mexico.

The soil in the Mississippi River valley is very fertile. The river carries rich black soil full of minerals. It drops the soil before it flows into the Gulf of Mexico. This rich soil forms a very fertile area called a **delta.** Many crops are grown in the rich delta soil. Sometimes, the river overflows before it reaches the ocean. Then it leaves some of the rich soil along its banks.

Forests cover much of the land in the Southern States. Many kinds of pine trees grow in this region. Swamps are also found

FUN FACTS

Five Southern states were named for rulers in Europe. Virginia was named for Queen Elizabeth I of England. She was known as the Virgin Queen. North and South Carolina were named for King Charles I of England. King George II of England gave his name to Georgia. Louisiana was named for King Louis XIV of France.

Ponce de León named Florida. Florida means "full of flowers." The names of the other Southern states come from American Indian languages. Mississippi means "big river." Kentucky means "level land, or plain." Arkansas means "downstream from the Kansas River." Oklahoma means "red people." Texas means "allies, or friends."

North Carolina was the first place in America where English people lived. In 1587, Sir Walter Raleigh sent men, women, and children to settle there. They built a fort on Roanoke Island. A baby, Virginia Dare, was born. Then the leader of the colony sailed back to England for supplies. When he returned, the colonists were gone. Did all of them die? Did some move away? The Lost Colony remains a mystery to this day.

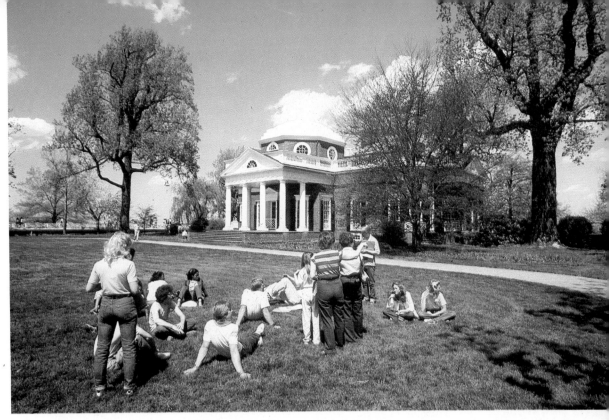

This is Monticello, which means "little mountain." It was the home of Thomas Jefferson, our third President. Jefferson built his home in the foothills of the Blue Ridge Mountains of Virginia.

along the coastal plains. **Swamps** are low, wet lands largely covered with water. Trees and grasses grow in the swamps. Many birds, fish, and small animals live there.

The states farthest south are often called the Sunbelt. This region gets a lot of light and heat from the sun all year. Most states in the South have long, hot summers. They have short, mild winters. They get a lot of rain in all seasons. Snow has sometimes fallen in every Southern state. Winters in western Texas and Oklahoma can be very cold and

windy. But winters in the South are milder and shorter than winters in New England.

Long summers and heavy rains are good for crops. In the states farthest south, crops can grow almost all year. No other part of the nation has a better climate for farming. The warm, sunny climate also saves energy. Less fuel is needed for heat and light.

Resources

Fertile soil, sunshine, and rain are natural resources. So are minerals that can be burned

The Oklahoma state capitol building has an oil well in its yard.

for energy. Texas is famous for oil wells. Texas and Louisiana lead the nation in producing petroleum and natural gas. The state of Oklahoma also has these fuels. Coal is found in Kentucky, Tennessee, and Virginia. Alabama has both coal and iron ore. So steel can be made in Alabama.

Farming is very important in the Southern States. Once, cotton was the South's main crop. The South was known as "the land of cotton." Cotton is still the leading crop in Texas and Mississippi. It is important in many states of the South. But now, many farmers raise cattle or soybeans instead of cotton. Texas and Oklahoma have huge cattle and sheep ranches. There, cattle are raised for meat and sheep for wool. Many Southern farmers also raise cattle on dairy farms. Poultry farms in the South supply many of the nation's chickens. Some farmers raise hogs for ham. Kentucky is famous for its beautiful racehorses.

All over the South, farmers grow fruits, vegetables, and grains. Corn, wheat, and soybeans grow in many Southern states. Along the Gulf Coast, farmers grow rice and sugar cane. They grow peanuts and pecans in Georgia and Alabama. They raise tobacco in North Carolina, South Carolina, Virginia, and Kentucky. Florida oranges and Georgia peaches are famous all over the nation.

Southern forests are a big source of wood and paper. Many Southern towns have furniture factories and paper mills. Once, farmers burned trees to clear land for farming. Now, they plant trees and harvest them like crops.

Manufacturing

Today in the South, more people are living in towns and cities. Fewer people are living on farms. Large machines do much of the farm work. There are more jobs for people in towns. Many factories have moved to the Southern States. The Southern States make cloth and clothing. They prepare and package foods. They make paper and furniture. They produce chemicals and make machines. Alabama manufactures steel. Texas and Louisiana **refine** petroleum. That means they make it into useful products such as gasoline and heating oil. Atomic energy is produced in Oak Ridge, Tennessee.

Places to Go

You can visit the past and the present in the Southern States. On Roanoke Island in North Carolina, you can see a play about Sir Wal-

ter Raleigh's Lost Colony. In Virginia, you can visit Jamestown and see how the early settlers lived. Then you can go on to nearby Williamsburg. This city was rebuilt to look as it did 200 years ago. You will find the grace and charm of the past in many Southern cities. St. Augustine, Florida, is the oldest city in the United States.

Williamsburg, Virginia, is near Jamestown. In Williamsburg, you can see what life was like in a Southern city 200 years ago.

In Louisiana, you will not want to miss New Orleans. There, past and present come together in the French Quarter. It is an old part of the city that has been preserved. In Texas, remember the Alamo! The Alamo is a church and fort in San Antonio. In 1836, brave Texans died there fighting for their freedom.

You may want to visit some of the beautiful cities on the Gulf Coast. Mobile (moh BEEL), Alabama, and Biloxi (buh LOK see), Mississippi, are two of these.

The Southern States are also an important part of the space age. The Kennedy Space Center is in Florida. There, United States space rockets blast off. Mission control for the flights is in Houston, Texas, at the Lyndon B. Johnson Space Center. The Alabama Space and Rocket Center is in Huntsville, Alabama. There, visitors can find out how it might feel to travel to the moon.

Today, the cities of the South are growing. Seventeen Southern cities are among the 50 largest cities in the United States.

Atlanta, Georgia, is one of the great cities of America. It is a major center of transportation. Railways and highways come together there. Many major airlines also fly through Atlanta. Recently, Atlanta opened one of the largest, busiest, most modern airports in the world.

FUN FACTS

Tennessee supplies electric power to a whole region. It is the home of the Tennessee Valley Authority. The TVA was set up by the federal government. Dams were built to stop the Tennessee River from flooding. Then the force of moving water was used to make electricity. Now coal and nuclear energy are also used to make electric power.

Alabama is the home of a famous college, Tuskegee Institute. It was founded by Booker T. Washington. The great scientist George Washington Carver worked there. He developed hundreds of new products from peanuts, sweet potatoes, and soybeans. Both Booker T. Washington and George Washington Carver were born slaves.

Virginia is known as "the Mother of Presidents." Four of the first five Presidents were from Virginia. They were George Washington, Thomas Jefferson, James Madison, and James Monroe.

South Carolina is a safe place to visit today. But once, its ships and coastal towns were attacked by pirates such as Blackbeard.

Oklahoma is called "the Sooner State." In 1889, the United States opened up some Oklahoma lands to settlers. At noon on April 22, settlers could rush into the state. The first to reach each piece of land could claim it. Some settlers sneaked in early to claim the best lands. They were called "Sooners" because they got there first.

THE SOUTHERN STATES

State name and nickname		Date state entered union	Area square miles	Area square kilometers	Number of people	State capital
Virginia (Old Dominion)		1788	40,815	105,711	5,346,279	Richmond
North Carolina (Tar Heel State)		1789	52,586	136,198	5,874,429	Raleigh
South Carolina (Palmetto State)		1788	31,055	80,432	3,119,208	Columbia
Georgia (Empire State of the South)		1788	58,876	152,489	5,464,265	Atlanta
Florida (Sunshine State)		1845	58,560	151,670	9,739,992	Tallahassee
Kentucky (Bluegrass State)		1792	40,395	104,623	3,661,433	Frankfort
Tennessee (Volunteer State)		1796	42,244	109,412	4,590,750	Nashville
Alabama (Yellowhammer State)		1819	51,609	133,667	3,890,061	Montgomery
Mississippi (Magnolia State)		1817	47,716	123,584	2,520,638	Jackson
Arkansas (Land of Opportunity)		1836	53,104	137,539	2,285,513	Little Rock
Louisiana (Pelican State)		1812	48,523	125,675	4,203,972	Baton Rouge
Oklahoma (Sooner State)		1907	69,919	181,090	3,025,266	Oklahoma City
Texas (Lone Star State)		1845	267,339	692,408	14,228,383	Austin

REVIEW

WATCH YOUR WORDS

1. A ___ is formed by soil that a river drops just before it flows into the sea.
   swamp prairie delta

2. ___ are low, wet lands.
   Sierras Swamps Plateaus

3. A ___ is wild land where no one lives.
   coast peninsula wilderness

4. A ___ is a long, flat boat.
   barge canal delta

5. Petroleum is made into gasoline by ___.
   conservation refining pollution

CHECK YOUR FACTS

6. List the 13 states in the Southern region.

7. The Louisiana Purchase (did/did not) double the size of the United States.

8. Which Southern state was once an independent nation?

9. Which Southern state was once an American Indian territory?

10. List three landforms found in the Southern States.

11. Where is the Piedmont Plateau?

12. What causes a delta to form?

13. What important mineral resources are found in Texas? In Alabama?

14. List four crops that are raised in the Southern States.

15. List three of the products made in Southern factories.

USE YOUR CHART

16. What Southern states joined the Union in the 1700s? List them.

17. Which Southern state has the most land?

18. Which two Southern states have the most people?

USE YOUR MAP

19. Which Southern states are on the Atlantic Coast?

20. Which Southern states are on the Gulf Coast?

21. Which Southern states are on the Mississippi River?

CLOSE THE MAP GAP

22. Add the Southern States to your map of the United States. Label each state and its capital. Also label the Mississippi River, the Ohio River, the Rio Grande, and the Gulf of Mexico.

THINK ABOUT IT

What three places in the South would you most like to visit? Tell why.

Lesson 5: The Midwestern States

**Ohio   Michigan   Indiana   Wisconsin   Illinois
Minnesota   Iowa   Missouri   North Dakota
South Dakota   Nebraska   Kansas**

FIND THE WORD

breadbasket

There are 12 states in the Midwestern region. This region is sometimes called the Middle West. Do not be fooled by this name. Some of these states are in the middle of the United States. But none of them is in the West. The Middle West was named long ago by people in the East. To them, the land around the Great Lakes was the West. Later, the land near the Pacific Ocean was called the Far West. So the Great Lakes region became the Middle West.

Look at the map of the Midwestern States on page 121. Six of these states border on the Great Lakes. The Missouri and Mississippi rivers flow through the states west of the lakes. About 59 million people live in the Midwestern States. That is 26 out of every 100 Americans.

The six Great Lakes states were once part of the Northwest Territory. The United States won the Northwest Territory from Great Britain in the Revolution. It included Ohio, Indiana, Illinois, Michigan, Wisconsin, and eastern Minnesota. Find these states on the map on page 121.

Missouri, Iowa, Kansas, Nebraska, and South Dakota were part of the Louisiana Purchase. So was western Minnesota and part of North Dakota.

During the 1800s, the lands of the Midwest were settled and became states. Ohio entered the Union first, in 1803. The Dakotas did not have enough people to be states until 1889. New settlers came there when the railroad was built. Many came all the way from Norway, Sweden, and Germany.

These people settled on the Great Plains 100 years ago. They built this sod house there. Sod is earth held together by roots of grass.

Land and Climate

Almost all the land in the Midwestern States is level. East of the Missouri River is the Central Lowland. This great area of level land is very fertile. The soil is rich and deep. The climate is good for crops. The summers are usually hot and wet. The winters are cold and snowy. Many crops grow in the Central Lowland.

West of the Missouri River are the Great Plains. The western parts of Kansas, Nebraska, and the Dakotas are on these plains. Much of the land on the Great Plains is dry grassland. Not enough rain falls there to grow crops. Farmers can use pipes and ditches to bring water to the land. Instead, many use the land to raise cattle and sheep.

There are two areas of hilly land in the Midwest. The Black Hills of South Dakota are mountains. Harney Peak in the Black Hills is higher than any Appalachian mountain. The Ozarks in Missouri are a region of hills and valleys. Actually, this area is a plateau.

The Midwestern States are not on the ocean. This makes their lakes and rivers very important. Waterways and canals link the rivers with the Great Lakes. Then the St. Lawrence Seaway provides an outlet to the Atlantic Ocean.

FUN FACTS

Minnesota reaches farther north than any other state except Alaska.

Michigan is a land of 11,000 lakes. Four of the five Great Lakes wash Michigan's shores.

Indiana is famous for auto racing. The Indianapolis 500 is a 500-mile auto race. The race cars drive on the Indianapolis Motor Speedway. This speedway was built in 1909 to test new cars.

South Dakota has a dry region called the Badlands. Here, the forces of nature have worn the land into strange hills and hollows. The Badlands got their name because they were hard to cross.

Missouri was the home of Mark Twain. He wrote about the adventures of Tom Sawyer and Huck Finn on the Mississippi River. Mark Twain was once the pilot of a riverboat on the Mississippi.

Kansas is famous for corn. Actually, it grows more wheat than any other state. Most of the United States lies between Canada and Mexico. The center of these 48 states is Kansas.

Iowa was covered with tall prairie grass 100 years ago. Pioneers crossed the state in covered wagons. Now Iowa's prairies have become fields of corn.

Wisconsin was settled by the French 300 years ago. Later, people came from Germany to live there. Today, you will still hear German spoken in Wisconsin.

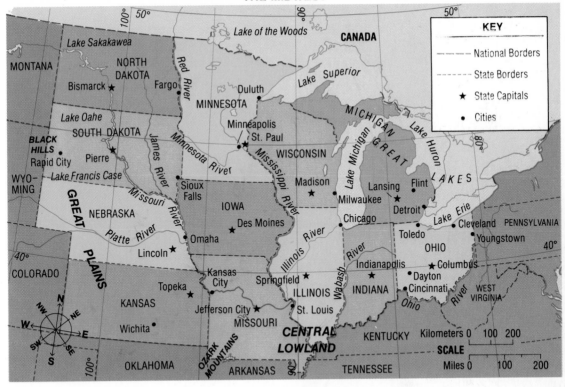

Many rivers in the region flow into the Mississippi. The Missouri flows into it from the west. The Ohio joins it from the east. Then the Mississippi keeps flowing south to the Gulf of Mexico.

Resources

The Midwest is the nation's most important farming area. It is called the breadbasket of the nation. A **breadbasket** is a region where much grain is grown. Farmers in the Midwestern States grow huge amounts of wheat and corn. So much food is grown here that some is sold to other nations. Soybeans, oats, and hay are other leading crops. In the Great Lakes states, farmers raise many fruits and vegetables.

Trees are still an important resource in northern Minnesota and Michigan. But these states used up much of their forests 100 years ago. Once, great forests covered much of the land around the lakes. Then settlers cut the trees down. Some were clearing the land to plant crops. Others worked for companies that sold wood. Now, Minnesota and Michigan are having to plant more trees.

Farmers in the Midwest also raise animals. Hogs, beef cattle, chickens, and turkeys are raised

121

Chicago, Illinois, is on Lake Michigan. The Chicago River flows through the city. Many tall buildings are on the river banks.

for their meat. Around the Great Lakes, many dairy farms are found. Wisconsin leads the nation in producing milk, butter, and cheese. Michigan, Minnesota, and Ohio are also dairy states.

Some states in the Midwest have important mineral resources. Illinois and Indiana produce large amounts of coal. Minnesota and Michigan are the nation's leading producers of iron ore. Missouri mines large amounts of lead. North Dakota produces petroleum. There are even gold mines in the Black Hills of South Dakota!

Manufacturing and Trade

Suppose you could fly in an airplane over the Midwestern States. You would see miles and miles of flat farmland. But you would also pass over great cities with large factories. Even in the Midwest, there are more jobs in factories than on farms.

Many states in this region prepare and package food. They pack meat and can vegetables. They grind grain to make flour and breakfast food. Metals and other minerals also provide factory jobs.

Illinois and Indiana make steel and refine petroleum.

Most of the nation's cars are made in the Midwest. Detroit, Michigan, is the center of the auto industry. Airplanes are built in Kansas. Space vehicles are made in Missouri. The Midwestern States also make mining equipment and farm machines.

The Midwestern States have very good transportation. Ships sail from the Atlantic Ocean through the St. Lawrence Seaway. That brings them to the Great Lakes. The Illinois waterway connects Lake Michigan with the Mississippi River. Goods can travel on this waterway from Chicago to St. Louis. Then they can go down the Mississippi River to the Gulf of Mexico. Goods can also be shipped north and east on this great water highway. Another important shipping route is the Ohio River.

Some of the nation's largest cities are on the Great Lakes. Find Chicago, Detroit, Milwaukee, and Cleveland on the map on page 121. What states are these cities in? What lakes are they on?

The largest carved figures in the world are on Mount Rushmore in South Dakota. George Washington's head is 18 meters (60 feet) tall.

Places to Go

Chicago is the second-largest city in the United States. Chicago is a port city on Lake Michigan. It is a center for shipping, railways, highways, and airlines. It has the busiest airport in the United States. Transportation provides many jobs in Chicago. There are also jobs in factories, offices, and city government. The world's tallest building is in Chicago. Goods made in this great city are sold all over the world.

123

THE MIDWESTERN STATES

State name and nickname		Date state entered union	Area		Number of people	State capital
			square miles	square kilometers		
Ohio (Buckeye State)		1803	41,222	106,765	10,797,419	Columbus
Michigan (Wolverine State)		1837	58,216	150,779	9,258,344	Lansing
Indiana (Hoosier State)		1816	36,291	93,994	5,490,179	Indianapolis
Wisconsin (Badger State)		1848	56,154	145,439	4,705,335	Madison
Illinois (Land of Lincoln)		1818	56,400	146,076	11,418,461	Springfield
Minnesota (Gopher State)		1858	84,068	217,736	4,077,148	St. Paul
Iowa (Hawkeye State)		1846	56,290	145,791	2,913,387	Des Moines
Missouri (Show Me State)		1821	69,686	180,487	4,917,444	Jefferson City
North Dakota (Flickertail State)		1889	70,665	183,022	652,695	Bismarck
South Dakota (Sunshine State)		1889	77,047	199,552	690,178	Pierre
Nebraska (Cornhusker State)		1867	77,227	200,018	1,570,006	Lincoln
Kansas (Sunflower State)		1861	82,264	213,064	2,363,208	Topeka

St. Louis, Missouri, is very different from Chicago, Illinois. It is more like the cities in the Southern States. Just north of St. Louis, the Missouri River flows into the Mississippi. Fur traders and French people from New Orleans settled St. Louis. Today, visitors to

St. Louis can take a steamboat trip on the Mississippi. They can also go to the top of the Gateway Arch. For many pioneers, St. Louis was the "Gateway to the West." More recently, space capsules have been built in St. Louis.

Native peoples lived in North America long before the Europeans came. In Ohio, Indiana, Iowa, and Illinois, you can see great mounds of earth. They were built by American Indian peoples over 2000 years ago. The mound builders were the first Midwestern farmers. In Ohio, they built one mound in the shape of a giant snake!

One of the most famous sights in the Midwest is Mount Rushmore in South Dakota. There, you can see George Washington, Thomas Jefferson, Theodore Roosevelt, and Abraham Lincoln. The faces of these Presidents are carved into the rock.

REVIEW

CHECK YOUR FACTS

1. List the 12 states in the Midwestern region.
2. Almost all the land in the Midwest is (level/hilly).
3. Why is the Midwest called the breadbasket of the nation?
4. List four crops grown in the Midwestern States.
5. Which state produces the most milk and cheese?
6. Which Midwestern states produce the most iron ore?
7. What rivers come together just north of St. Louis?

USE YOUR CHART

8. Which Midwestern state has the most land?
9. Which Midwestern state has the most people?
10. Which was the first Midwestern state to join the Union?

USE YOUR MAP

11. Which six Midwestern states border on the Great Lakes?
12. The Mississippi River forms part of the border of five Midwestern states. List them.
13. Name at least two rivers that flow into the Mississippi.
14. The Ohio River forms the southern border of three Midwestern states. List them.

CLOSE THE MAP GAP

15. Add the Midwestern States to your map of the United States. Label each state and its capital. Also label the Mississippi, Missouri, and Ohio rivers and Lake Erie, Lake Huron, Lake Michigan, and Lake Superior.

THINK ABOUT IT

Can you think of a better name for this region than the Middle West?

Lesson 6: The Mountain States

Montana Wyoming Colorado New Mexico
Idaho Utah Arizona Nevada

FIND THE WORDS

canyon geyser irrigate dam

The eight Mountain States are huge. They are among the largest states in the nation. They are also in a region of great beauty. Here, you can see high mountains and deep valleys. You can see great forests and wide deserts. You can even see boiling water shoot out of the ground. Millions of people visit the Mountain States to see these sights. But only 11 million people live in this region. All six New England States would fit into any one of the Mountain States. And there would be room to spare! Yet a million more people live in New England.

Even so, many people are moving to the Mountain States. Between 1970 and 1980, Nevada and Arizona were the fastest-growing states in the nation.

MOUNTAIN STATES

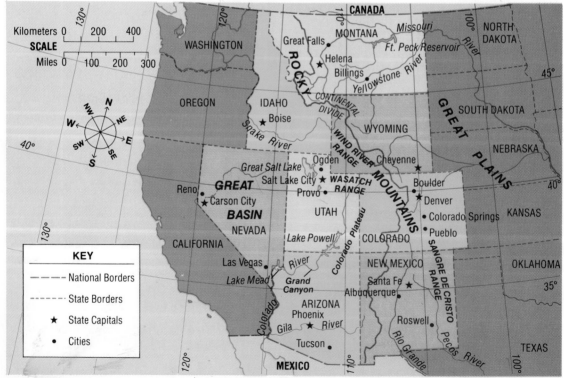

126

Land and Climate

Mountains and plateaus are the main landforms of the Mountain States. The Rocky Mountains stretch north to Alaska. They go through parts of Idaho, Montana, Wyoming, Utah, Colorado, and New Mexico. The highest mountain in this part of the Rockies is Mount Elbert. It is in Colorado. Mount Elbert is 4400 meters (14,431 feet) above sea level.

Like the Appalachians, the Rockies have many different ranges. That means the mountains have different names in different places. The Bitterroot Range is between Idaho and Montana. The Wind River Range is in Wyoming.

A high ridge passes through the Rocky Mountains. It is like the backbone of the continent. This ridge is called the Continental Divide. All the rivers west of it flow toward the Pacific Ocean. All the rivers east of it flow toward the Atlantic Ocean.

East of the Rockies are the Great Plains. West of the Rockies is an area called the Great Basin. This area is a desert. Mountains and plateaus surround it.

One plateau in the area is called the Colorado Plateau. It is famous all over the world for the Grand Canyon. The Colorado River flows through the bottom of the canyon. From the rim of the canyon, the river seems small and

The Rocky Mountains stretch from Alaska to New Mexico. This is a scene near Sun Valley, Idaho.

far away. Actually, the river carved the Grand Canyon out of the rock! It took many long ages for this to happen. The force of the running water wore part of the rock away. It cut a long, deep valley into the plateau. A deep, narrow valley with steep sides is called a **canyon.** The Grand Canyon is more than a mile deep.

The Grand Canyon is part of a national park in Arizona. Most of our largest national parks are in the Mountain States. Yellowstone National Park is in Wyoming, Montana, and Idaho. There, hot springs called **geysers** (GY zurz) shoot water and steam into the air. Yellowstone also has great forests. Animals such as buffaloes, moose, and bears live in the park.

These people are in Yellowstone National Park. They are watching water shoot up from a geyser.

In the Mountain States, the climate is mostly dry. Summers are hot and dry. Winters are cold except in southern Arizona and New Mexico. There is snow in the mountains. To grow most crops, farmers in the Mountain States need irrigation. To **irrigate** land is to bring water there from somewhere else. Water flows to the fields through pipes and ditches.

To save water, large dams have been built on many rivers. A **dam** is a wall that blocks river water. It stops the water from flowing on to the ocean. Behind a dam, a lake will form to hold the water.

Resources

There are valuable minerals in the Mountain States. These states have silver and gold. They have copper and lead. Copper and lead are important in manufacturing.

Some mineral resources are burned for energy. Wyoming, Colorado, Montana, and Utah have large amounts of coal. Several of these states also have petroleum and natural gas. Water and sunlight are other sources of energy. Dams provide waterpower as well as water for irrigation. Both waterpower and energy from the sun can be used to make electricity.

Thanks to irrigation, crops can grow in the Mountain States. Most of these states grow wheat, hay, potatoes, and sugar beets. With irrigation, Arizona and Nevada can even grow cotton and fruit. Still, animals are more important than crops in most of this region. Many farmers raise sheep and cattle on large ranches. Wood from the forests is another natural resource.

Manufacturing, Business, and Trade

Mining and ranching are very important in the Mountain States. These states sell minerals and pack meat. They make wood products and sell wool. Their dairy cows supply milk and cheese. Factories make aircraft, spacecraft, and missiles in Utah and Arizona. In New Mexico, scientists study atomic energy and energy from the sun.

Places to Go

There are many exciting things to do in the Mountain States. You can visit the national parks. You can ski, swim, hike, camp, or canoe. You can see natural wonders such as canyons, caves, and deserts. You can go to places where American Indians lived hundreds of years ago. The Indians were pioneers in irrigation. They worked out very good ways to get water to their fields. Some built homes on the sides of cliffs.

Some of the nation's fastest-growing cities are in the Mountain States. Here, the city with the most people is Phoenix (FEE niks), Arizona. Phoenix is a city in the desert. Thanks to irrigation and air-conditioning, many people can live there. Second in population is Denver, Colorado. Denver is at the foot of the Rockies. It is on a mile-high plateau. Denver has a suburb called Aurora. In 1980, Aurora had over twice as many people as it had in 1970!

THE MOUNTAIN STATES

State name and nickname		Date state entered union	Area		Number of people	State capital
			square miles	square kilometers		
Montana (Treasure State)		1889	147,138	381,087	786,690	Helena
Wyoming (Equality State)		1890	97,914	253,597	470,816	Cheyenne
Colorado (Centennial State)		1876	104,247	270,000	2,888,834	Denver
New Mexico (Land of Enchantment)		1912	121,666	315,115	1,299,968	Santa Fe
Idaho (Gem State)		1890	83,557	216,413	943,935	Boise
Utah (Beehive State)		1896	84,916	219,932	1,461,037	Salt Lake City
Arizona (Grand Canyon State)		1912	113,909	295,024	2,717,866	Phoenix
Nevada (Silver State)		1864	110,540	286,299	799,184	Carson City

129

FUN FACTS

Many Mountain states were wild and lawless in the early mining days. Tombstone, Arizona, was a well-known mining camp. There, Wyatt Earp fought the famous gunfight at the O.K. Corral. Later, many booming mining towns turned into ghost towns. When mines closed down, people left.

Wyoming is called the Equality State. Wyoming women got the vote in 1869. The United States did not give women the right to vote until 1920.

Idaho has more national forest land than any state except California.

In Arizona, one out of every five people is American Indian.

Colorado means "red" in Spanish. The state was named for the Rio Colorado, or "Red River." Montana means "mountain country."

Utah has the second-saltiest body of water on Earth. Only the Dead Sea is saltier than the Great Salt Lake.

New Mexico was the place where the first atomic bomb was exploded. This state has twice as many sheep and cattle as it has people.

Nevada has the smallest capital city in the United States. Carson City, Nevada, was named for Kit Carson. He used to guide explorers and armies through the West.

REVIEW

WATCH YOUR WORDS

1. To ____ land is to bring water there.
   dam   irrigate   conserve
2. A ____ stops river water from flowing to the sea.
   canal   harbor   dam
3. Water and steam shoot out of a hot spring called a ____ .
   canyon   geyser   swamp
4. A river can cut a ____ out of rock.
   swamp   delta   canyon

CHECK YOUR FACTS

5. List the eight Mountain States.
6. What are the main landforms of the Mountain States?
7. What national park has geysers?
8. How do farmers in the Mountain States get water?
9. List four mineral resources of the Mountain States.

USE YOUR CHART

10. Which was the first Mountain state to join the Union?
11. Which Mountain state has the most land?
12. Which two Mountain states have the most people?

USE YOUR MAP

13. In what state is the Grand Canyon?
14. What rivers flow through New Mexico?
15. In what state is the Great Salt Lake?

CLOSE THE MAP GAP

16. Add the Mountain States to your map of the United States. Label each state and its capital. Also label the Rocky Mountains, the Great Salt Lake, and the Colorado River.

Lesson 7: The Pacific States

Alaska   Washington   Oregon
California   Hawaii

FIND THE WORDS

mission   volcano   earthquake

The Pacific Ocean borders the West Coast of the United States. It is the largest ocean in the world. Five states have coasts that are washed by the Pacific waters. They are Alaska, Washington, Oregon, California, and Hawaii (huh WAH yee). Four of these states are on the continent of North America. The islands of Hawaii are far out in the ocean.

The Pacific States are special in many ways. California has more people than any other state in the nation. Alaska has the most land of any state. It also has the fewest people. Alaska is the state closest to the North Pole. Hawaii is the state closest to the equator.

History

California was discovered by a Spanish explorer in 1542. Spain started a colony there over 200 years later, in 1769. This colony was at San Diego (dee A goh).

THE PACIFIC STATES

State name and nickname	Date state entered union	Area square miles	Area square kilometers	Number of people	State capital
Alaska (Last Frontier)	1959	586,400	1,518,776	400,481	Juneau
Washington (Evergreen State)	1889	68,192	176,617	4,130,163	Olympia
Oregon (Beaver State)	1859	96,981	251,181	2,632,663	Salem
California (Golden State)	1850	158,693	411,014	23,668,562	Sacramento
Hawaii (Aloha State)	1959	6,450	16,706	965,000	Honolulu

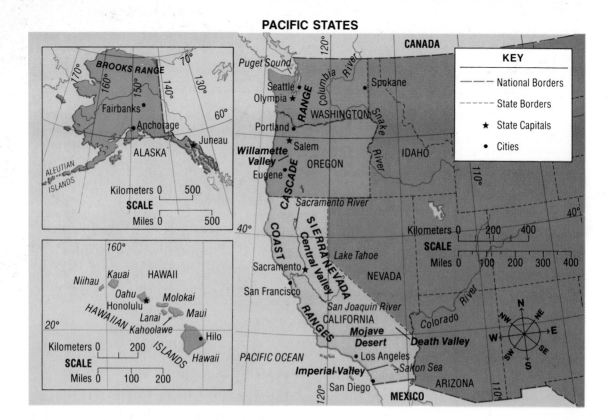

PACIFIC STATES

KEY
- – – – National Borders
- - - - - State Borders
- ★ State Capitals
- • Cities

Soon, Spanish priests were starting many religious settlements, called **missions.** Missions and forts were built from south to north along the coast. Then, in 1777, the first California town was started. It was San Jose (hoh ZAY).

Later, California was ruled by Mexico. Then, in 1848, it became part of the United States. That same year, gold was discovered in California. The great California Gold Rush began. People came to California from all over the world. The population grew very fast. By 1850, California became a state.

In the 1840s, many settlers had begun to come to Oregon. They came in horse-drawn wagons along the Oregon Trail. It took them 6 months to travel from Kansas City, Missouri, to Oregon. By 1859, Oregon had enough people to become a state. Washington had to wait another 30 years. By 1889, the railroad had brought many new settlers there.

Alaska and Hawaii were the last states to come into the Union. In 1867, the United States bought Alaska from Russia. In 1900, Hawaii became a U.S. territory.

Waikiki (WY kee KEE) is a famous beach in Honolulu, Hawaii.

Hawaii used to be a kingdom. Then, for a few years, it was a nation with a president. Next, it became a territory. Finally, in 1959, both Alaska and Hawaii became states.

Land and Climate

No two states are more different than Alaska and Hawaii! On a globe, you can clearly see where these states are. Find them on the map of the world on pages 10 and 11. On smaller maps, Alaska and Hawaii are often put at the bottom. Then, everything on the map can be shown in more detail.

Alaska is the largest state. It is more than twice the size of Texas. Alaska juts out from North America in the northwest. At about 168° west longitude, it almost touches the Soviet Union. The upper part of Alaska is north of the Arctic Circle. There, the ground is always frozen. For most of the year, the Arctic Ocean is covered with ice. In the far southeast, Alaska gets more rain than snow. But most of Alaska has cold, snowy winters.

Hawaii is one of the smallest states. It is made up of eight large islands and many small ones. The island farthest south reaches to about 19° north latitude. That means it is close to the equator. Hawaii has a warm, sunny climate. It has palm trees and broad beaches of white sand. It has great tropical forests of ferns. Flowers bloom and fruits grow all year in the state of Hawaii.

Both Alaska and Hawaii have high mountains. Mount McKinley in Alaska is the highest mountain in North America. Both states also have volcanoes. A **volcano** is an opening in the earth. Hot, melted rock can shoot out of such an opening. So can ashes, smoke, and gases. The melted rock can build up around the opening. That way, it forms a mountain around the volcano. Material from a volcano can also push up from under the ocean. Then, it forms an island. Many of the islands of Hawaii were formed by volcanoes.

Washington, Oregon, and California share some of the same geography. Along the Pacific Coast are ranges of low mountains. They are called the Coast Ranges. Farther east are higher mountains. These higher mountains are called the Cascade Range in Washington and Oregon. In California, they are called the Sierra Nevada. Between the Coast Ranges and the higher mountains are three fertile valleys. The one farthest south is the great Central Valley of California. These valleys between the mountains have rich farmland.

FUN FACTS

Point Barrow, Alaska, is farther north than any other point in the United States. It is just beyond 71° north latitude. There, the Arctic Ocean is frozen 9 or 10 months of the year. Ka Lae (kah LAH a), Hawaii, is farther south than any other point in the nation. It is at 19° north latitude.

The highest point in North America is in Alaska. Mount McKinley is 6194 meters (20,320 feet) above sea level.

The lowest point in North America is in California. Death Valley is 86 meters (282 feet) below sea level. It is one of the hottest, driest places in the world. California also has the highest waterfall in North America. This is Yosemite (yoh SEM uh tee) Falls.

The place in the world where it rains most often is in Hawaii. It is Mount Waialeale (wy AH lee AH lee) on the island of Kauai (KOW eye). Sometimes it rains there as much as 350 days a year!

Crater Lake, Oregon, is the deepest lake in the United States. Oregon also has the continent's deepest canyon.

Washington has an active volcano. It is Mount St. Helens in the Cascade Range. Mount St. Helens used to have an elevation of 2950 meters (9677 feet). Now, it is only 2530 meters (8300 feet) above sea level. On May 18, 1980, the top of the mountain blew off! Steam and ashes shot up into the sky. The blast had more force than an atomic bomb. The great heat burned down forests. It killed millions of fish. Rushing rivers of mud buried people's homes. Towns in three states were covered with ashes. Mount St. Helens had really blown its top!

The top of Mount St. Helens is in the clouds. This volcano is in the state of Washington.

Along the Pacific Coast, Washington and Oregon have a marine climate. This climate area goes as far south as San Francisco. Warm, wet winds blow in from the ocean. These winds keep the air from getting very hot or cold. They bring a lot of rain to the coast. Then, at the snow-capped Cascade Range, the winds are cooled. Rain falls on the western side of the mountains. But the areas east of the mountains are dry. There, farmers have to irrigate their fields.

Great forests grow in Washington and Oregon because of the rain. California's northern coast has giant redwood trees. These trees have huge trunks. They can grow as tall as 117 meters (385 feet). They are among the oldest living things on Earth.

Here, Mount St. Helens is no longer quiet. It is creating its own clouds. You can see the heavy smoke shooting up into the air.

Farther south, the California coast has a Mediterranean climate. Cities like Los Angeles have warm, dry summers and warm, wet winters. In the dry southeast, California has deserts. Death Valley and the Mojave (moh HAH vee) Desert are there.

Resources

California produces more farm products than any other state. In the valleys, the land is irrigated. That way, California can grow huge crops of vegetables and fruits. No other state grows as much lettuce or as many tomatoes, carrots, and strawberries. Grapes, oranges, and lemons are major California crops. Cotton also grows in California.

Farther north, Oregon and Washington grow apples, peaches, pears, and cherries. They also grow many vegetables and raise wheat. Out in the Pacific, Hawaii grows pineapples and raises sugar cane. Only Alaska is not a farming state. But cattle are raised in all the states in the Pacific region.

There are also rich mineral resources in the Pacific States. California and Alaska have large amounts of petroleum and natural gas. In Alaska, petroleum is found in the northern part of the state. So a pipeline had to be built across the state. Oil can flow through the pipeline to an ice-free southern port. In California, much petroleum is found under the ocean close to the shore. Many people do not want to drill for this petroleum. They are afraid the oil might spill and spoil the beaches. Other people say that the nation needs the petroleum. They believe drilling is worth the risk.

Manufacturing, Business, and Trade

The Pacific States make money from the food they produce. They freeze, pack, or can fruit, vegetables, fish, and meat. They package and sell dairy products. They also manufacture wood and paper products from the forests. Redwood is used for building. It is valued for its beauty. Also, it does not easily rot.

Many jobs in Alaska depend on petroleum, wood, and fish. Many

The Alaska pipeline carries petroleum across fields of snow. The oil flows from the Arctic coast to an ice-free port near Anchorage.

There is much rich farmland in California's valleys. California produces more farm products than any other state.

people in Hawaii make their living on large farms. In Washington, Oregon, and California, airplanes and ships are built. In California, movies and television shows are made. Films from Hollywood are watched all over the world.

Places to Go

The Pacific States have many places to see. There are beaches, forests, lakes, and deserts. There are flat, fertile valleys. There are steep cliffs bordering the sea. In some parts of California, you can swim and ski on the same day!

Cities are growing in the Pacific States. The largest cities in this region are in California. Look at the map on page 132. Find Los Angeles, San Diego, and San Francisco. All these cities have Spanish names. Other large cities on the West Coast are Portland, Oregon, and Seattle, Washington.

San Francisco is a beautiful city in northern California. It is built on steep hills. The Golden Gate Bridge stretches across the entrance to the harbor. A great earthquake and fire destroyed San Francisco in 1906. In an **earthquake**, the ground shakes and trembles. This can cause buildings to fall down. But the people of San Francisco quickly built their city again. A famous part of San Francisco is called Chinatown. More Chinese-Americans live there than anywhere else in the nation.

People from all over the Earth live in the Pacific States. The native Alaskans are the Innuit (Eskimos). The native Hawaiians are the Polynesians. Later, people came to Hawaii from Japan, China, and the Philippines. Now people from Asia also live in Washington, Oregon, and California. People who speak Spanish live in California, too. American Indians, Mexicans, Europeans, Blacks, and Asians all helped to build the Pacific States.

REVIEW

WATCH YOUR WORDS

1. Hot, melted rock can shoot out of a ____.
   geyser volcano swamp
2. A(n) ____ makes the ground shake and tremble.
   earthquake geyser dam
3. The first religious settlements in California were called ____.
   forts territories missions

CHECK YOUR FACTS

4. List the five states that make up the Pacific region.
5. Which Pacific states are on the continent of North America?
6. Which state has more people than any other state?
7. Which state has the most land?
8. How are Alaska and Hawaii different? How are they alike?
9. What is a volcano?
10. Why do great forests grow in Washington and Oregon?
11. The land east of the Cascade Mountains is (wet/dry).
12. List five of the crops that grow in California.
13. Which Pacific state raises sugar cane and pineapples?
14. Which Pacific states raise apples, peaches, and pears?
15. Which Pacific states have a lot of petroleum?

USE YOUR CHART

16. Which is the smallest Pacific State?
17. Which Pacific state has the fewest people?

USE YOUR MAP

18. A river forms most of the border between Washington and Oregon. What river is it?
19. What large lake is northeast of the capital of California?
20. What range of mountains crosses northern Alaska?
21. On what island is Honolulu, Hawaii, found?

CLOSE THE MAP GAP

22. Add the Pacific States to your map of the United States. Label each state and its capital. Also label the Coast Ranges, the Cascade Range, the Sierra Nevada, the Columbia River, and the Pacific Ocean. Then label Canada and Mexico. Now your map of the United States is complete!

THINK ABOUT IT

Why do so few people live in Alaska? Why do so many live in California?

CHAPTER REVIEW

WATCH YOUR WORDS

1. The Pilgrims anchored their ship in a
   ___.
   delta   swamp   bay

2. The Statue of Liberty is on an island
   in New York___.
   wilderness   harbor   territory

3. The Middle Atlantic States have
   many___.
   ports   volcanoes   geysers

4. A___tree loses its leaves.
   softwood   hardwood   pine

5. The Mississippi River drops fertile
   soil to form a___.
   harbor   bay   delta

6. The Midwest is called the ___ of the
   nation.
   breadbasket   wilderness   delta

7. The Grand ___ is more than a mile
   deep.
   Geyser   Volcano   Canyon

8. There are hot springs called ___ in
   Yellowstone National Park.
   geysers   swamps   volcanoes

9. In 1906, a(n) ___ and fire destroyed
   San Francisco.
   volcano   earthquake   geyser

10. Mount St. Helens is a___.
    geyser   delta   volcano

CHECK YOUR FACTS

11. How many states are there in the
    United States?

12. What is the difference between a cap-
    ital and a capitol?

13. Where are the New England States?

14. Name three large cities in the Middle
    Atlantic States.

15. Is the land better for farming in the
    South or in New England?

16. Are the Southern States gaining or
    losing population?

17. Is most land in the Midwestern
    States hilly or flat?

18. How do the Mountain States compare
    with the New England States in size?
    In population?

19. How can farmers in a dry region
    grow crops?

20. Name two living and two nonliving
    resources of the Pacific States.

KNOW YOUR STATES

21. What was the first state to join the
    Union?

22. What were the last two states to join
    the Union?

23. What are the largest and smallest
    states?

24. What state has the most people?

25. In what state was the first lasting
    English colony?

USE YOUR MAPS

26. List the states on the Atlantic Coast.

27. List the states on the Gulf Coast.

28. List the states on the Pacific Coast.

29. List the states that border on one or
    more of the Great Lakes.

30. List the states on the Mississippi
    River.

GET CHART SMART

31. Make a chart about the 50 states. List
    the six groups of states down the left
    side. Write these things across the
    top: *Landforms, Farm Products, Min-
    erals, Manufactured Goods*. Then fill in
    the chart for each group of states.

UNIT REVIEW

WATCH YOUR WORDS

Use the words below to fill in the blanks. Use each term only once.

canal	Congress	geysers	Lakes
canyons	dams	Gulf	Seaway
capital	delta	irrigate	states
Capitol	federal district	isthmus	volcano

The United States is a nation made up of 50____. Washington, DC, is the____ Washington is not in a state but in a(n) ____. The____ is in Washington, DC. It is the building in which____meets.

Most of the United States is on the continent of North America. A narrow strip of land, called a(n)____, links North and South America. There, a(n)____ connects the Atlantic and Pacific oceans. Farther north, the St. Lawrence____links the Atlantic Ocean with the five Great____. Another waterway connects the lakes with the Mississippi River. The Mississippi flows south to the____of Mexico. It

drops rich soil to form a(n)____before it flows into the sea.

North America has many natural wonders. Rivers have cut deep____out of solid rock. Water shoots out of the ground from hot springs called ____ . When a(n)____explodes, it can cover the land with ashes or melted rock. But other wonders have been made by human beings. People have built cities, highways, railroads, airports, and canals. They have built____across rivers to hold the water back. Then they use the water to____dry land. That way, they can live and grow food in the desert!

CHECK YOUR FACTS

1. What are the two major mountain systems of North America?

2. The highest mountains on the continent are in the (east/west).

3. List three areas of plains in North America.

4. What two rivers form the longest river in North America?

5. List two resources that can be renewed and two that cannot.

6. What three large nations take up most of North America?

7. Where is Central America?

8. The United States (is/is not) the world's largest nation.

9. How many states were there when the United States began?

10. Who were the first colonists to come to New England?

11. Where in the Middle Atlantic States do most people live?

12. Where is the Statue of Liberty? The Liberty Bell? Independence Hall?

13. Where was the first lasting European settlement in the United States?

14. What was the Wilderness Road?

15. Which region is called the breadbasket of the nation? Why?

16. What is the shape of the land in the Midwestern States?

17. What are the main landforms in the Mountain States?

18. What is the Continental Divide?

19. List five different groups of people who live in the Pacific States.

140

KNOW YOUR EARTH

Match the word with the clue.

20. gulf   A. flat or rolling grassland

21. peninsula   B. range of steep mountains

22. prairie   C. part of an ocean near land

23. sierra   D. land almost surrounded by water

KNOW YOUR STATES

24. What two states were once nations?

25. Which state is not on the continent of North America?

26. Which state produces the most farm products?

27. Which two states produce the most petroleum and natural gas?

28. Which state is split into two parts by a lake?

USE YOUR MAPS

29. Look at the physical map of North America on page 73.
    a. Give the latitude of Barrow, Alaska, and Houston, Texas.
    b. Give the longitude of Portland, Maine, and Portland, Oregon.
    c. Give the latitude and longitude of Reno, Nevada, and the Panama Canal.

30. Look at the political map of North America on page 87. Give the right intermediate direction: *northeast, northwest, southeast, southwest.*
    Alaska is ___ of Cuba. The Great Lakes are ___ of Alaska. Puerto Rico is ___ of Ottawa.

CLOSE THE MAP GAP

31. On a separate sheet of paper, draw an outline map of North America. Put these things on your map:
    a. United States, Canada, Mexico, Central America
    b. Rocky Mountains, Appalachian Mountains, Sierra Madres
    c. Mississippi River, Missouri River, St. Lawrence River, Rio Grande
    d. Great Plains, Central Lowland, coastal plains
    e. Atlantic Ocean, Pacific Ocean, Arctic Ocean
    f. Gulf of Mexico, Caribbean Sea
    g. Great Lakes, Great Salt Lake, Mexican Plateau, Panama Canal
    h. Washington, DC, Ottawa, Mexico City
    i. your state and its capital

32. Answer these questions. Show the answers on your map.
    a. How can goods travel by water through the middle of the United States?
    b. Where in Canada do most people live?
    c. Where in Mexico do most people live?

THINK ABOUT IT

33. Suppose you had to move to another region of North America. What region would you choose? Describe the climate and landforms.

34. Many people in North America speak English, Spanish, or French. Some people speak two languages. What languages are spoken in your state?

35. Many factories have left the North and moved to the South. What reasons can you find for this?

STUDYING YOUR STATE

You have studied your continent. You have learned about your government. And you have found out many things about all 50 states. Now, you may want to learn more about your own state. Here is a way to go about it.

Look for books and articles about your state in the library. You can find many facts in an encyclopedia or almanac. Also write to departments in your state for free materials. Your teacher has the addresses. Your state historical society can help you learn about state history. Your state department of transportation may send you a road map. Many states have a department of travel or tourism. It sends out leaflets to attract visitors to the state. You may be able to visit a state or local museum.

Be a detective. Try to find the answers to these questions. Soon, you will be an expert on your state.

HISTORY OF YOUR STATE

1. What early American Indian peoples lived in your state? What kinds of homes did they have? What artifacts did they leave behind?
2. Who were the first people from Europe to settle in your state? When did these settlers first arrive?
3. What part of your state was settled first? What attracted people to that region?
4. What is the oldest town or city in your state?
5. Was your state once a colony? Was it ever a territory or part of a territory? Was it ever part of Canada or Mexico? Was it once ruled by Great Britain, France, or Spain?
6. In what year did your state become a state?
7. What were the most important things that happened in your state? Make a time line. Put on the dates when these events happened.
8. Were any important battles fought in your state? If so, what were they?
9. Were any Presidents born in your state? What other great leaders lived there? Can you still visit the places where these leaders lived?
10. What are the people of your state like? From what parts of the world did they come?

GEOGRAPHY OF YOUR STATE

11. What landforms are found in your state?
12. Is your state on the Atlantic Ocean or Pacific Ocean?
13. What important rivers or lakes are in your state?
14. What are the highest and lowest points in your state?
15. What climate or climates does your state have? How does the weather change from season to season?
16. Does your state get much rain? If not, do farmers irrigate their fields?

NATURAL RESOURCES OF YOUR STATE

17. What crops are grown in your state?
18. Are animals raised in your state for milk, eggs, meat, or wool? Are horses raised there?
19. What important minerals are found in your state?
20. What sources of energy are found in your state? Does it have coal, petroleum, natural gas, waterpower, or nuclear power? Is sunshine used for solar energy?
21. Does your state have large forests?
22. Does the land, the water, or the climate attract visitors to your state?
23. What is your state doing to conserve its natural resources?

BUSINESS, TRANSPORTATION, AND TRADE

24. What kinds of factories are found in your state? What products are made there?
25. What are some other businesses in your state that make goods or supply services?
26. What kinds of jobs do people have who work for the city, county, or state?
27. What kinds of transportation are used to move people and goods in your state?
28. What products and resources does your state sell to other states?

GOVERNMENT OF YOUR STATE

29. What is the capital of your state?
30. What is the legislature called? How many members does it have?
31. Who is the governor of your state?

FUN FACTS ABOUT YOUR STATE

32. How did your state get its name? Its nickname?
33. What is the state motto? The state bird? The state flower? Is there a state animal?
34. Where and when is your state fair held?
35. What colleges, museums, and parks are in your state?
36. What places in your state attract the most visitors?

USE YOUR STATE MAP

37. How far does your state extend from north to south? From east to west? Use the distance scale to measure.
38. What two towns in your state are farthest apart? What roads would you take to get from one to the other?
39. How far is the state capital from where you live? In what direction would you travel to get there?
40. What U.S. highways go through your state?
41. What other states or nations border your state?
42. List the state parks, national parks, and national forests in your state.
43. Does your state map tell about places to visit?

PUT IT ALL TOGETHER

44. Draw or trace an outline map of your state.
45. Put the state capital and the five largest cities on the map.
46. Label important mountains, deserts, valleys, plains, and plateaus. Also label important bodies of water, such as oceans, lakes, and rivers.

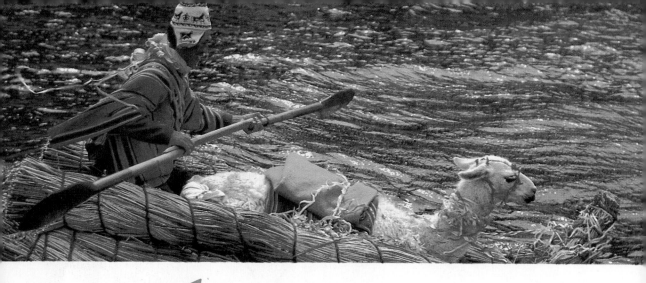

CHAPTER 1

SOUTH AMERICA AND ITS PEOPLE

Lesson 1: Land and Climate

FIND THE WORDS

altiplano   jungle
llanos   pampas

"Towering, snow-capped mountains seem to rise out of the sea."

"There are rivers so wide you can't see across them!"

"There are forests so thick that the sun never shines on the ground!"

"One desert is so dry that sometimes it doesn't rain there for 10 years!"

Suppose friends told you about a land like that. Would you believe them? Would it even sound like a place on this planet? Well, it is. All these things describe the continent to the south of us. All of them are true of South America.

North America and South America share the Western Hemisphere. In many ways, these two continents are alike. Each of them has high mountains in the west. Each has lower mountains in the east. Look at the elevation maps on pages 73 and 147. Find the western and eastern mountains on each continent.

SOUTH AMERICA AND CENTRAL AMERICA

WEST INDIES

Havana

Caribbean Sea

Lake Nicaragua

Caracas

Panama Canal

Bogotá

LLANOS

Orinoco River

GUIANA HIGHLANDS

ATLANTIC OCEAN

EQUATOR

EQUATOR

A N D E S

Amazon River

PACIFIC OCEAN

Lima

Lake Titicaca

La Paz

ALTIPLANO

BRAZILIAN HIGHLANDS

M O U N T A I N S

ATACAMA DESERT

Rio de Janeiro

São Paulo

Mt. Aconcagua

Paraná River

Uruguay River

Santiago

P A M P A S

Montevideo

Buenos Aires

N
NW NE
W E
SW SE
S

Kilometers 0	500
SCALE	
Miles 0	500

KEY

– – – National Borders   • Cities

ELEVATION

Meters	Feet
over 4,000	over 13,100
2,000 to 4,000	6,600 to 13,100
1,000 to 2,000	3,300 to 6,600
200 to 1,000	660 to 3,300
sea level to 200	sea level to 660
below sea level	below sea level

147

Each continent also has huge plains in the middle. And each has big rivers that flow through the plains. The rains that fall on the plains drain into the rivers.

These are some ways North America and South America are alike. In other ways, the two continents are very different. It is easier to live in North America than in South America. Only in the far north does North America have a harsh climate. In South America, much of the land and climate makes life difficult. As you read on, you will see why this is so.

Highlands of South America

South America has three main areas of highlands. They are the Andes Mountains, the Guiana Highlands, and the Brazilian Highlands.

The Andes Mountains run down the west coast of South America. On a map, this long line of mountains looks like a curving spine. Find the Andes (AN deez) on the elevation map on page 147.

The Andes are the longest system of mountains in the world. They are over 8045 kilometers (5000 miles) long. They are also the second-highest mountains in the world. Only the Himalayas (HIM uh LAY uhz) in Asia are higher. More than 45 peaks in the Andes are over 6098 meters (20,000 feet) high.

The Andes Mountains are close to the Pacific coast. There is only a narrow plain between the ocean and the mountains. Part of this plain is the Atacama (AH tuh KAH muh) Desert. Find this desert on the climate map on page 151. The Atacama Desert is the driest place in South America. In fact, it is one of the driest deserts on Earth. Sometimes, no rain falls there for 10 years. That means it might not have rained there from the time you were born until now!

The Andes Mountains are very steep and rugged. This makes it hard for people to cross the mountains. It is hard to build roads and railroads there. It is also hard for people to live there.

The Andes Mountains are the longest system of mountains on Earth. They are also the world's second-highest mountains.

Look at the elevation map again. Find the *altiplano* (AHL tee PLAH noh) in Bolivia. The **altiplano** is a plateau. It is a large area of high, flat land. In Spanish, *altiplano* means "high plain." People who live in the Andes live on plateaus like the *altiplano*. Or they live in valleys between the mountains. Plateaus and valleys are areas of flat land.

In the mountains, the climate changes as you climb up. The higher you go, the thinner the air gets. Remember, thin air holds less heat and wetness than heavier air does. So the higher you go, the cooler the climate is. Look at the climate map on page 151. Find the equator. It passes through the top part of South America. This means that most of South America is in the tropics. In the lowlands, the climate is very hot. So people prefer to live in the highlands. In the really high areas, the weather is cool all year.

Along the east coast of South America are two other areas of highlands. Look at the elevation map. Find the Guiana (gee AN uh) Highlands in the north. Then find the Brazilian Highlands to the south. Look at the map key. How high are these highlands? Are they as high as the Andes? How close to the Atlantic coast are they? Between these highlands and the ocean, do you see a narrow coastal plain?

Now look at the climate map. The Guiana Highlands are just north of the equator. Angel Falls, the highest waterfall on Earth, is there. Parts of the Guiana Highlands are covered by thick forests.

The Atacama Desert is the driest place in South America.

Other parts are grasslands. The Guiana Highlands are not high enough to have cool air. So both the forests and the grasslands are very hot. Few people can make a living there.

In the Brazilian Highlands, much of the land is dry grassland. Few people live there, either, except along the coast. Most of South America's people live on plateaus or fertile plains along the coasts.

Lowlands of South America

South America also has three main areas of lowlands. They are the Amazon River valley, the llanos, and the pampas.

Look at the elevation map. Between the Andes, the Guiana Highlands, and the Brazilian Highlands is a huge area of lowlands. This great area is the Amazon River valley. Here the climate is hot and wet all year round.

The Amazon is the second-longest river in the world. It is almost 6400 kilometers (4000 miles) long. Only the Nile River in Africa is longer. But the Amazon carries more water than any other river on Earth. When the Amazon flows into the Atlantic, the river is 322 kilometers (200 miles) wide. You cannot even see across it!

The land in the Amazon River valley is covered by a thick rain forest. It is the largest rain forest in the world. Along the river banks, the underbrush is very thick. In the tropics, a very thick growth of plants and trees is called a **jungle.** To reach land from the river, people have to chop through the jungle with big knives. Then, when they get through the jungle, the rain forest seems strange. Tall trees grow so close together that no light reaches the forest floor. Without light, no small plants can root in the ground. Instead, there are huge tree trunks. There are also ferns and tangled vines.

The weather in the Amazon valley is always hot and wet. Because of this, few people live there. The soil in the Amazon valley is not good. The heavy rains wash out many of the minerals that crops need. The heat makes it hard for people to work. It makes

This picture shows the valley of the Amazon River. The Amazon is the second-longest river in the world.

CLIMATES OF SOUTH AMERICA

CARIBBEAN SEA

VENEZUELA

Orinoco River

GUYANA

FRENCH GUIANA

SURINAME

COLOMBIA

Guiana Highlands

Equator

ECUADOR

Amazon River

SOUTH AMERICA

PERU

Madeira River

BRAZIL

Andes Mountains

Mt. Ancohuma

Brazilian Highlands

Lake Titicaca

BOLIVIA

ATLANTIC OCEAN

PACIFIC OCEAN

Altiplano

Atacama Desert

Salado River

PARAGUAY

Parana River

CHILE

Uruguay River

ARGENTINA

URUGUAY

KEY

– – National Boundaries

0 200 400 600
Kilometers

Miles
0   200   400   600

N

CLIMATES

Warm and Wet: Hot wet summer, mild wet winter

Dry Grassland: Hot summer, hot to cold winter, variable rainfall

Desert: Hot summer, hot to cold winter, dry year round

Mediterranean: Warm dry summer, mild wet winter

Marine: No dry season, mild winter, cool summer

Highlands: Rainfall varies, cool summer, dry winter

Rain Forest: Hot and wet year round

Tropical Grasslands: Hot wet summer, hot dry winter

This man is using a bulldozer to clear the rain forest.

Cowboys in Argentina round up cattle on the pampas.

them get tired easily. People can try to clear the land. But the forest keeps growing back. People have to keep fighting the forest.

There is a second area of lowlands in northern South America. This is an area of treeless plains called the **llanos** (YAH nohs). In Spanish, *llano* means "plain." The Orinoco (OR uh NOH koh) River flows through these plains. Find the llanos on the map on page 147. They are in Venezuela.

On the llanos, the weather is hot all year. Most rain falls in the summer. Then, the grass grows fast. Cattle and sheep can feed on it. But during the winter, little rain falls. Then, the heat burns up the grass. Few people live in the llanos. There are not many ways to make a living there.

South of the Amazon River valley is a third large area of flat land. This is a region of grassy plains called the **pampas** (PAM puz).

In a South American Indian language, *pampa* means "plain." The pampas are in Argentina and Uruguay. They are one of the flattest, most fertile areas on Earth. The climate there is good for growing crops and raising animals.

Look at the map on page 147. Find the pampas. The Paraná and Uruguay rivers flow through these fertile plains. On the pampas, the climate is mostly warm all year. Winters are mild. Ranchers raise cattle and sheep on the pampas. Farmers grow huge crops of wheat, rice, oats, and corn.

Look again at the climate map on page 151. Notice that much of South America is warm or hot. Find the desert along the Pacific coast. Then find the desert in the south. It borders on the Atlantic.

Now you can see why much of South America is hard to live in. Many places are too high or too steep. Others are too hot, too wet, or too dry. The people of South America live where the land is flat and the soil is fertile. They live where the climate is comfortable. Soon, you will learn more about how they make a living.

REVIEW

WATCH YOUR WORDS

1. A high plain is a____.
   jungle plateau rain forest
2. The high plain in Bolivia is called the____.
   llanos pampas *altiplano*
3. A very thick growth of tropical plants and trees is a____.
   llanos jungle *altiplano*
4. The hot, treeless plains in Venezuela are called the____.
   llanos *altiplano* pampas
5. The fertile plains in Argentina are called the____.
   llanos pampas jungle

CHECK YOUR FACTS

6. Name two ways in which North America and South America are alike. Name two ways in which they are different.

7. Name the three highland areas of South America. Where are they?
8. Name three lowland areas in South America. Which lowland area is best for growing food?
9. Describe the climate of the Amazon valley. Why do few people live in this river valley?
10. Where in the Andes Mountains do people live? Why?

THINK ABOUT IT

Why do people in South America call a plateau an *altiplano*? Why do they say *llanos* and *pampas* instead of plains?

TRY SOMETHING NEW

"Highest, longest, widest, strongest . . ." Pretend you are writing about South America for the *Guinness Book of World Records*. In what features is South America first or second in the world?

Lesson 2: Resources of South America

FIND THE WORDS

cacao   llama   alpaca
export   import

Much of South America's land may be hard to live on. But the continent is very rich in natural resources. Nonliving resources include fertile land and mineral wealth. Living resources include crops, animals, and products that grow in the forests.

Some land in the highlands and plains of South America is fertile. Fertile soil contains the minerals plants need to grow. On their fertile land, the South Americans grow large crops. Coffee trees produce beans used to make coffee. **Cacao** (kuh KAY oh) trees produce seeds used to make chocolate and cocoa. Sugar cane has thick stems from which we get sugar. And bananas also grow in South America. In places with mild climates, people grow wheat, oats, and corn. You could have a good breakfast with cereal, bananas, and cocoa from South America!

Some people in South America raise animals for a living. They raise cattle and sheep for milk,

Some South Americans grow bananas. They make money by selling bananas to other nations. Bananas are a South American export.

RESOURCES OF SOUTH AMERICA AND CENTRAL AMERICA

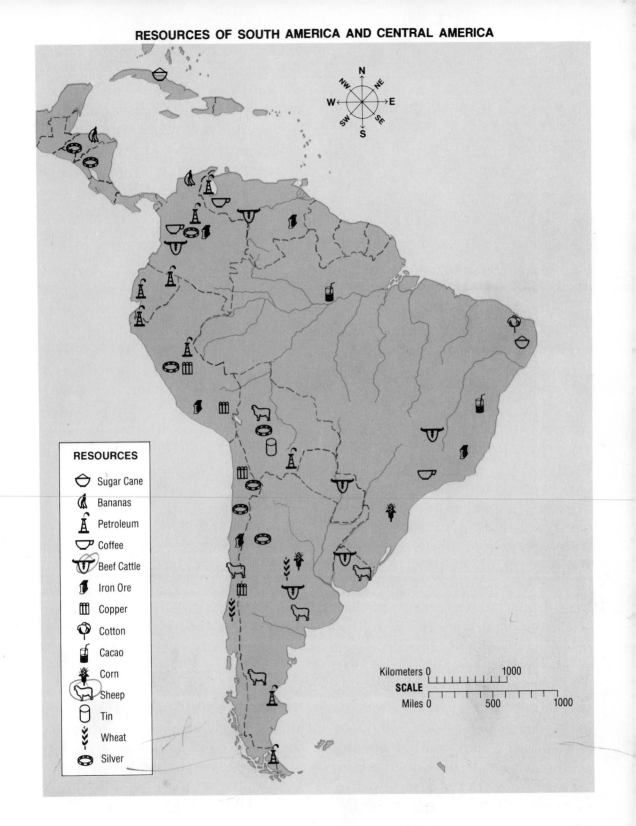

RESOURCES

- Sugar Cane
- Bananas
- Petroleum
- Coffee
- Beef Cattle
- Iron Ore
- Copper
- Cotton
- Cacao
- Corn
- Sheep
- Tin
- Wheat
- Silver

SCALE

Kilometers 0 ____ 1000

Miles 0 ____ 500 ____ 1000

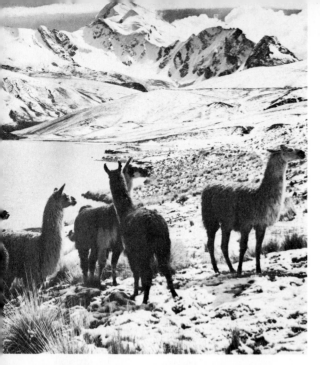

Llamas live in the Andes Mountains. Their soft wool is used to make cloth and clothing.

meat, leather, and wool. They also raise llamas and alpacas. A **llama** (LAH muh) looks like a little camel without a hump. An **alpaca** (al PAK uh) looks like a sheep. Both llamas and alpacas have soft wool. South American farmers grow cotton, too.

Natural resources help South American people earn money. Much of what they raise is sold in other parts of the world. To sell goods to other countries is to *export* (ek SPORT) them. Goods sold to other countries are called **exports** (EK sports). Goods bought by one country from another are **imports** (IM ports). The United States *imports* (im PORTS) almost all its coffee from South America. Coffee is an export that helps South Americans earn money.

South Americans also grow crops for their own use. Corn, potatoes, and onions are among the crops they grow for themselves. Other living resources grow in the Amazon rain forest. Rubber trees grow there. Other trees produce nuts and furnish valuable wood for building.

Much of the best land in South America is owned by large landowners. A few landowners may own huge areas of land. Workers and their children live on this land. The workers are mostly poor. Many of them are South American Indians. Some small farmers in South America own their own land. But usually this is not good land.

Metals and other minerals are important South American resources. The first Europeans in South America were looking for gold and silver. They found great amounts of those metals in the Andes. But gold and silver are only a small part of South America's mineral wealth. There are also diamonds and emeralds on the continent. Tin is found in Bolivia. There is copper in Chile and Peru. There is iron in Brazil, Venezuela, and Colombia.

There is petroleum in Peru, Venezuela, Ecuador, and Colombia. This thick, dark-colored liquid is sometimes called black gold. Gasoline and fuel oil are made from petroleum. That is why this mineral is so valuable.

Look at the map on page 155. It shows the resources of South America. You can see that metals and other minerals are found throughout the continent. But most minerals are found in the highlands.

Unfortunately, there are problems with the mineral wealth of South America. First, the continent does not have much usable coal. Also, many countries do not have enough petroleum. Coal and petroleum can provide the energy to run factories and mines. Buying coal and petroleum from other countries is very costly.

Second, many minerals are in places that are hard to reach. Or they are far from places where people live. It is hard to get those minerals out of the ground. That means the minerals cost more to use. These two problems have made it hard for South Americans to develop their continent.

REVIEW

WATCH YOUR WORDS

1. ___ and ___ are South American animals with soft wool.
   Cattle   Llamas   Kangaroos
   Alpacas

2. Chocolate and cocoa come from ___ seeds.
   alpaca   coffee   cacao

3. We get gasoline and fuel oil from ___.
   alpacas   petroleum   rubber

4. Coffee, bananas, and cacao are South American ___.
   exports   imports
   nonliving resources

5. In the United States, coffee is a(n) ___.
   export   import   natural resource

CHECK YOUR FACTS

Look at the Map

6. Is silver found in the east or the west?

7. Are more sheep and cattle raised in the north or the south?

8. Are cotton and sugar cane grown on the west or the east coast?

9. Is more petroleum found in the northwest or the southeast?

10. Where do bananas grow?

Look at the Lesson

11. What are exports? What are imports?

12. List three crops that South America exports.

13. List three animals that South Americans raise.

14. What is petroleum? Why is it so valuable?

15. What are two problems in developing South America's resources?

Lesson 3: People of South America

FIND THE WORDS

conquer conquistador empire
descendants ancestors

It is the year 1531. A small group of Spanish soldiers sails down the west coast of South America. Their leader is Francisco Pizarro (fran SIS koh pi ZAH roh). He has heard of a rich Indian empire. He and his soldiers are on their way to conquer it.

In 1532, the Spanish soldiers reach Peru. High in the Andes, they find the empire of the Incas (ING kuz). The Spanish soldiers have horses, swords, and guns. They capture the emperor. The Incas bring them a great treasure in gold and silver to set the emperor free.

Even so, Pizarro and his soldiers kill the emperor. Then they go on to conquer the Incan empire. To **conquer** is to defeat in battle. A Spanish conqueror was called by a Spanish word—**conquistador** (kohn kees tah DOR).

Afterward, the Spanish sent gold and silver back to Spain. They forced the Indians to work for them in mines and fields. And they set up certain ways of living in South America. Those ways of living are still followed today.

Earliest Peoples

People lived in the Western Hemisphere long before the Spanish came. Experts believe that the first Americans came from Asia. They think these people crossed at the Bering Sea. Look at the map of Earth on pages 10 and 11. Find the Bering Sea. It is where Asia and North America almost touch.

The first peoples from Asia were bands of hunters. They were following herds of animals. Some of these people settled in North America. They lived in forests, deserts, and plains. Others kept going south. They traveled to Central America and South America.

Five thousand years ago, people in Central America had learned to farm. Some of these peoples went on to build great cities and nations. About 550 years ago, two groups began to build empires. An **empire** is a group of lands or nations under one government. The Aztecs built a great empire in Mexico. The Incas stretched their empire across the Andes Mountains. The Incan empire grew until it was 4000 kilometers (2500 miles) long!

To the Incas, riches were workers, crops, animals, and land. They used gold and silver for decoration. But gold and silver were

The Incas made this statue of a llama out of gold.

This is a South American Indian settlement. It is in the Andes Mountains of Peru.

riches to the Spanish. For this glittering wealth, the Spanish conquered the Incas' lands.

People from Many Lands

Today, the descendants of the first Americans live in North America and South America. We call them American Indians or Native Americans. Actually, each group has its own name and language. The American Indians are descendants of the early peoples from Asia. People's **descendants** are like their great-grandchildren. The early peoples from Asia were the ancestors of the American Indians. People's **ancestors** are like their great-grandparents.

Most South American Indians live in the highlands of the Andes Mountains. They live in the nations of Bolivia, Ecuador, and Peru. That is where the empire of the Incas used to be. At least half the people in these nations are American Indians. Other South American Indians live in the rain forests of the Amazon River. Find these places on the climate map on page 151.

About 450 years ago, people from Europe began to come to South America. They came first from Spain and Portugal. These nations set up colonies in the new land. Nine South American nations used to be colonies of Spain. They are Venezuela, Colombia, Ecuador, Peru, Bolivia, Chile, Argentina, Uruguay, and Paraguay. Find these countries on the map on page 163. Then find Brazil. Brazil used to be a colony of Portugal. Today, many people in South America speak Spanish. But people in Brazil speak Portuguese.

People from Great Britain, the Netherlands, and France also came to South America. They, too, set up colonies in the new world. Guyana used to be a British colony. Suriname was Dutch. French Guiana was a colony of France. Today, it is a department of France. France's departments are like our states. Can you name the overseas state of our country?

Some Europeans came to South America to search for gold and silver. Others started businesses or farms. Today, people with European ancestors live all over South America. Most people in Argentina and Uruguay are descendants of people from Italy and Spain.

Some European settlers brought people from Africa to their colonies. They forced the Africans to work as slaves. Many Africans worked in sugar cane fields on the east coast. Others worked in mines. The Africans had to do the heavy work that Indians did elsewhere. Slavery went on for hundreds of years. Finally, in the nineteenth century, slavery was ended. Today, the descendants of the early Africans live all over South America. But most of the people with African ancestors live in Brazil.

Look at the pictures on page 159. Notice the many different faces of South Americans. People have come to South America from all over the Earth.

REVIEW

WATCH YOUR WORDS

1. Pizarro and his Spanish soldiers ___ the Incas.
   colonized conquered founded

2. What was a Spanish conqueror called?

3. The ___ of the Incas was 4000 kilometers long.
   road canal empire

4. The American Indians are ___ of Asian peoples.
   ancestors conquerors descendants

5. Many people in Brazil have African ___.
   descendants ancestors landowners

CHECK YOUR FACTS

6. Where did the first Americans come from?

7. Why did Francisco Pizarro go to South America?

8. What happened to the Indians when the Spanish came?

9. How did Africans first come to South America?

10. Why did Europeans come to South America?

TRY SOMETHING NEW

Look at the map on page 163. Where were the colonies of Spain? Write your answers. Use the cardinal and intermediate directions.

Lesson 4: Nations and Cities of South America

FIND THE WORDS

- middle class
- progress

Twelve nations and one state occupy the land of South America. You already know something about the land, climate, and people of each. You can learn more by looking at the map on page 163.

Find Brazil on the map. You can see that Brazil is the biggest country in South America. It takes up almost half the continent. Look at the borders of Brazil. How many countries touch Brazil?

Now find Chile. It is a long, narrow country. It is tucked between the Andes Mountains and the Pacific Ocean. Then go north and find Colombia. Colombia has coasts on both the Caribbean Sea and the Pacific Ocean. Play a game using the map for a treasure hunt. See how many other interesting facts you can find. Can you find the second-largest country? Can you find any countries that do not touch Brazil?

The chart on page 164 gives you more information about each nation. Which nations have more than 10 million people?

Where the People Live

Look at the population map of South America on page 164. Use your finger to trace around the edges of the continent. Most South Americans live along the coasts.

Much of the middle of South America is wilderness. Wilderness is wild or empty land where no one lives. There are few roads or railroads in the middle of South America. The middle of North America is very different. It has many big cities, such as Chicago, St. Louis, and Denver. It also has many roads and railroads.

About half of South America's people live in cities. South American cities are as big and busy as cities anywhere in the world. Find the cities on the population map. They are the largest cities in South America. Most of these big cities are near the ocean.

Common Problems

The nations and cities of South America share many problems. The most important problem is poverty. Many people in South American countries are poor. In South America, being poor can mean many things. It can mean

NATIONS OF SOUTH AMERICA AND CENTRAL AMERICA

BAHAMAS

Havana ★

CUBA

DOMINICAN
REPUBLIC

PUERTO RICO
(U.S.)

GUATEMALA

JAMAICA

BELIZE

HONDURAS

HAITI

ANTIGUA
AND
BARBUDA

EL
SALVADOR

NICARAGUA

CARIBBEAN SEA

DOMINICA

ST. LUCIA

BARBADOS

ATLANTIC OCEAN

Lake Nicaragua

GRENADA

ST. VINCENT AND
THE GRENADINES

COSTA RICA

PANAMA

Caracas ★

TRINIDAD AND TOBAGO

N
NW NE
W ★ E
SW SE
S

Panama Canal

VENEZUELA

★ Bogotá

Orinoco River

GUYANA

SURINAME

FRENCH GUIANA

COLOMBIA

EQUATOR

EQUATOR

★Quito

ECUADOR

Amazon River

PERU

BRAZIL

Lima ★

Cuzco ●

BOLIVIA

Lake Titicaca

★ La Paz

★ Brasília

★ Sucre

PACIFIC OCEAN

PARAGUAY

São Paulo ●

Rio de Janeiro

Asunción ★

River

Uruguay River

Paraná

URUGUAY

Santiago ★

Buenos Aires ★

CHILE

ARGENTINA

Montevideo

KEY

– – – National Borders

★ National Capitals

● Cities

Kilometers 0   500   1000

SCALE

Miles 0   500   1000

POPULATION OF SOUTH AMERICA

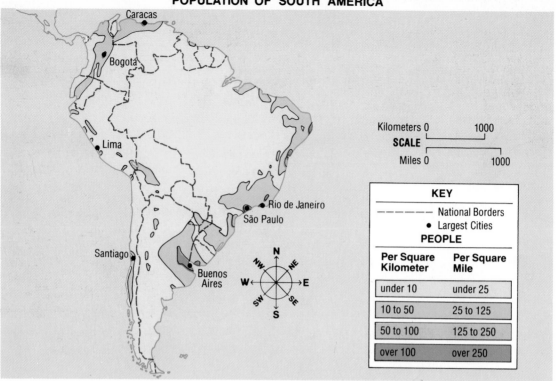

SOUTH AMERICAN NATIONS

Nations	Area		Number of people	Capital	Official language
	square miles	square kilometers			
ARGENTINA (AHR jun TEE nuh)	1,072,157	2,776,889	26 million	Buenos Aires	Spanish
BOLIVIA (buh LIV ee uh)	424,162	1,098,581	5 million	Sucre and La Paz	Spanish
BRAZIL (bruh ZIL)	3,286,470	8,511,965	115 million	Brasília	Portuguese
CHILE (CHIL ee)	292,256	756,945	11 million	Santiago	Spanish
COLOMBIA (kuh LUM bee uh)	439,735	1,138,914	26 million	Bogotá	Spanish
ECUADOR (EHK wuh DOR)	109,483	283,561	8 million	Quito	Spanish
GUYANA (gy AN uh)	83,000	214,969	1 million	Georgetown	English
PARAGUAY (PAR uh GWY)	157,047	406,752	3 million	Asuncíon	Spanish
PERU (puh ROO)	496,220	1,285,210	17 million	Lima	Spanish
SURINAME (SUR uh NAM)	63,037	163,266	1 million	Paramaribo	Dutch
URUGUAY (YUR uh GWY)	68,536	177,508	3 million	Montevideo	Spanish
VENEZUELA (VEN uh ZWAY luh)	352,143	912,050	13 million	Caracas	Spanish
Department of France					
FRENCH GUIANA (french gee AN uh)	35,135	91,000	1 million	Cayenne	French

Rio de Janeiro is a port city in Brazil. Many people enjoy Rio's beautiful beaches.

The city of Santiago is the capital of Chile.

having no running water or electricity in your home. It can mean having tattered clothes and no shoes. It can mean not being able to go to the doctor when you are sick. If you are poor, there may not be a school for you to go to. Your parents may not have jobs. You may not have enough food.

Outside the cities, most of the people are small farmers. They work on land owned by big landowners. Many people move from the farm to the city to find better jobs. But most cannot find work.

The governments of all the countries want to develop their resources. They build public works, such as highways, railroads, dams, and power plants. They encourage people to start businesses and build factories. In these ways, the governments help provide jobs.

For many years, there were only two classes of people in South America. There were the rich and the poor. The rich owned the land. They ran the businesses and the government. The poor did the hard work. They had little to say about how their government was run. There was only a tiny middle class.

The **middle class** is made up of people who are neither rich nor poor. They are mostly people with good jobs. They work in offices, factories, shops, banks, and other businesses. Some of them are doctors, lawyers, and teachers. They are able to earn enough money to meet their needs.

165

FUN FACTS

The driest place in the world:
Calama, in Chile, is in the Atacama Desert. Calama is the driest place in the world. No one has ever seen it rain there. In fact, in the Atacama Desert in Chile, it did not rain for about 400 years! Finally, in 1971, some rain fell there.

The river with the most water:
The Amazon River carries more water than any other river in the world. Only the Nile River in Africa is longer than the Amazon. This mighty river was named for the Amazons. In Greek myths, they were a nation of women who were warriors.

Earth's largest rain forest:
The largest rain forest on Earth is in the Amazon River valley. Trees grow so close together there that sunlight never reaches the ground.

Earth's longest mountains:
The Andes are the longest system of mountains in the world. They are over 8045 kilometers (5000 miles) long. Only the Himalayas in Asia are higher than the Andes.

Earth's highest waterfall:
Angel Falls in Venezuela is the highest waterfall on Earth. This waterfall was named for James Angel. He was an American pilot who found the falls in 1935. Angel Falls drops 979 meters (3212 feet).

Earth's largest high-altitude lake:
Lake Titicaca is on the *altiplano* of Bolivia. It is 3813 meters (12,506 feet) above sea level. It is also 209 kilometers (130 miles) long.

Many people in South American cities are poor.

Here is a good way to tell how well a country is doing. Look at the size of the middle class. In the United States, most of the people are in the middle class.

Argentina, Uruguay, Chile, and Brazil are doing well. These countries have many people in the middle class. Also, the middle class in these countries is growing. That means that fewer people are poor.

Other countries in South America have a very small middle class. Bolivia, Ecuador, Peru, Suriname, and Paraguay are some of these countries. Many people in these countries cannot read and write. The governments of these countries are having trouble providing work. All over South America, the population is increasing. There are more people looking for work than there are jobs. So most people in poor countries will probably be poor for a long time.

The countries with a growing middle class are making progress. **Progress** (PROG res) is improvement. It is action taken to reach a goal. Jobs for people are a sign of progress. Electricity, running water, schools, and doctors are signs of progress, too.

REVIEW

WATCH YOUR WORDS

1. A ___ is a wild region where no people live.
   plain   wilderness   coast
2. The ___ is growing in Argentina and Brazil.
   poverty   wilderness   middle class
3. Jobs that allow people to meet their needs are signs of___.
   poverty   progress   wealth

CHECK YOUR FACTS

Look at the Maps

4. What is the largest country in South America?
5. List the countries that touch the borders of Brazil.
6. Where do most South Americans live?

Look at the Chart

7. What five countries have the most people?
8. What five countries have the fewest people?

Look at the Lesson

9. What is it like to be poor in South America?
10. Why do people move from the farm to the city?
11. What is the middle class?
12. How can a government help provide more jobs?
13. What are some signs of progress in South America?

THINK ABOUT IT

Many people live in the middle of North America. Why do so few live in the middle of South America?

CHAPTER REVIEW

WATCH YOUR WORDS

1. The ___ is a plateau in Bolivia, high in the mountains.
   pampas *altiplano* llanos

2. Hot chocolate comes from the ___ bean.
   coffee cacao alpaca

3. In Brazil, coffee is an ___ . In the United States, coffee is an ___ .
   import export artifact

4. Many people in Brazil are ___ of African peoples.
   ancestors artifacts descendants

5. Many people in Argentina had Spanish ___.
   descendants ancestors llamas

6. Jobs and education are signs of ___.
   progress resources empire

CHECK YOUR FACTS

7. Why is much of South America's land hard to live on?

8. List three important facts about the Andes Mountains.

9. List two important facts about the Amazon River.

10. What is the Amazon rain forest like?

11. What is the climate like in the Amazon River valley?

12. List three important things about the pampas.

13. South America has many resources. Name three animals, three plants, and three minerals.

14. Who was Francisco Pizarro?

15. Name three continents from which people came to South America.

16. Name four European countries that had colonies in South America.

USE YOUR CHART

Look at the chart on page 164. Then answer these questions.

17. How many nations are there in South America?

18. Which nation has the most land? Which has the most people?

19. Which nation is smallest in size? How many people live there?

20. How many nations have Spanish as their official language?

21. Which nation has Portuguese as its official language?

CLOSE THE MAP GAP

22. Draw or trace an outline map of South America.

23. Label the Andes Mountains, the Atacama Desert, the Amazon River, the Amazon rain forest, and the pampas.

24. Color the Andes brown, the Atacama yellow, the Amazon blue, the rain forest green, and the pampas green.

25. Put red dots on the map to show where most of the people live.

26. Label these cities: São Paulo, Caracas, Rio de Janeiro, Buenos Aires, Lima, Santiago, and Bogotá.

THINK ABOUT IT

27. Where would you rather live—the *altiplano*, the pampas, or the rain forest? Why?

28. Why is it hard for South Americans to develop their resources?

29. Why don't people live in the middle of South America?

30. Do you think it is good for a country to have a large middle class? Why, or why not?

2 LIVING IN A HIGH LAND

Lesson 1: Bolivia

FIND THE WORDS

coastline   seaport   high-altitude

Bolivia is one of the nations in South America. It is about the size of Texas and California combined.

There are several special things about Bolivia. First, this country has no coastline. A **coastline** is a natural boundary next to the ocean. Bolivia is not on the ocean. It has to ship its products from a seaport in Chile. A **seaport** is a town on the coast where ships can load and unload. One other nation in South America has no coastline and no seaports. Look at the political map on page 163. Can you find that other nation? What is it? Find Bolivia on the map, too.

Here is another special thing about Bolivia. Most of the people live on a very small part of the land. Look at the physical map on page 171. There are two very different kinds of land in Bolivia. There are high mountains in the

169

Lake Titicaca is the largest high-altitude lake in the world. It is 3813 meters (12,506 feet) above sea level.

west. There are grassy plains and rain forests in the east. Where do you think most Bolivians live?

Did you guess that they live in the west? If so, you guessed right! Most Bolivians live on a plateau high in the Andes Mountains. That plateau is called the *altiplano*. Most of the *altiplano* is about 3660 meters (12,000 feet) above sea level. So most Bolivians live in a high land.

Another special thing about Bolivia is this. Bolivia has two capital cities! By law, the capital is Sucre (SOO kray). It is in the middle of the country. The other capital is La Paz (lah PAHZ). It is north and west of Sucre. Bolivia's courts of law are in Sucre. The congress and most of the government buildings are in La Paz.

La Paz is on the *altiplano*. It is Bolivia's largest city. La Paz is also one of the highest cities in the world. La Paz is 3600 meters (11,800 feet) above sea level. At that elevation, the air is cold and thin. Visitors find it hard to breathe. But Bolivians are very comfortable living there.

The *altiplano*'s main resources are minerals. Tin, silver, and copper are found there. Minerals are Bolivia's most important exports. Land on the *altiplano* is not very fertile. A cereal grass called millet grows there. So do potatoes, onions, and some other vegetables.

Fish are another resource found on the *altiplano*. They come from Lake Titicaca (TEE tee KAH kah). Lake Titicaca is the largest high-altitude lake in the world. The term **high-altitude** means "high above sea level."

Bolivia has mountain valleys that are much more fertile than

170

BOLIVIA

ELEVATION

Meters	Feet
over 4,000	over 13,100
2,000 to 4,000	6,600 to 13,100
1,000 to 2,000	3,300 to 6,600
200 to 1,000	660 to 3,300
sea level to 200	sea level to 660
below sea level	below sea level

PERU

BRAZIL

Madre de Dios River

Beni River

San Martín River

Mamoré River

San Miguel River

Lake Titicaca

La Paz

Cochabamba

BOLIVIA

Santa Cruz

Oruro

Lake Poopó

Sucre

Potosí

ALTIPLANO

ANDES MOUNTAINS

PARAGUAY

ARGENTINA

CHILE

Kilometers 0   300

SCALE

Miles 0   300

KEY

• Cities   ⭐ Capitals

– – National Borders

Coffee grows in Bolivia's fertile valleys.

who live on the eastern plains raise cattle and goats. There is much fertile soil in the east. But little of the land is being farmed. There are also rich forests. And there are valuable minerals, such as iron ore, petroleum, and natural gas.

To use these rich lands, Bolivia needs better transportation. Now, there are few highways and railroads in the east. It is hard to get food and cattle from the east to the cities in the mountains. So it is hard for people in the east to sell their products. Many of the goods that are sold in Bolivia travel by air. Moving goods by airplane costs more than sending them by train, ship, or truck. Why do you think this is so?

the *altiplano*. Coffee, sugar, fruit, and grains grow in the valleys. Sucre is in one of these valleys.

Bolivia needs to develop its resources in the east. The few people

REVIEW

WATCH YOUR WORDS

1. Every country that has the ocean as a boundary has a(n)____.
   altiplano   coastline   import

2. A(n) ____ is a town on the coast where ships can load and unload.
   export   *altiplano*   seaport

3. Lake Titicaca is the largest____lake in the world.
   fishing   high-altitude   polluted

CHECK YOUR FACTS

4. What are three special things about Bolivia?

5. Where do most Bolivians live?

6. What natural resources are found on the *altiplano*?

7. What natural resources do the mountain valleys have?

8. What natural resources are in the east of Bolivia? Why aren't these resources being used?

THINK ABOUT IT

9. Why would not having a coastline be a problem for a nation?

10. Why would it be hard to build roads and railroads across Bolivia?

Lesson 2: The People of the Altiplano

FIND THE WORDS

plantation ranch hacienda
criollos campesino

Imagine a time over 1400 years ago. At that time, a great city was built on the *altiplano*. This city was in Bolivia, near Lake Titicaca. It was about 4000 meters (13,000 feet) above sea level. It was called Tiahuanaco (tee uh wuh NAH koh).

The people of Tiahuanaco built huge stone palaces and temples. They carved statues from great blocks of stone. One statue is called *Gateway to the Sun*. Pictures of the sun, of gods, and of giant birds are carved on it. The people of Tiahuanaco also wove beautiful cloth. They painted pottery. And they knew how to work with metals. Tiahuanaco lasted about 600 years as a great city. Experts think it was a religious center. Today, only its ruins remain.

Who built Tiahuanaco so long ago? Many think the ancestors of the Aymara built it. The Aymara (eye MAH ruh) are South American Indians. They lived on the *altiplano* long before the Incas came.

The Incas

Around the year 1100, the Incas came to the *altiplano*. They built their capital at Cuzco (KOOS koh) in Peru. Look at the political map of South America on page 163. Find Cuzco. You can see it is not far from Lake Titicaca.

Over 300 years went by. Then, in the 1400s, the Incas started to build their empire. They conquered other Indian groups in the Andes region. After a long struggle, they conquered the Aymara.

The Incas learned a lot from the people who lived on the *altiplano* before them. They also taught the Aymara some new ways of doing things. The Incas

The people of Tiahuanaco carved the *Gateway to the Sun*. The running figure at right is one of many carvings on the gateway.

The Incas wove wool and cotton cloth. Incan women knew almost all of the weaving methods and patterns used today.

were expert at planning and organizing. They counted their people. They made maps of their land. They built one road through the mountains and another along the coast. They dug canals to carry water to dry fields. They grew crops on the sides of mountains. They built stone cities that not even earthquakes could destroy. They wove wool and cotton cloth. They mined gold and silver. They knew how to make bronze from copper and tin. They were expert farmers and excellent soldiers. By the 1500s, the Incas ruled much of South America's west coast.

Some Aymara escaped to the mountains when the Incas came. Others stayed and learned Incan ways of fighting and farming. They helped build canals and roads. But most refused to learn the Incan language and religion. The Incas ruled the Aymara. But the Aymara way of life went on.

The Spanish

Then, in 1532, the Spanish came. Francisco Pizarro and his soldiers conquered the Incas. In 1538, his two brothers conquered the Aymara. Now the Spanish ruled all the American Indians of the *altiplano*.

Soon, the Spanish found the rich silver mines that the Incas had used. To get this silver, the Spanish forced Indians to dig in the mines. Many Indians died from too much work and too little food. Others died from European diseases. They caught these diseases from the Spanish.

The Spanish in South America made the Spanish in Europe rich. They sent silver and other treasure back to Spain. In return, the rulers of Spain gave the Spanish settlers land. The settlers used their lands to raise crops and animals.

A large farm where crops are raised is called a **plantation**. A large farm used to raise animals is called a **ranch**. In South America, a Spanish ranch or plantation was called a **hacienda** (HAH see EN duh). The Spanish settlers owned the haciendas. They had the best, most fertile land. They forced the Indians to work for them. Some hacienda owners became very rich.

Spain ruled the *altiplano* for almost 300 years. The king and queen of Spain lived far away.

WHERE WE ARE IN TIME AND PLACE

THE INCA EMPIRE

500–1000 A.D.	1100	1438–1532	1532	1538
People lived at Tiahuanaco	Incas founded Cuzco in Peru	Incas built their empire in the Andes	Francisco Pizarro conquered Incas	Pizarro's brothers conquered Aymara

THE INCA EMPIRE

Caribbean Sea

Isthmus of Panama

Quito

ANDES MOUNTAINS

Machu Picchu
Cuzco
Lake Titicaca
Tiahuanaco

PACIFIC OCEAN

Maule River

Kilometers 0 500 1000

SCALE

Miles 0 500 1000

KEY

Extent of the Inca Empire
• Cities

In 1911, Hiram Bingham made a great discovery. He was the son and grandson of missionaries. He taught at Yale University. And he had come to South America to explore Incan ruins.

He found what he called "the lost city of the Incas." It was the city of Machu Picchu (MAH choo PEEK choo). It was near the Incan capital of Cuzco in Peru.

Machu Picchu was built on a high ridge between mountain peaks. Bingham had never seen anything like it before. The city looked almost as if the Incas had just left it. It was built on many levels. More than 3000 steps led from one level to another. Like other Incan cities, it had homes, temples, and palaces. It also had government buildings and a lookout tower. It was 2058 meters (6750 feet) above sea level.

To build this mountain city, the Incas first made models of clay. Then they cut and shaped large blocks of stone. They used ramps and rollers to move the stones. Then they fitted the stones very carefully together. Because they built so well, Machu Picchu has lasted for more than 800 years! People still visit it. How would you like to live there, on top of the world?

They sent Spanish officials to govern the *altiplano* for them. These officials made laws. They collected taxes. They controlled the army. The Spanish rulers and officials made decisions for the people of South America.

Independence

Many Spanish settlers wanted to make their own decisions. Many of them had been born on the *altiplano*. The *altiplano*—not Spain—was their home. They called themselves **criollos** (kree OHL yohs).

In 1809, fighting broke out between the Spanish soldiers and the criollos. The fighting lasted 16 years. Finally, the Spanish were defeated. The armies of the criollos won. These armies were led by two great generals. They were Simón Bolívar (see MOHN boh LEE vahr) and Antonio de Sucre (an TOH nee oh duh SOO kray).

A new, independent nation was born in 1825. It was called Bolivia in honor of General Bolívar. Its capital city was called Sucre after General de Sucre. Sucre was Bolivia's first president.

Independence for Bolivia made little difference to the Aymara. The Indians still dug silver in the mines. They still worked on the haciendas. They received little or no pay. Their lives were still ruled by others.

The *patrón* (pah TROHN), or boss, owned the land. The Indians

Left: Aymara mothers carry young children with them on their backs.
Right: These Aymara students go to school on the *altiplano*.

had to farm the land for the *patrón*. Indian families also took turns working as servants in the *patrón*'s home. They cooked meals and cleaned house. They milked cows and herded sheep and cattle. They cleaned the stables. They fixed the hacienda buildings. The *patrón* let the Indian families use small plots of ground. There, they could grow food for themselves. In some places, the *patrón* provided a school for the children. But the *patrón* could also beat the Indians and take their land away. Life was hard for these American Indians.

Finally, in 1952, the people of the *altiplano* won their freedom.

Workers from the haciendas and the mines joined with poor people from the cities. They put their own leaders in charge of the government. This new government made many changes. Most of the hacienda lands were divided up. Now, families could own their little plots of land. New schools were built. Everyone over 21 got the right to vote. And the Indians got a new name. They were no longer the *patrón*'s servants. They were **campesinos** (KAM puh SEE nohz), or "small farmers."

Today, the *campesinos* are the largest group in Bolivia. About half of them are Aymara.

REVIEW

WATCH YOUR WORDS

1. A large farm where workers grow crops is a____.
   campesino   plantation   ranch

2. A large farm where herds of animals are raised is a ____.
   plantation   ranch   *campesino*

3. A large Spanish farm in South America was a____.
   hacienda   *campesino*   *patrón*

4. Some Spanish settlers on the *altiplano* fought for independence from Spain. They were____.
   campesinos   Incas   criollos

5. The Aymara people who became small farmers are____.
   criollos   *patróns*   *campesinos*

CHECK YOUR FACTS

6. How did the Incas change life on the *altiplano*? Name five things they did.

7. What happened to the Aymara and the Incas when the Spanish came?

8. Why did some Spanish settlers fight Spain?

9. Who was Simón Bolívar? Who was Antonio de Sucre? How did their people honor them?

10. What did an Indian family on a hacienda do for the *patrón*?

TRY SOMETHING NEW

Pretend you are a *campesino*. You used to work for a *patrón*. Tell how your life changed in 1952.

Lesson 3: The Future of the Aymara

FIND THE WORDS

adapt   pack animal
memorize   civics

Since Incan times, the Aymara have kept their own culture. In their villages, they still follow customs from the old days. They pass on their dances, songs, and beliefs. They speak the Aymara language of their ancestors. They make artifacts, such as colorful blankets and shawls.

Over the years, the Aymara learned to live under many different rulers. To do this, they had to adapt. To **adapt** is to change when the conditions around you change. Aymara life is still changing.

The Village

In this lesson, we will visit an Aymara village. This village is on the shore of Lake Titicaca. Long ago, village people built their houses of mud brick, with roofs of straw. Now, most live in

In the villages, some Aymara follow their old ways. They cut wool from their llamas. Then they spin the wool into thread. After that, they use hand looms to weave the thread into cloth.

Once, the Aymara used llamas to carry goods to market. Now, they use trucks.

Bottom Left: Aymara farmers plant potatoes. Their ancestors were the first people in the world to grow potatoes.

Bottom Right: The Aymara sell their onions at a market in La Paz.

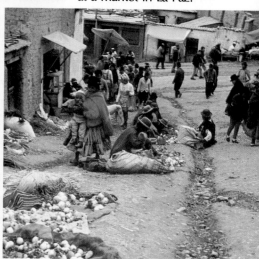

two-story houses with metal roofs. Once, people wove their cloth from the wool of llamas. Then, they sewed their clothes by hand. Now, they often buy their cloth. Many make clothes on sewing machines. Many also buy ready-made clothes in stores. Some are proud that they can dress the same way city people do.

This Aymara village is about 80 kilometers (50 miles) from La Paz. Once, the trip to La Paz was long and hard. Then, village people used llamas to carry their goods to market. An animal that carries a load on its back is called a **pack animal.** In Incan times, the armies used llamas to carry their supplies. Now, trucks carry goods between the village and the city. Many families in the village hope to own a truck someday. Village people can also get to the city on bicycles or on the bus.

Market Women

Most of the people in the village are small farmers. Their ancestors were the first people in the world to grow potatoes. Now, onions are the most important crop in the village. Both onions and potatoes grow well at high altitudes. The teenage village girls sell the onions in the city markets. Village families get most of their money from the onion sales.

Dolores Santiago always wanted to be a market woman. This is her story.

"I can still remember my childhood days. We were very poor. One day, a market woman came to our house. She wore new shoes and a brightly colored shawl. She had shiny black hair. Her eyes twinkled. She carried a big package. In it was my first pair of real shoes. I decided that I wanted to be a market woman.

"By the time I was 14, I was taking things to market for many families. I had to learn how to get the best price for their vegetables and weaving. It took a lot of work. People came to the market from many places. I had to learn how to speak Spanish.

"At first, my business was bad. People passed me by. I thought it was because I was new.

"One day, I watched the best market woman. She wore bright clothes. She sat in front of the prettiest building. She placed her goods so that they all looked interesting to shoppers.

"The next day, I wore my prettiest clothes. I left early and got there before the others. I sat in front of a big blue-and-white building. Then, I took extra time to fix my goods.

"That day, I sold more things than ever before!"

Market women learn how to arrange their fruits and vegetables. An attractive display helps a market woman make more sales.

Tin is one of Bolivia's most important resources. Here, a woman sells tin goods at the market.

At the village school, students learn to read and write in Spanish. They also learn arithmetic.

The Village School

In 1958, the people of the village built a school. There, students learn to read and write in Spanish. In Bolivia, people need to know Spanish to get good jobs.

The village school has no maps or globes. There are not many books. The teacher teaches the lesson and writes things on the board. Often, students say things over and over until they know them. To learn this way is to **memorize.** Students also learn to write down what the teacher says. They see and say what they have to learn.

The class spends most of its time on arithmetic and civics. **Civics** is the study of the rules and rights of people in a nation. The class also studies history, geography, and health.

Sometimes, parents visit the school. While they watch, the teacher asks the students questions. The students give the answers. Then the parents know that their children are learning.

Many young Aymara have left their quiet villages. They look for jobs in busy modern cities like La Paz.

Life in the City

Life has changed for the Aymara in many ways. The village people are still poor. But now they own land. They take their own crops to market. They learn to read and write. They own radios and other products from all over the world. They take a greater part in their local government. They also learn more about their country and the world.

Life in the villages has gotten better. Still, most young people are moving to La Paz. They want to find jobs in the city. This is not easy. Some cannot find work. Others get jobs that pay very little. They clean streets, carry heavy boxes, or work as servants. Many of them have not yet learned Spanish.

Other village people learn new ways of living in the city. They learn Spanish. They dress like city people. Some drive taxis and trucks. Others work in factories or stores. Many start businesses, making clothes or baking bread. Often, people already in the city help others from their village. They help newcomers get a job and find a place to live. They visit their village often. That way, they stay close to their families.

For thousands of years, the Aymara have been farmers. Much of their culture is built on farming life. Their way of life has lasted through Incan rulers. It has lasted through Spanish conquerors. It has lasted through haciendas and *patrones*. Will the Aymara way of life last in the city?

City life for the Aymara is a mixture of old and new. Even in the city, many Aymara keep their rich culture alive.

REVIEW

WATCH YOUR WORDS

1. To change when conditions around you change is to____.
   conquer escape adapt

2. The Incan armies used the llama as a(n)____.
   export pack animal nonliving resource

3. To say something until you know it is to____it.
   memorize repeat forget

4. ____ is the study of rights people have and rules they follow.
   History Civics Science

6. How did the Aymara get their clothes in the past? How do they get their clothes today?

7. How did the Aymara take their goods to market in the past? How do they get their goods to the city now?

8. The Aymara's ancestors were the first people to grow a certain vegetable. What was it?

9. List three things that students study in the Aymara village school.

10. Why is it important for a market woman to know Spanish?

CHECK YOUR FACTS

5. What were Aymara houses like in the past? What are they like now.

THINK ABOUT IT

How is the Aymara school like your school? How is it different?

CHAPTER REVIEW

WATCH YOUR WORDS

1. Bolivia and Paraguay do not have ____ .
   resources   exports   coastlines
2. Sheep and cattle are raised on a ____ .
   plantation   ranch   *campesino*
3. Sugar cane is raised on a ____ .
   ranch   llano   plantation
4. Small farmers, or ____ , are the largest group in Bolivia.
   campesinos   conquistadores   criollos
5. The Aymara survived because they could ____ .
   conquer   adapt   memorize

CHECK YOUR FACTS

6. Where in Bolivia do most people live?
7. How high is the *altiplano?*
8. What is Sucre? For whom was it named?
9. What is La Paz? Tell three special things about it.
10. What resources are found on the *altiplano?* Name three living resources and three nonliving resources.
11. Where was the empire of the Incas? List five things the Incas did.
12. What work did the American Indians do for the Spanish?
13. Why did the criollos fight the Spanish army?
14. Who was Simón Bolívar?
15. When was Bolivia born as a nation? When did the Aymara get the vote?

FIND THE TIME LINE

16. List the events below in the right order. Start with the one that happened first. End with the one that happened last.
    —The Spanish conquered the Incas and the Aymara.
    —The Indians got votes and land.
    —People built Tiahuanaco.
    —The criollos won their independence from Spain.
    —The Incas conquered the Aymara.

TRY SOMETHING NEW

17. Write the story of the Aymara. First, tell who they are and where they live. How long have they lived there? Then, tell about their history. Who conquered them? What work did they have to do? How did they win their freedom? Finally, tell how their life changed in 1952.

THINK ABOUT IT

18. How could Bolivia develop its resources in the east?
19. How did the Aymara keep their culture alive?
20. Have you ever learned to do something by watching someone who did it well? Is this a good way to learn?
21. How can your parents tell that you are learning?
22. Why is it important for people in Bolivia to learn Spanish? Why is it important for you to learn English?

UNIT REVIEW

WATCH YOUR WORDS

Use the words below to fill in the blanks.
Use each term only once.

adapt   cacao   conquistador
altiplano   coastline   descendants
ancestors   conquer   empire

exports   llamas   petroleum
haciendas   middle class   progress
imports   pack animals   seaport

High in the Andes Mountains is a plateau called the ___ . There, long ago, the city of Tiahuanaco was built. We think the ___ of the Aymara built it. Then, about 500 years ago, the Aymara were defeated by the Incas. They became part of the great Incan ___ . The Incas built long roads. They used woolly___as ___ ___ to carry loads. Then, Francisco Pizarro came with his Spanish soldiers to ___ the Incas. Pizarro was a conqueror, or___ . The Spanish settlers made the Indians work for them on large farms called ___ . The ___ of those Indians still live in Bolivia. The Aymara survived many rulers because they could ___ , or change.

Products that South American nations sell to other countries are ___ . One such product is ___ , from which we get cocoa and chocolate. Another such product is coffee. The United States brings in, or ___ , coffee from South America. Bolivia sells tin to other nations. But Bolivia does not have a ___ . Therefore, it has to ship its goods from a ___ in Chile. Many South American nations do not have enough ___ to meet their energy needs. The nations making the most ___ , or improvement, have a growing___ .

CHECK YOUR FACTS

1. What are the longest, and second-highest, mountains in the world?
2. What is the driest place in South America?
3. What is the climate like in the highlands of South America?
4. What river carries the most water?
5. Name three plants and three animals that South Americans raise.
6. Name three minerals that are found in South America.
7. What are exports? What are imports?
8. What five European countries had colonies in South America?
9. Where are most of the big cities in South America?
10. Name three signs of progress.

KNOW YOUR PEOPLE

Match the name with the clue.

11. The Aymara

12. The Incas

13. Francisco Pizarro

14. Simón Bolívar

15. Antonio de Sucre

A. conquered the peoples of the Andes in the 1500s.

B. was the first president of his country.

C. ruled an empire in the Andes.

D. lived on the altiplano before the Incas.

E. had a country named for him.

GET CHART SMART

16. Copy the chart below on a separate sheet of paper. Then fill in the blanks.

Nations	Area	Number of people	Capital	Official language
ARGENTINA	1,072,157 sq. mi.		Buenos Aires	
BOLIVIA		5 million		Spanish
BRAZIL	3,286,470 sq. mi.		Brasília	
COLOMBIA		26 million		Spanish
PERU	496,220 sq. mi.		Lima	
VENEZUELA		13 million		Spanish

17. Answer these questions based on your chart.
  a. Which two nations have the most land?
  b. Which three nations have the most people?
  c. Which nation has two capitals?

USE YOUR MAPS

18. Look at the elevation map of South America on page 147. What is the elevation of the Andes Mountains? Of the pampas?

19. Look at the resource map of South America on page 155. In what places is petroleum found?

20. Look at the map of Earth on pages 10 and 11. Where did early peoples cross from Asia to North America?

21. Look at the political map of South America on page 163. How many countries do not touch Brazil?

22. Look at the population map of South America on page 164. Which areas have the most people?

TRY SOMETHING NEW

Make a Time Line

23. Make a time line for Bolivia. Put these dates on it. Then write what happened on each date.
1100   1538   1825   1952

Word Games

24. Which thing in the list below is not a plant?
cacao   coffee   alpaca   banana

25. Which thing in the list below is not an animal?
cow   sheep   llama   llano

26. Which thing in the list below is not land?
pampas   llanos   *campesino*   *altiplano*

27. Which thing in the list below is not a farm?
plantation   criollo   hacienda   ranch

28. Which place in the list below is not hard to live in?
jungle   wilderness   desert   pampas

PUT IT ALL TOGETHER

29. On a separate sheet of paper, draw an outline map of Bolivia. Use the map on page 171 as a guide. Put these things on your map:
  a. the Andes Mountains
  b. the *altiplano*
  c. the eastern plains
  d. La Paz and Sucre
  e. Lake Titicaca
  f. the border with Peru
  g. the border with Chile
  h. the border with Argentina
  i. the border with Paraguay
  j. the border with Brazil

1 AFRICA AND ITS PEOPLE

Lesson 1: Land and Climate

FIND THE WORDS

rapids inland barren
source silt mouth
rainy season dry season

More than 500 years ago, ships left Portugal, a country in Europe. They sailed down the Atlantic coast of Africa. The captains of those ships were looking for a way to the riches of India. They were trying to find a way around Africa.

Along the coast of Africa, they found few harbors for their ships. A harbor is a place on a coast protected from the open sea. There, ships can anchor safely. There, people and goods can be easily moved between ship and shore.

The land in Africa seemed to rise very steeply from the shore. Often, there were deserts or rain forests along the coast. Also, the rivers often had **rapids,** or rocky places. The rocks make the water flow very fast. Rapids and water-falls kept ships from sailing up the rivers very far.

These were the kinds of land and rivers the explorers found. Thus, it was hard for them to travel inland in Africa. **Inland** means beyond the coast, toward

AFRICA

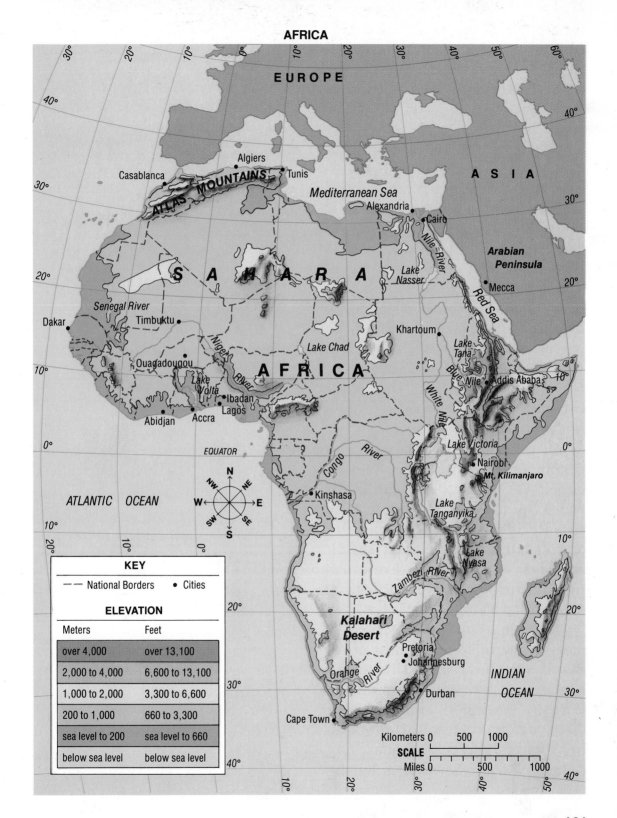

EUROPE

ASIA

Algiers
Casablanca
ATLAS MOUNTAINS
Tunis

Mediterranean Sea

Alexandria
Cairo

Arabian Peninsula

S A H A R A

Lake Nasser

Nile River

Red Sea

Mecca

Senegal River

Dakar

Timbuktu

Khartoum

Lake Tana

Niger River

Lake Chad

A F R I C A

Blue Nile

Addis Ababa

Ouagadougou

White Nile

Lake Volta

Ibadan
Lagos

Abidjan
Accra

EQUATOR

Lake Victoria

Nairobi
Mt. Kilimanjaro

ATLANTIC OCEAN

Congo River

Kinshasa

Lake Tanganyika

N
NW NE
W   E
SW SE
S

Lake Nyasa

Zambezi River

Kalahari Desert

Pretoria
Johannesburg

Orange River

INDIAN OCEAN

Durban

Cape Town

KEY

- - - National Borders • Cities

ELEVATION

Meters	Feet
over 4,000	over 13,100
2,000 to 4,000	6,600 to 13,100
1,000 to 2,000	3,300 to 6,600
200 to 1,000	660 to 3,300
sea level to 200	sea level to 660
below sea level	below sea level

Kilometers 0   500   1000
SCALE
Miles 0   500   1000

the middle of the land. Europeans couldn't get to the middle of Africa. So they called Africa the Dark Continent. They called it that because they knew little about it.

Not until the 1800s did Europeans begin to explore all of Africa. But Africa had great empires long before the Europeans came. You will learn about two empires of west Africa in the next lesson.

Look at the elevation map of Africa on page 191. Notice that most of the continent is made up of plateaus. Sometimes there are narrow plains along the coast. But Africa's coast has few natural harbors. It has few rivers that ships can sail. This is because the highlands are close to the ocean.

Africa is the second-largest continent on Earth. Only Asia is larger. Yet much of the land in Africa is not useful to people. The climate is either too hot and dry or too hot and wet. Even so, almost 500 million people live in Africa. In this lesson, we will look at Africa's land and climate.

The equator crosses Africa almost in the middle. So most of Africa lies in the tropics. This makes Africa the hottest continent on Earth. Remember, climates near the equator are tropical climates. In tropical deserts, savannas, and rain forests, the weather is hot almost all year.

An oasis is a place in a desert with water and fertile land.

At the mouth of the Nile is a fertile delta. The delta was formed from silt dropped by the Nile.

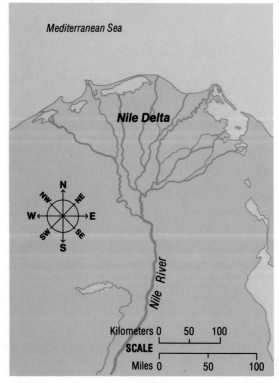

NILE RIVER DELTA

Mediterranean Sea

Nile Delta

Nile River

Kilometers 0   50   100

SCALE

Miles 0   50   100

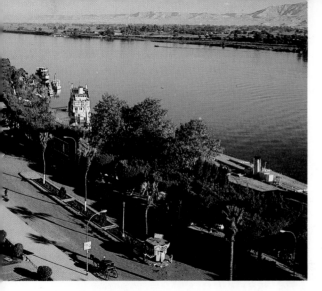
The Nile is the longest river on Earth.

The Sahara

A great desert, the Sahara, stretches across most of northern Africa. In the language of the Arabs, *Sahara* (suh HAR uh) means "desert." The Sahara is the largest desert on Earth.

On the Sahara, days are very hot. Nights are cool. Almost no rain falls in the Sahara. The land is mostly barren. **Barren** land is land on which no plants will grow. Here and there in the desert are sand dunes. There are also some mountains in the Sahara.

Few people live in the Sahara. Most of those who do live there live in oases (oh A seez). An *oasis* (oh A sis) is a place in a desert with water and fertile land. In Africa, the Nile River flows through the Sahara. The valley of the Nile is the largest oasis in the world.

The Nile

The Nile River is the longest river on Earth. The Nile has two branches, the White Nile and the Blue Nile. The White Nile begins at Lake Victoria at the equator. The Blue Nile begins at Lake Tana in Ethiopia (EE thee OH pee uh). That means Lake Victoria and Lake Tana are the sources of the Nile. The **source** of a river is the place where it starts. The two branches of the Nile join at Khartoum (kahr TOOM) in the Sudan. From there, the Nile flows north to the Mediterranean Sea.

Notice that the Blue Nile starts in the eastern highlands. In the summer, heavy rains fall there. Then the river carries the rain water north. So, once a year, the Nile in Egypt would fill up and overflow. The river also carries along soil that is full of minerals. This rich soil is called **silt.** When the river flooded the land, it left this rich soil on top. That made the banks of the Nile very fertile.

Still, the river carried some of the floodwater on to the sea. That water was lost. To save it, the people of modern Egypt built a dam. Now, the Aswan High Dam holds back the floodwaters. Now, farmers can get water for their fields all year long. But their fields no longer get the Nile River silt.

The place where a river flows into the ocean is called the **mouth.** Sometimes, at the mouth of a river, there is a delta. A delta is an area of rich soil, or silt. It is usually shaped like a triangle. The delta of the Nile is north of Cairo (KY roh) in Egypt.

The Savannas

Now look at the climate map on page 195. Suppose you are traveling from north to south in Africa. First, you cross a narrow strip of land along the Mediterranean Sea. There, the land is fertile and the climate is comfortable. Next, you go through the desert. Then, you come to tropical grasslands, or savannas. Almost half of Africa is savanna land. Savannas have a few trees and bushes.

Savannas have only two seasons. In the **rainy season,** the weather is hot and wet. The land is green. The rivers fill up and sometimes overflow. The farmers grow their crops during the rainy season. In the **dry season,** the weather is hot and dry. Little or no rain falls. The grass dies, and the fields turn brown. Some of the rivers dry up.

The Rain Forests

South of the savannas are tropical rain forests. Rain forests cover much of the Atlantic coast near the equator. They also stretch far inland. Find the rain forest area on the climate map. The weather is hot and wet there all year. It is hard for people to live and work in such a climate.

Elephants and zebras visit a water hole on the African savanna. Savanna lands are grasslands.

CLIMATES OF AFRICA

EUROPE

ASIA

Mediterranean Sea

Sahara

AFRICA

Nile River

Red Sea

Senegal River

Niger River

Lake Chad

Blue Nile

Benue River

White Nile

ETHIOPIAN HIGHLANDS

ATLANTIC OCEAN

Congo River

Lake Victoria

Equator

Lake Tanganyika

Mt. Kilimanjaro

Lake Nyasa

Zambesi River

Orange River

N

INDIAN OCEAN

0 200 600
Kilometers

Miles
0 200 600

KEY

Rain Forest:
Hot and wet year round

Savanna:
Hot wet summer,
hot dry winter

Dry Savanna:
Hot summer, hot to cold
winter, variable rainfall

Desert:
Hot summer, hot to cold
winter, dry year round

Warm and Wet:
Hot wet summer,
mild wet winter

Mediterranean:
Warm dry summer,
mild wet winter

Highlands:
Various local climates
generally cool or cold
all year

Mount Kilimanjaro is the highest mountain in Africa. It is near the equator. Even so, there is snow on top all year.

The South

South of the rain forests are more savannas. Still farther south, you come to the Kalahari (KAH luh HAH ree) Desert. Finally, you reach the southern tip of Africa. There, the weather changes more from season to season. There are more areas of fertile land.

The Highlands

All along the eastern part of Africa are highlands. They stretch from the Red Sea down the whole continent. In the highlands are plateaus with fertile land. The climate on the plateaus is cool and comfortable. It is not too wet or too dry. People can grow grain crops, such as wheat. Coffee also grows in the eastern highlands. On the highland plains of Kenya, there are many wild animals. Lions, elephants, zebras, giraffes, and leopards are found there.

Running through the eastern highlands is the Great Rift Valley. This valley is a huge break in the land. It is very wide and deep. It is also 2900 kilometers (1800 miles) long.

Some large, deep lakes have formed in this valley. Among them are Lake Nyasa (ny AS uh) and Lake Tanganyika (TANG guh NYEE kuh). Lake Tanganyika is almost a mile deep. Other important lakes in Africa are Lake Victoria and Lake Chad. Find these lakes on the elevation map. These are natural lakes. Then find Lake Nasser. It is an artificial lake. Lake Nasser formed behind the Aswan High Dam. It holds the floodwaters of the Nile.

Near Lake Victoria is Mount Kilimanjaro (KIL uh mun JAHR oh). It is the highest mountain in Africa. Mount Kilimanjaro is almost 5900 meters (19,340 feet) high. Even though it is near the equator, there is snow on top all year. Why do you think this is so?

REVIEW

WATCH YOUR WORDS

1. The place where a river starts is its ___.

   mouth   source   rapids

2. The place where a river flows into the ocean is its ___.

   rapids   source   mouth

3. The rocky places in rivers are called ___.

   highlands   mouths   rapids

4. The rich soil a river carries is called ___.

   sand   silt   savanna

5. A ___ is a protected place on a coast where ships can anchor.

   plateau   harbor   valley

6. The ___ of the Nile is shaped like a triangle.

   source   valley   delta

7. Land on which no plants will grow is ___.

   barren   fertile   rain forest

8. To go toward the middle of a continent is to go ___.

   inland   east   south

9. Farmers grow crops in the savannas during the ___.

   dry season   rainy season
   baseball season

10. The grass on the savannas dies during the ___.

    rainy season   floods   dry season

CHECK YOUR FACTS

11. Name three kinds of land in Africa that have tropical climates.

12. What is the largest desert on Earth? Where is it?

13. What is the longest river on Earth? Where is it? What are its branches?

14. What large lake in Africa lies on the equator?

15. Why did the people of Egypt build the Aswan High Dam?

TRY SOMETHING NEW

Plan a trip down the west coast of Africa. Start at the Mediterranean Sea. Go to the tip of the continent. What climates will you pass through? What clothes and supplies will you need?

THINK ABOUT IT

How would a ship sail from Portugal to India today? Would it have to sail around Africa? Is there now a shorter way?

Lesson 2: People: Past and Present

Many different peoples live in Africa. This makes it hard to talk about Africans in a general way.

Even so, it is possible to divide Africans into five main groups. These groups are Blacks, Arabs, Hamites, Europeans, and Asians.

Blacks

Blacks are by far the largest group of Africans. In fact, we often use the word *African* to mean *Black*. Most Black Africans live south of the Sahara. Some live in small villages. Others live in large, modern cities. Blacks are a majority in almost all the countries where they live.

There are many important Black peoples in different parts of Africa. Bantu peoples live in central and southern Africa. The San live in the Kalahari Desert. White settlers in South Africa called the San the Bushmen.

These peoples, and many more, are Blacks. But they often look very different from one another. More important, different Black peoples in Africa have different beliefs. They speak many different languages. Their histories differ. They follow different ways of life.

Most Africans are Blacks. But there are many different Black peoples in Africa. Each group has its own language, customs and beliefs.

Arabs

Most of the Arabs in Africa live north of the Sahara. Their ancestors conquered this area over a thousand years ago. Most Arabs are Muslims. Many Blacks in Africa are Muslims, too. A **Muslim** (MUZ lum) is someone who believes in the religion called **Islam** (IS lam). This religion was founded in the 7th century by the prophet Muhammad (moh HAM uhd). Muhammad lived in southwestern Asia 1400 years ago. He was born in the city of Mecca (MEK uh). Today, many people in Africa and Asia are Muslims.

Hamites

The Hamites live in north Africa. They were named for Ham, a son of Noah in the Bible. These people came to Africa from Asia long ago. They look much like Europeans. Some Hamites are Muslims. Most Hamites in Ethiopia are Christians. The Christian Hamites belong to the Coptic Church.

Europeans

Europeans began coming to Africa about 150 years ago. In most of the continent, they are a very small minority. Only in the nation of South Africa are there very many Europeans. There, 4 million of the 28 million people have European ancestors.

There are many Arabs in northern Africa. These Arabs are trading in a market in Morocco. They dress in loose, light-colored robes to protect themselves from the sun.

Asians

Asians live in east Africa. Most came to Africa from India and Pakistan. They form a minority in many countries that border the Indian Ocean.

Three Empires

You have probably heard of the most famous African empire. It was the kingdom of ancient Egypt in the valley of the Nile. The ancient Egyptians were Hamites. Their empire lasted for 3000 years.

The Egyptians built great stone **pyramids** (PIR uh midz) in the desert. These pyramids were tombs where kings, queens, and nobles were buried. A king of ancient Egypt was called a **pharaoh** (FEHR oh). Ancient Egyptians believed in life after death. They thought people could take things with them to the afterlife. Important people had their jewelry, furniture, dishes, and statues buried with them. The ancient Egyptians also had a system of picture writing. Their writing, paintings, and artifacts tell us what their life was like.

Two other great empires were founded in west Africa. They were Black African empires. The first was the empire of Ghana (GAH nuh). It lasted for over 700 years. Traders met in Ghana to trade salt and other goods for gold. They did this by the "silent trade." The traders never met face to face. First, one set of traders left piles of goods by the river. Then, the second set of traders left gold beside the goods they wanted. If the price was right, the first traders took the gold. They left the goods they had sold. If the gold wasn't enough, they took away some goods. Then they tried the trade again. The two sets of traders trusted each other. They were on their honor to be honest.

The king of Ghana charged a tax on the trade. That way, he made his empire rich. He also built a great army. In 1066, William the Conqueror defeated England with 25,000 soldiers. That same year, Ghana had 200,000 soldiers. Suppose William had gone to Ghana. His army would have been outnumbered eight to one!

Right: The ancient Egyptians carved this huge stone statue of a sphinx. It has a human head and a lion's body.

Below: The people of ancient Egypt built great pyramids in the desert. Egyptian pyramids were tombs. Kings, queens, and nobles were buried there.

WHERE WE ARE IN TIME AND PLACE

THREE AFRICAN EMPIRES

3100–1300 B.C. **1200s** **332** **4**

First six
periods of
ancient Egypt

Moses led the
Hebrew people
out of Egypt

Alexander the Great
conquered Egypt

Birth of
Jesus Christ

300s–1000s A.D. **1066** **1312–1337**

Empire of
Ghana

William I
and the Normans
conquered England

Mansu Musa
was emperor
of Mali

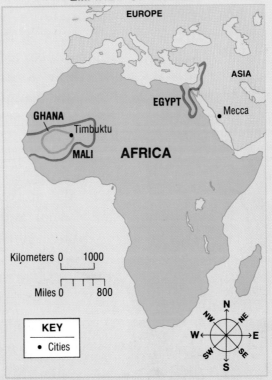

EMPIRES OF AFRICA

EUROPE

ASIA

EGYPT

Mecca

GHANA

Timbuktu

MALI

AFRICA

Kilometers 0   1000

Miles 0   800

KEY
• Cities

N
NE
NW
W   E
SW
SE
S

Next, the empire of Mali (MAH lee) became great. Mali had rich gold mines. One emperor of Mali was named Mansu Musa. He lived in the city of Timbuktu (TIM buck TOO). Look at the elevation map on page 191. What river flows through Timbuktu? Where does this river join the ocean?

In 1324, Mansu Musa went to Mecca. Mecca is the most holy city of the Muslims. Mansu Musa took huge amounts of gold to Mecca. He brought many teachers back to Timbuktu. That way, he made his empire a center of learning and trade.

Making a Living

Today, over three out of every four Africans live by farming. Most do **subsistence farming.** To subsist is to stay alive. Subsistence farmers grow just enough food for their own needs. They usually have little or nothing left over to sell. They use old and simple ways of farming. They do not have modern farm machinery. Most of these people are poor.

In the drier parts of Africa, **herding** is very important. Groups of people raise herds of cattle, goats, or sheep. A herd is a group of large animals that are all the same kind. To herd animals is to keep them together while they find grass to eat.

Some herders who live in dry places are called nomads. A **nomad** (NOH mad) is a person who travels from place to place. Family groups of nomads travel together. They live in tents, which they fold up and carry with them. They move about, looking for grass and water for their animals. The nomads herd sheep and goats. On the desert, they use camels to carry loads. They get milk from their goats and camels. They can drink the milk or use it to make cheese. They also make their clothes from sheep wool and camel hair. Now, not many nomads are left in the desert. Long dry spells left no grass for their animals to eat.

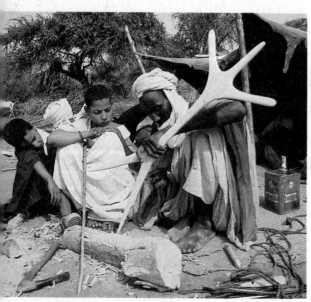

Families of nomads stop at oases for food and water. Here, a father shows a child how to carve a camel saddle.

AFRICA'S LARGEST CITIES	
City	**Number of people**
Cairo, EGYPT	5,084,463
Alexandria, EGYPT	2,318,655
Kinshasa, ZAIRE	2,008,352
Casablanca, MOROCCO	1,371,330
Addis Ababa, ETHIOPIA	1,196,300
Lagos, NIGERIA	1,060,848
Algiers, ALGERIA	903,530
Ibadan, NIGERIA	847,000
Nairobi, KENYA	818,000
Dakar, SENEGAL	798,792
Cape Town, SOUTH AFRICA	691,296
Johannesburg, SOUTH AFRICA	654,682
Accra, GHANA	564,194

Not all of Africa's people are farmers or herders. Many millions of Africans live in cities. Some African cities are among the largest in the world. Cairo is the largest city in Africa. It is the capital of Egypt. This great city is thousands of years old. Most other African cities are very young. Nairobi (ny ROH bee) was started less than 100 years ago. It is the capital of Kenya. Now, Nairobi is a center of manufacturing and trade.

Dakar, Senegal

Cairo, Egypt

FUN FACTS ... about Africa

The hottest place in the world:
Africa is the hottest continent on Earth. The hottest place in the world is Dallol, Ethiopia. For 6 years, the average yearly temperature there was 34°C (94°F). It was hot in the summer and in the winter, too!

The largest desert in the world:
The Sahara is the largest desert on Earth. At its longest, it stretches more than 4830 kilometers (3000 miles) from the Atlantic Ocean to the Red Sea. At its widest, it covers more than 1930 kilometers (1200 miles) from north to south. Overall, the Sahara covers more than 9,065,000 square kilometers (3,500,000 square miles).

The longest river in the world:
The Nile is the longest river on Earth. It is about 6695 kilometers (4160 miles) long. For hundreds of years, the source of the Nile was a mystery. Long ago, people thought this great river began in the "Mountains of the Moon."

The largest oasis in the world:
The valley of the Nile is the largest oasis on Earth. The most fertile part of the valley is the Nile delta.

REVIEW

WATCH YOUR WORDS

1. Egyptian kings, or ___ , were buried in tombs called ___ .
   pyramids   savannas   artifacts
   pharaohs

2. The religion that Muhammad founded is called ___ .
   Hamite   Coptic   Islam

3. A person who believes in Islam is a ___ .
   Coptic   Muslim   Kalahari

4. Herders who keep moving from place to place are called ___ .
   Hamites   traders   nomads

5. In ___ , farmers usually grow only the food they eat.
   subsistence farming   herding
   the Sahara

CHECK YOUR FACTS

6. Which is the largest group of Africans? Where do most of these people live?

7. Name four other groups of African peoples.

8. Who was Muhammad? What did he do?

9. Name two empires that were founded in west Africa. Which one was ruled by Mansu Musa?

10. What is the largest city in Africa? What country is it in?

THINK ABOUT IT

Most African farmers are poor. Many farm the same way their ancestors did. How could African farmers raise more food?

TRY SOMETHING NEW

Mansu Musa traveled from Timbuktu to Mecca. How far is Timbuktu from Mecca if you cross the Red Sea? How far is it if you go by land? Use your distance scale.

Lesson 3: Resources and Their Use

FIND THE WORDS

fertilizer   commercial farming
raw material   finished goods

The continent of Africa has many resources. But they are not spread evenly over the continent. Some parts of Africa are rich in resources. Other areas have very few resources.

One important mineral resource is petroleum. Fuel oil comes from petroleum. We use petroleum to heat our homes and to run our cars.

In north Africa, there is a lot of petroleum in Algeria and Libya.

South of the Sahara, petroleum is found in Nigeria. Algeria, Libya, and Nigeria sell petroleum as an export. The money they earn is helping them become modern. Some petroleum is also found farther south, in Angola. Look at the resource map on page 206. Find the petroleum on the map.

Phosphates (FOS fayts) are also mineral resources. They are salts used to make fertilizers. A **fertilizer** is spread on the soil. It adds minerals to help crops grow. Phosphates are found in Morocco.

Look again at the resource map of Africa. It shows where the mineral wealth of Africa is found.

Petroleum is found along the coast of Nigeria. These Africans are collecting petroleum from wells in the ground.

RESOURCES OF AFRICA

RESOURCES

- Cacao
- Beef Cattle
- Cotton
- Coffee
- Sheep
- Corn
- Petroleum
- Phosphates
- Iron Ore
- Tin
- Copper
- Coal
- Gold
- Diamonds

SCALE

Kilometers 0 — 1000

Miles 0 — 500 — 1000

There is copper in southern Africa, in Zambia and Zaire (zah IR). South Africa is rich in gold, diamonds, and coal. Find the parts of Africa that have the most minerals. Then look at the part of Africa just south of the Sahara. The nations here do not have much mineral wealth.

All African nations are trying to make better use of their mineral resources. However, most of Africa's minerals are exported. Only South Africa has enough industry to use its mineral resources at home.

Another natural resource is farmland. In north Africa, people farm the land along the Mediterranean Sea. This is the only part of north Africa that gets enough rain for crops. Here, farmers grow fruits such as olives, dates, and grapes.

Most of the farmland in Egypt is in the delta and valley of the Nile. That is where most of Egypt's people live. Cotton is grown there. In the Nile valley, much of the land is irrigated. To irrigate dry land is to bring water there from somewhere else. The water is used to wet the land so crops will grow. People dig ditches or lay pipes to carry the water. In north Africa, they get the water from the Nile. Remember that the Aswan High Dam holds back the Nile's floodwater. This water is

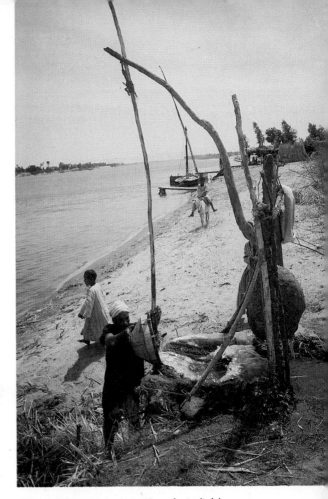

These farmers are irrigating their fields in an old-fashioned way. They take water from the Nile and empty it into a canal.

stored in Lake Nasser. It can be used all year to irrigate dry land.

South of the Sahara, Africans do two kinds of farming. One kind is called **commercial farming.** It is done on large farms called plantations. In commercial farming, crops are grown to be sold. Cacao beans, from which we get cocoa and chocolate, are grown in Ghana. Coffee is raised in the highlands of east Africa. Peanuts

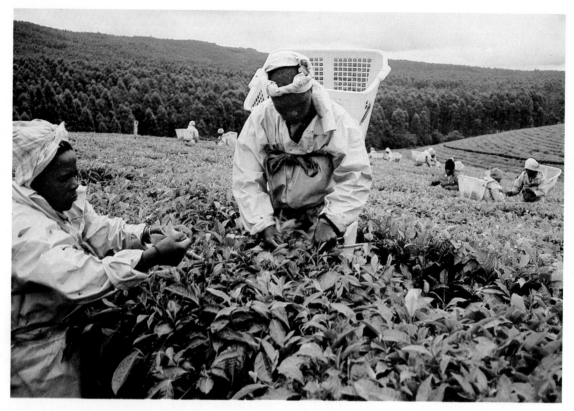

In commercial farming, large crops are grown to be sold. Tea is grown on this farm in South Africa.

and cotton are grown in some savanna lands. All these crops are African exports.

The other kind of farming is subsistence farming. It is done on small, family farms. In subsistence farming, families grow food to feed themselves. They do not raise crops to sell. Most of the farming south of the Sahara is subsistence farming.

Many resources in Africa are not used in ways that improve people's lives. This is so because of the kinds of products Africa exports. Most African nations sell their resources as raw materials. A **raw material** is a natural product that has not been improved by manufacturing. Resources are worth less as raw materials than as finished goods. **Finished goods** are products that have been manufactured. They are in the form in which you can use them. For example, logs are raw materials. Tables made from the logs are finished goods.

Iron comes from a mine in the form of iron ore. Iron ore is a raw material. It is not very useful as it is. In a steel mill, the ore is melted down. It is made into steel sheets or pipes. The steel sheets or pipes can then be used in cars or buildings. These finished goods are worth much more than the raw material.

Here is another example. Cotton picked from a plant is a raw material. People use it to make cotton thread and cotton cloth. The thread and cloth are worth more than the raw cotton. A shirt made from the cloth and thread is worth even more. At each of these steps, people had to do work. This work added value to the material. So, after each step, the material was worth more.

Nations would rather sell finished goods than raw materials. Selling finished goods gives them more value for their resources. Manufacturing more finished goods will help African nations meet two of their goals. They can provide more work for their people. And they can get more money for what they sell.

REVIEW

WATCH YOUR WORDS

1. A____adds minerals to soil.
   raw material   fertilizer   resource
2. To ____ dry land is to bring water to it.
   fertilize   farm   irrigate
3. In____, farmers raise crops to sell.
   subsistence farming   herding
   commercial farming
4. Logs, cotton, and iron ore are____.
   finished goods   nonliving resources
   raw materials
5. Shirts and tables are____.
   finished goods   raw materials
   natural resources

CHECK YOUR FACTS

Look at the Map

6. Are there more minerals in middle Africa or southern Africa? In the west or the east?

7. Where in Africa are gold and diamonds found?
8. Where in Africa are both sheep and cattle raised?

Look at the Lesson

9. How do farmers in the Nile River valley get water to grow crops?
10. What is the difference between commercial farming and subsistence farming?
11. Name three crops that African farmers export.

THINK ABOUT IT

What makes finished goods worth more than raw materials? In your answer, give an example. Choose a raw material. Then tell what finished goods people make from it.

Lesson 4: Nations of Africa

FIND THE WORDS

unity   culture group
civil war

Almost 500 million people live in Africa. They live in 51 different nations. Each nation has its own land and people. Each has its own capital city and government leaders. At one time, most African nations were European colonies. That meant they were ruled by nations in Europe. Today, most of these colonies have become independent nations. This means the people rule themselves, just as people do in the United States.

Most African nations have small populations. Look at the chart below. First, it shows the five African nations that have the most land. Then, it shows the five African nations that have the most people. One nation is on both lists. Which is it? Find these nine nations on the map of Africa on the next page.

NINE AFRICAN NATIONS

Nations with the most land	Area		Number of people
	square miles	square kilometers	
SUDAN (soo DAN)	967,494	2,505,813	17 million
ALGERIA (al JIR ee uh)	919,590	2,381,741	18½ million
ZAIRE (zah IR)	905,000	2,344,000	28 million
LIBYA (LIB ee uh)	679,358	1,759,540	3 million
NIGER (NY jur)	489,189	1,267,000	5 million

Nations with the most people	Area		Number of people
	square miles	square kilometers	
NIGERIA (ny JIR ee uh)	356,667	923,768	72 million
EGYPT (EE jipt)	386,659	1,001,449	40 million
ETHIOPIA (EE thee OH pee uh)	471,776	1,221,900	30 million
ZAIRE (zah IR)	905,000	2,344,000	28 million
SOUTH AFRICA (south AF ruh kuh)	471,442	1,221,037	28 million

NATIONS OF AFRICA

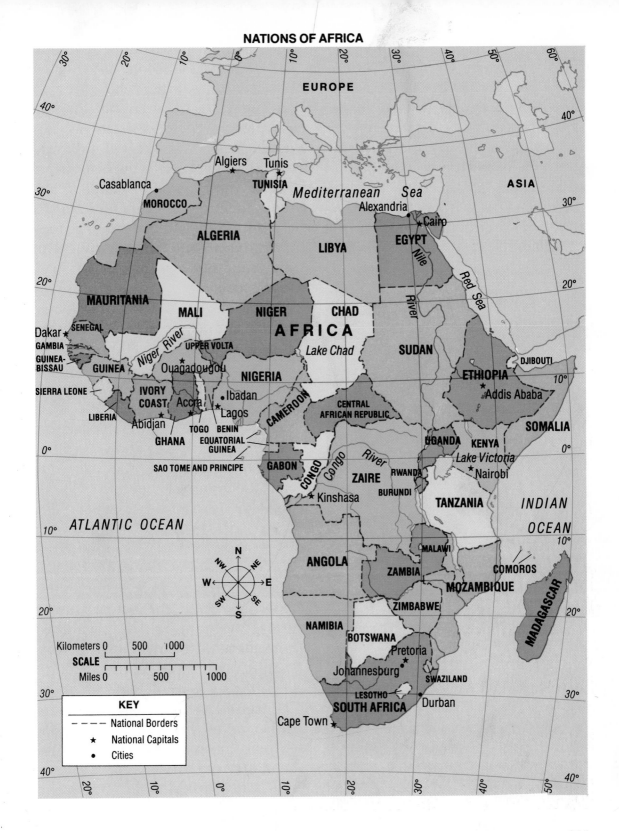

EUROPE

Algiers ★ Tunis ★
Casablanca ● **TUNISIA**
MOROCCO *Mediterranean   Sea*
ASIA
Alexandria ●
★ Cairo
ALGERIA **LIBYA** **EGYPT**
Nile
MAURITANIA *Red Sea*
MALI **NIGER** **CHAD**
A F R I C A River
Dakar ★ **SENEGAL** *Niger River* **UPPER VOLTA** *Lake Chad* **SUDAN** **DJIBOUTI**
GAMBIA
GUINEA- Ouagadougou ★ **ETHIOPIA**
BISSAU **GUINEA** **NIGERIA** ★ Addis Ababa
SIERRA LEONE **IVORY** ● Ibadan
COAST Accra ● Lagos **CENTRAL** **SOMALIA**
LIBERIA **AFRICAN REPUBLIC**
Abidjan ★ **CAMEROON** **UGANDA** **KENYA**
GHANA **TOGO** **BENIN** *Congo* River *Lake Victoria*
EQUATORIAL **CONGO** **ZAIRE** **RWANDA** ★ Nairobi
GUINEA **GABON** *Congo* **BURUNDI**
SAO TOME AND PRINCIPE ★ Kinshasa **TANZANIA** **INDIAN**

ATLANTIC OCEAN **OCEAN**
MALAWI
ANGOLA **ZAMBIA** **COMOROS**
MOZAMBIQUE
N **ZIMBABWE** **MADAGASCAR**
NW ★ NE
W ●━●━● E **NAMIBIA**
SW ★ SE **BOTSWANA**
S Pretoria ★
Johannesburg ●
SWAZILAND
Kilometers 0   500   1000 **LESOTHO** Durban ●
SCALE **SOUTH AFRICA**
Miles 0   500   1000 Cape Town ★

KEY
- – – – National Borders
- ★ National Capitals
- ● Cities

211

African nations share many of the same goals. They are working for a better future for their peoples. One important goal is national unity. Many African nations are trying to increase unity within the nation. **Unity** is a feeling of oneness or togetherness. Government leaders want people to feel that they belong to their nation and their nation belongs to them. But sometimes people do not feel like part of a larger whole.

There are hundreds of different peoples in Africa. These peoples are sometimes called culture groups. People in a **culture group** speak their own language. They have their own beliefs and way of living. Different culture groups may live in the same nation. But they may not feel that they belong together.

Here is one reason. Language can keep people apart. Africans speak more than 800 different languages. Within a single nation, 20 different languages may be used. It is hard for people to work together if they do not speak the same language. A nation needs at least one language that everyone can understand.

Here is another reason. The people of Africa did not draw up their own national boundaries. Europeans drew those boundaries years ago when they set up their colonies. Then the colonies won their freedom. Even so, most boundaries did not change. Now, members of the same culture group may live in two or more different nations. They would rather be in the same nation. Also, culture groups that were always enemies may be in the same nation. They would rather be apart.

Government workers in Africa want to get people to try new ways.

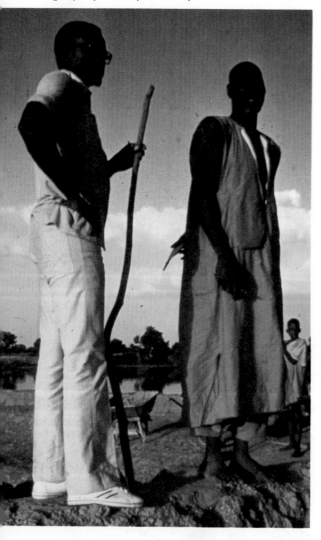

These problems have caused several civil wars in Africa. A **civil war** is a war between different groups in the same nation.

Unity is not the only goal of African nations. Another goal is to develop Africa's resources. Some African nations are among the poorest countries in the world.

Other African nations make money from petroleum or other exports. Among these nations are Nigeria, Libya, Algeria, and Zaire. South Africa is the richest nation in Africa. It has gold, diamonds, and coal mines. It also has huge farms and many factories.

All over Africa, governments are trying to make life better for their people. To do this, they are building schools and roads. They are trying to improve farming. They want businesses to build more factories and to open more mines. But all these things cost money. And most African nations do not have much money. To help African nations, other nations could lend them money. They could also send people to help.

African peoples value their past. They are loyal to their culture groups. They are proud of their beliefs. They honor their ancestors. Becoming more modern will change their way of life. Do you suppose all Africans want this to happen?

CHAPTER REVIEW

WATCH YOUR WORDS

1. The coast of Africa has few___.
   rapids harbors beaches

2. People exploring Africa found it hard to travel___.
   north west inland

3. Much land in the Sahara is___.
   barren fertile savanna

4. In dry areas, people ___ cattle, goats, and sheep.
   export import herd

5. Herders who move from place to place and live in tents are___.
   ancestors subsistence farmers
   nomads

6. Lake Victoria and Lake Tana are the ___of the Nile River.
   mouths sources deltas

7. The delta of the Nile is at the ___ of the river.
   mouth savanna source

8. More money can be made from ___ than from___.
   raw materials rain forests
   sand dunes finished goods

9. Islam is the religion of the___.
   Muslims Hamites Christians

10. People who feel like part of a larger whole have___.
    civil war culture groups unity

CHECK YOUR FACTS

11. Why was it hard for Europeans to explore Africa?

12. What kind of land is most of northern Africa?

13. Which way does the Nile River flow? What are its branches?

14. Savannas have two seasons. What are they?

15. What are the five main groups of people in Africa?

16. How do subsistence farming and commercial farming differ?

17. Name three African nations that have petroleum.

18. Why do people irrigate land? How do they do it?

19. Name three great African empires of earlier times.

20. Name two goals that the nations of Africa share.

CLOSE THE MAP GAP

21. Draw or trace an outline map of the continent of Africa.

22. Africa is surrounded by two oceans and two seas. Label them.

23. Label the Sahara, the equator, the rain forests, and the eastern highlands.

24. Label the Nile River and its branches. Also label Lake Victoria and Lake Tana.

25. Draw in boundaries for nations with coasts on the Mediterranean Sea. Label these nations.

THINK ABOUT IT

26. Why are harbors useful?

27. Lands near the equator get a lot of sunlight. Why did Europeans once call Africa the Dark Continent?

28. Why did ancient Egyptians have their furniture buried with them?

29. Why isn't the southern tip of Africa the hottest part?

30. Suppose every state in the United States was an independent nation. Suppose people in every region spoke a different language. How would your life change?

CHAPTER 2 LIVING ON A SAVANNA

Lesson 1: Upper Volta

FIND THE WORDS

landlocked   warrior   assembly
sorghum   baobab

Upper Volta (VOL tuh) is a nation in west Africa. It is near the equator. It lies between the modern nations of Mali and Ghana. Find Upper Volta on the map of Africa on page 211. What hemispheres is it in?

Like Bolivia in South America, Upper Volta has no coastline. It is **landlocked.** That means it is completely surrounded by land. Upper Volta is surrounded by six other African nations. Four of those nations are on the coast.

The climate in Upper Volta is hot, dry, and sunny for much of the year. There are deserts in the north. Some grasses and a few small trees and bushes grow there. There are savannas and small forests in the south.

Once, Upper Volta was a colony of France. Then, in 1960, it became an independent nation. Upper Volta is a small nation. It is the same size as one of our states: Colorado. It has fewer people than New York City has. About 6½ million people live in

Upper Volta. Most of them are farmers and live in villages. But about 170,000 people live in the capital city, Ouagadougou (WAH guh DOO goo).

Upper Volta is a poor nation. The soil is thin and does not hold water well. This makes it hard for people to farm. There are few factories in the cities. This makes it hard for people to find jobs.

Upper Volta imports food, clothes, metals, and machines. That means it buys these goods from other nations. It exports cotton, peanuts, and live animals. That means it sells these things to other nations. Upper Volta has to pay for what it imports. It does not earn nearly as much for what it exports. This is another reason why the nation remains poor.

UPPER VOLTA

Many people leave Upper Volta to work in other nations. They go south to the Ivory Coast and Ghana to find jobs. Then they send money home to help their families.

Several culture groups live in Upper Volta. The Mossi (MAW see) people are the largest group. About half the people in the country are Mossi. Each culture group has its own language. The language of the Mossi people is called Moré (muh RAY).

Many people in Upper Volta speak two or more languages. Besides their own language, they may also speak French. Sometimes, people also speak the language of groups that live nearby. That way, neighbors can understand each other.

The Mossi people have their own leaders and ways of doing things. The Mossi once ruled over a large kingdom. They had strong armies. Other people feared their **warriors,** or fighters. The Mossi king lived in Ouagadougou. He was called the Moro Naba (MOH roh NAH buh). Later, the Mossi became part of the Mali empire.

When Upper Volta became independent, the people elected a National Assembly. An **assembly** is a group of people who meet to make laws. In the United States, we call such a group a *legislature.* Upper Volta has a president, too.

In the villages, most Mossi people work in the fields. Families do subsistence farming. They grow the food they eat. They do not have much left over to sell. Village

A Mossi market is a place for buying and selling goods. It is also a place for friends to meet.

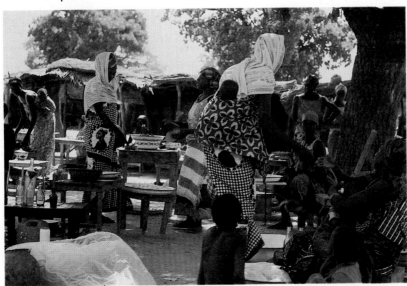

The Mossi sell fruit and vegetables in the market.

Do these baobab trees look upside down to you?

The Mossi like to help each other. These young Mossi are carrying a new roof.

people make thread out of the cotton they grow. They dye the thread different colors. Then they weave it into cloth.

Since the weather is usually hot, the Mossi are almost always outdoors. In the hottest part of the day, they sit under sun shelters. That way, they have some shade.

Mossi children are like all children. They like to play games. One game they play is like hopscotch. They play a string game like our game of cat's cradle. They also play ball and guessing games.

In a Mossi village, a person almost never feels alone. Everyone knows everyone else. The Mossi like to do things together and help each other. Members of a family work together. Groups of families sometimes work together, too.

The Mossi sit under sun shelters during the hottest part of the day.

A favorite meeting place is the market. The market is a place for buying and selling. There, people can buy and sell fruit, vegetables, and grain. Thread and cloth are also sold at the market. Mossi women sell a drink called *dolo*. It is made from **sorghum** (SOR gum), a grain that tastes like corn. Syrup is also made from the sorghum plant. Have you ever heard of sorghum molasses?

At the market, the Mossi talk with friends. They meet people from other villages. They tell stories and make each other laugh. One story they tell is about the **baobab** (BAY oh bab) tree. The branches of this tree are bare and twisted. They look more like roots than branches. The Mossi say that one day God became angry with the baobab. They say God pulled the tree up and put it back upside down!

REVIEW

WATCH YOUR WORDS

1. A ____ country is surrounded by land.
   barren   independent   landlocked
2. The Mossi kingdom once had strong armies of____.
   farmers   warriors   pharaohs
3. Another name for a legislature is an____.
   assembly   empire   export
4. *Dolo* and syrup are made from ____ .
   cotton   sorghum   peanuts
5. The ____ tree looks like it is upside down.
   baobab   softwood   hardwood
6. Cotton and peanuts are ____ of Upper Volta.
   imports   exports   seaports

CHECK YOUR FACTS

Look at the Map

7. What is the capital of Upper Volta?
8. What six nations surround Upper Volta?
9. Name two ways you could get from Ouagadougou to Koudougou.

Look at the Lesson

10. Name three things that Upper Volta imports.
11. Give two reasons why Upper Volta is not rich.

THINK ABOUT IT

Each culture group in Upper Volta speaks its own language. Suppose each group also learned to speak French. How would this help Upper Volta?

Lesson 2: Life in the Village

Upper Volta has two seasons. It has a dry season. It also has a rainy season.

The period from November to May is the dry season. This is the time when people in the United States have fall, winter, and spring. In the first half of the dry season, the weather is cool. In the second half, the weather gets very hot. All the grass dies. Often the animals have very little to eat. They get thin and grow weak.

The dry season causes problems for people living on Africa's savannas. It is hard to farm land that is dry most of the year. The Mossi dig wells to find water. Digging a well is hard work. Several families may work together to dig a well. Then all of them use it.

In the dry season, the Mossi get water from their wells. With this water, they can grow vegetables in small gardens. But without rain, they cannot grow crops in the fields. This can be a hard time of year for the Mossi.

The rainy season begins in late May or early June. It ends in October. When the rains come, the weather gets cooler. The rains make the grass and the crops grow. The animals can find more food, and they get fatter. The people plant crops in the fields when the rains begin. They have to grow all their crops during the rainy season.

Growing food in Upper Volta is not easy. Farmers do most of the work by hand. When the rainy

In the dry season, the Mossi get water from their wells. Digging a deep well is hard work.

Top left: Preparing food. *Top right:* The rainy season. *Bottom right:* A family garden.

season starts, a farm family clears its fields. First, the Mossi wait for the rains to soften the hard ground. Then, they begin to loosen the soil. They do this with an iron blade on a short wooden handle. Then, they plant their seeds.

Families plant some crops near their homes. They plant other crops in fields far from the village. Family members walk to these fields during the rainy season.

Farmers in Upper Volta raise cereal plants and vegetables for their own use. They plant corn, millet, sorghum, and rice. They grow tomatoes, onions, eggplants, and beans. They also raise chickens and gather fruits and nuts.

Some farmers grow cotton and peanuts to sell. They may also sell sheep and goats. They use the money to buy seeds and other things they need.

As the crops grow, the Mossi families weed the fields. First, they pull up the weeds. Then, they loosen the soil around the crops. This is the hardest work of the growing season.

When the crops are grown, the people harvest them. To **harvest** crops is to gather them in. Harvesting the crops is the last job of the growing season. Again, the whole family works together. First, the men cut down the stalks of grain. Then, the women cut the heads of grain off the stalks. The children take care of the babies. They also carry water to the workers in the fields.

The women carry the grain home to be dried and stored. They take the stalks, too. They can burn stalks as fuel for cooking. They can also feed stalks to the animals during the dry season. The Mossi waste little of what they grow.

Drought

Sometimes, the rainy season does not come when it is due. Then there is a drought (DROWT). A **drought** is a long period of time with little or no rain. Upper Volta has had many droughts. So have many other nations in west Africa.

A drought causes many problems. Rivers dry up. Grass dies. Soil blows away. Animals die because they have no water to drink. Food will not grow without water to wet the soil. So the people become very hungry. A **famine** (FAM in) happens when people in a place do not have enough food for a long time. Then, many people get sick and weak. Some of them die. A long drought can even turn savanna land into desert. This is one way that nature's forces change the surface of Earth.

In the 1960s and 1970s, west Africa had a bad drought. Herders and farmers left their homes. They had to live in camps near the cities. Thousands of people died. The people who lived had to adapt. They had to change because conditions around them changed. Nomads had to settle down. Herders began to farm. Farmers and herders found work building roads. They began to ride bicycles. Many farmers and herders got used to city life. The change in their land and climate changed their ways.

The Compound

Members of a Mossi farm family live in a family compound. A **compound** is a group of houses built close together. Each house is made of mud brick and has a straw roof. Each house or group of houses has a **courtyard.** This is a roofless area with walls around it.

A compound has different work areas. Women cook in their own courtyards. There is a place to grind flour and make dough. There are other places to wash clothes. There may also be a place where women can make *dolo.* Outside the compound are places to keep animals and places to store grain. There is also a small family field around each compound.

223

This child is working in the compound. She has ground up grain to make flour. Now she is using flour to make dough.

cereal served with a vegetable sauce. To honor a special guest, the Mossi will serve chicken. But Mossi families eat very little meat.

All members of a Mossi compound have special jobs. Men and boys build the houses. Women pave the floors and put plaster on the walls. The children take care of the family's animals.

A Mossi village is made up of groups of family compounds. The compounds of a village are spread out over a wide area. The most important compound is that of the village chief. Visitors to a village go to see the chief as soon as they arrive. This is a Mossi custom.

A Mossi family usually has two meals a day. Breakfast might be cereal, fried cakes, or beans. The main meal might be a very thick

REVIEW

WATCH YOUR WORDS

1. A group of houses for a Mossi family is a____.
   compound   courtyard   village

2. A roofless area with walls around it is a____.
   village   compound   courtyard

3. To gather in crops is to____them.
   plant   weed   harvest

4. A____is a long time with no rain.
   desert   harvest   drought

5. When people do not have enough food to live, there is a____.
   rainy season   famine   desert

CHECK YOUR FACTS

6. When is the dry season in Upper Volta?

7. How do the Mossi find water during the dry season?

8. When do the Mossi plant their crops?

9. Name two crops that some Mossi farmers sell.

10. What is the last job of the growing season?

THINK ABOUT IT

Farmers in Upper Volta do most of their work by hand. How do most farmers plant, weed, and harvest in the United States?

Lesson 3: Cities and Change

Today, many Mossi young people are leaving their villages. They are moving to the cities. Why? There are several reasons.

Life in Mossi villages has been hard for many years. There has been very little rain and not enough food. Also, there are not many ways to earn money in the villages. Some young people sell crops that they raise on their own. But usually, they give all the money to their families. In the cities, young people hope to earn money for themselves.

Most people in the villages are **illiterate.** That means they do not know how to read and write. In Upper Volta, only 1 person in 14 can read and write. Many children do not get to go to school. There are not many elementary schools in Upper Volta. Children can go to school only if there is a school nearby.

There are about 40 high schools in Upper Volta. The high schools are in the cities. There is only one university. It is in the capital city, Ouagadougou. Ouagadougou has several other kinds of schools. One school trains people for government jobs. Another school trains nurses. Still another trains veterinarians, or animal

This is a French high school in Upper Volta. Does it look like schools you know?

doctors. There are also schools that teach people trades.

Many young people move to the cities hoping to go to school. All of them hope to find a job. Those who get jobs do not make much money. But they still send some money home to help their families. They also go home to visit as often as they can. On these visits, they tell friends about city buildings and traffic. They tell about the food in French and African restaurants. Some friends in the village cannot imagine movies and television. They want to visit stores in the city. They want to see the many things for sale.

After hearing such stories, more and more young people leave the

Young people who cannot read and write get jobs with long hours and low pay.

farms. This has caused the population of cities to grow very fast. Now there are more people in cities looking for jobs. But there are no more jobs than before.

It is hard to get a good job in the city. It is important to have gone to school. It is important to know French. But many young people have not been to school. They do not speak French. They cannot read and write. So they have to take jobs with long hours and low pay. Some young men load sacks of sugar on carts in the market. Others help build buildings. They dig with shovels and picks. They also push carts loaded with sand and cement.

Most young women work in *dolo* factories. Some find jobs in homes. Young men also work in homes. In homes, workers clean, wash, iron, and do errands. They may also cook and take care of the garden.

Some young people go into business for themselves. They buy goods at one price and sell them for more. That way, they make a profit. **A profit** is the extra money left from a sale after expenses are paid. Some young people sell magazines, newspapers, or cold sodas. Others sell vegetables that they grow in small gardens. Still others shine shoes on the streets.

Many young people try to find work but are not successful. They are **unemployed.** That means they

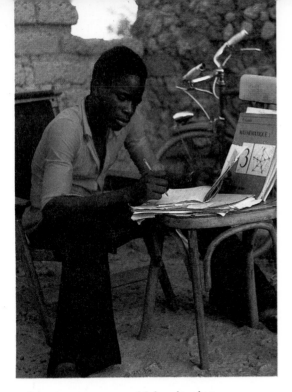

Kaboré Lazare goes to high school at night. He is preparing for the future.

Campaoré Poko owns a large *dolo* business. She also buys and sells cattle.

do not have a job. These people may become unhappy. They may wonder if coming to the city was a mistake.

Kaboré Lazare (kuh BAW ray luh ZAH ruh) is a young man about 19 years old. He left his family farm and moved to Ouagadougou. Now he works as a waiter 6 days a week. He works 8 hours a day. After work, he studies for 2 hours. Then he goes to high school in the evening. He is learning to speak French. He already knows English. Going to school is very important to Lazare. He is learning many new things. He is working hard to prepare himself for a better job.

Mossi women work and study in the cities, too. Women who go to school and learn French sometimes can get good jobs. Some are trained for jobs in government. Others become teachers or nurses. Sometimes, women in the cities have men working for them. In the villages, Mossi men are always in charge. In the cities, both men and women have to change old ways of thinking.

Campaoré Poko (CAHM pah oh ray POH koh) has a large *dolo* business in the city. She hires many young city women. They make and sell *dolo* for her. Compaoré Poko has become rich. She owns her own home. With the money from her *dolo* business, she buys and sells cattle. The Mossi people respect Campaoré Poko because she runs her business well.

Changing to new ways was good for Kaboré Lazare and Campaoré Poko. But change is hard for most people. The older Mossi like to do things as their ancestors did them. They think the young people should stay on the family farms.

Government leaders also want to change Upper Volta. They want Upper Volta to be a united nation.

They want the people to learn French. That way, everyone would have at least one language in common. The government has made French the official language of Upper Volta. The **official language** of a nation is the one used by the government and the schools.

The leaders also want the people to learn better ways of farming. They want the people to use better methods of health care. But the older Mossi want to see someone using the new ways, first. If the new ways make things better, they may try them, too.

REVIEW

WATCH YOUR WORDS

1. The ____ in the cities of Upper Volta is growing.
   famine   drought   population

2. A person who cannot read or write is ____.
   unemployed   landlocked
   illiterate

3. A person without a job is ____.
   illiterate   unemployed   inland

4. In Upper Volta, it is important to know the ____.
   pharaoh   official language
   unemployed

5. A ____ is the money left from a sale after expenses.
   profit   price   harvest

CHECK YOUR FACTS

6. Why do many Mossi young people move to the cities?

7. Why are many Mossi people not able to read and write?

8. What kinds of jobs can people from a Mossi village get in the city?

9. Why do the Mossi have respect for Campaoré Poko?

10. Name three things that government leaders want people in Upper Volta to do.

THINK ABOUT IT

Young people usually like new things. Older people sometimes prefer old ways of doing things. Why do you think this is true? Are new ways always better than old ways?

CHAPTER REVIEW

WATCH YOUR WORDS

Match each word to the right meaning.

1. assembly		A.	surrounded by land
2. compound		B.	to gather in the crops
3. courtyard		C.	a long period with no rain
4. drought		D.	a group that meets to make laws
5. famine		E.	without a job
6. harvest		F.	not able to read and write
7. illiterate		G.	a group of houses built close together
8. landlocked		H.	a lack of food that makes people sick and weak
9. profit		I.	a roofless area with walls around it
10. unemployed		J.	money left from a sale after expenses

CHECK YOUR FACTS

11. Where is Upper Volta? What is its capital city?
12. Why do many people leave Upper Volta?
13. What is the largest culture group in Upper Volta?
14. What is *dolo*? What is it made from?
15. How long does the dry season last in Upper Volta?
16. What happens during a drought? Name three things.
17. What are three jobs that Mossi children do in the compound or fields?
18. Name three jobs that people can train for in Ouagadougou.

19. How is Kaboré Lazare preparing himself for a good job?
20. Why do Upper Volta's leaders want the people to learn French?

FIND THE TIME LINE

21. List the events below in the right order. Start with the one that happens first.
   __1__ The families weed the fields.
   __2__ The rains soften the ground.
   __3__ The women carry the grain and stalks home.
   __4__ Farm families loosen the soil and plant seeds.
   __5__ The people harvest their crops.

USE YOUR MAP

Look at the map of Upper Volta on page 216. Use it to answer these questions.

22. Give the right cardinal direction (north, south, east, or west):
   Niger is ___ of Upper Volta. Upper Volta is ___ of Ghana. The railroad runs ___ and ___ from Ouagadougou to Ivory Coast.
23. Name two things on the map that were made by people.
24. Name two things on the map that are natural features.

THINK ABOUT IT

25. How does the climate of Upper Volta affect the way farm families live?
26. Why are the Mossi careful not to waste anything they grow?
27. Suppose all the young Mossi move to the cities? What will happen to the farms?
28. Think about life in a Mossi village. What might city people miss?
29. How could the Mossi learn to farm in better ways?

UNIT REVIEW

WATCH YOUR WORDS

Use the words below to fill in the blanks. Use each term only once.

commercial farming
deserts
drought
dry season
famine
finished goods
harbors

harvest
herding
inland
irrigate
nomads
pharaohs
profit

pyramids
rain forests
rainy season
rapids
raw materials
savanna
subsistence farming

Africa was hard for Europeans to explore. This continent had few ___ where ships could anchor. It was also hard to get past the coast and go ___ . Ships could not sail up rivers that had waterfalls and ___ . Hot, barren ___ and thick, wet ___ made it hard to cross Africa on foot.

Now, we know much more about Africa. We know that almost half of Africa is tropical grassland, or ___ . We know the savannas have two seasons. Farmers plant their crops during the ___ . They cannot grow crops in the fields during the ___ . Most farm families in Africa grow only enough food to feed themselves. This is called ___ . In places that are too dry to farm, people live by ___ animals. Herders who move from place to place are called ___ .

Sometimes, the rains do not come when they are due. A long time with no rain is called a ___ . Fields dry up and animals die. Food will not grow in the dry land. Sometimes there is a shortage of food that makes people sick and weak. This is called a ___ .

In the valley of the Nile, farmers ___ their fields. They use water from the Nile to wet the land. That way, crops will grow. Along the Nile, you will also see great ___ . These are the tombs in which the ancient Egyptian kings, or ___ , were buried.

There are also large farms in Africa. Here, crops are grown to be sold. This is called ___ . Africa needs more large farms and factories. Factories improve ___ , such as cotton and logs. These materials are worth much more as ___ , such as shirts and tables. Then, the goods can be sold for a ___ .

CHECK YOUR FACTS

1. What is the second-largest continent on Earth?
2. What is the hottest continent on Earth? Do you remember which continent is the coldest?
3. What is the Sahara? Where is it?
4. What is the Nile? How long is it?
5. What are savannas? How do the seasons change on savannas in Africa?
6. What is the climate like in Africa's rain forests? In the eastern highlands?
7. Name three animals found in Kenya.
8. What is the Great Rift Valley?
9. What is Africa's highest mountain?
10. Divide Africans into five main groups of people. Then name a part of Africa where each group lives.
11. Name three great African empires.

12. How do most Africans make a living?
13. Name three large cities in Africa.
14. Name three African nations that export petroleum.
15. Where in Egypt do most of the people live?
16. Name three crops that Africa exports.
17. What is the difference between raw materials and finished goods?
18. What is the richest nation in Africa?
19. Why is it hard to make a living in Upper Volta?
20. What does Upper Volta import? What does it export? Does Upper Volta make a profit? Why, or why not?

KNOW YOUR PEOPLE

Match the name with the clue.

21. Blacks   A. were kings of ancient Egypt.
22. Mansu Musa   B. founded a great religion.
23. The Moro Naba   C. are the largest group of Africans.
24. Muhammad   D. was the king of the Mossi.
25. Pharaohs   E. was emperor of Mali.

KNOW YOUR RIVERS

Match the word with the clue.

26. delta   A. rocky places in a river
27. mouth   B. the place where a river begins
28. rapids   C. a triangle of rich soil at a river mouth
29. silt   D. the place where a river flows into the sea
30. source   E. rich soil that a river carries

USE YOUR MAPS

31. Look at the elevation map of Africa on page 191. Where is most of the land at sea level?
32. Look at the political map of Africa on page 211.
   A. What African nations have coastlines on the Red Sea?
   B. What African nations does the equator pass through?

THINK ABOUT IT

33. In the United States, we say "up north" and "down south." But in Egypt, Upper Egypt is south. Lower Egypt is north. Why is this so?
34. Pretend you are president of a new African nation. The people of your nation belong to two culture groups. They speak different languages. They do not get along. You want them to work together. What will you do?

PUT IT ALL TOGETHER

35. Draw or trace an outline map of Africa. Put these things on the map and label them:
   A. the equator
   B. the Atlantic Ocean, Mediterranean Sea, Red Sea, and Indian Ocean
   C. the White Nile, the Blue Nile, the Nile, and the Nile delta
   D. Lake Victoria, Lake Tana, and Lake Nasser
   E. the Sahara
36. Color the climate areas north of the equator. Color the deserts yellow, the dry savanna brown, the savanna light green, the rain forest dark green, and the highlands purple.
37. Suppose the desert spread farther south. What would happen to the people, the animals, and the land?

EUROPE

ELEVATION

Meters	Feet
over 4,000	over 13,100
2,000 to 4,000	6,600 to 13,100
1,000 to 2,000	3,300 to 6,600
200 to 1,000	660 to 3,300
sea level to 200	sea level to 660
below sea level	below sea level

KEY

– – – National Borders

● Cities

★ National Capitals

Kilometers 0   500

SCALE

Miles 0   500

ICELAND

ARCTIC CIRCLE

ARCT

NW N NE
W   E
SW SE S

UNITED KINGDOM OF
GREAT BRITAIN
AND NORTHERN IRELAND

NORWAY
Oslo

SWEDEN
Stockholm

DENMARK
North Sea   Copenhagen ★

E U R O P E

IRELAND ★ Dublin

Thames River ★ London   Amsterdam
NETHERLANDS   EUROPEAN   Elbe River   PLAIN
Brussels ★   Berlin ★   POLA
BELGIUM   EAST GERMANY
★ Bonn   Prague ★
Paris ★   Seine River   WEST GERMANY   CZECHOSLOV
Loire   Danube   River
FRANCE   River   Vienna ●
SWITZERLAND   A   P   S   AUSTRIA
Rhône   Milan ●   HUN
River   Po River

ATLANTIC OCEAN

PYRENEES MOUNTAIN
Ebro River
Duoro River
PORTUGAL   Madrid ★
Lisbon ★
Tagus River
SPAIN

YUGOSL

ITALY
Rome ★

Naples

AFRICA

Mediterranean Sea

232

40° 60° 30° 20° 10° 70° 0° 10°

50°

40°

20°

30°

10°

0°

OCEAN

Barents Sea

30° 40° 70° 50° 60° 70° 60° 80°

URAL MOUNTAINS

PHYSICAL MAP OF EUROPE

50°

FINLAND

Helsinki
★

• Leningrad

ASIA

★ Moscow

UNION OF SOVIET SOCIALIST REPUBLICS

Volga River

saw

Dnieper River

40°

RATHIAN MOUNTAINS

est

CAUCASUS MOUNTAINS

Caspian Sea

ROMANIA

de

Bucharest
★

Black Sea

Mt. Elbrus

BULGARIA

Sofia
★

60°

LKAN MOUNTAINS

Istanbul

EECE

Athens

30°

30° 40° 50°

1 EUROPE AND ITS PEOPLE

Lesson 1: Land and Climate

FIND THE WORDS

**mainland   island   peninsula
sea   uplands**

Europe! What do you think of when you hear that name? Castles in Spain? April in Paris? The isles of Greece? Skiing in the Alps? London fog? Maybe you think of the capitals of Europe—great cities like London, Paris, and Rome. In fact, Rome gave us our word *romance*. And Europe is full of romantic, faraway places. Many Americans have ancestors who came from Europe. Much of our history is there.

234

Europe and Asia are part of the same big mass of land. Even so, we think of Europe and Asia as two continents. Those two continents are separated by the Ural Mountains. Find the Ural Mountains on the map of Europe on pages 232 and 233.

Europe is only one of seven continents of Earth. Yet, when writers from Great Britain and Ireland say "the Continent," they mean Europe. Actually, they mean the mainland of Europe.

The **mainland** of a continent or country is the chief mass of land. Islands may be counted as part of a continent. But islands are not part of the mainland.

Some people call Europe "a continent of peninsulas and of islands." What do you suppose this means?

An **island** is a piece of land completely surrounded by water. It is smaller than a continent. Australia is completely surrounded by water, but we call it a continent. It is a large mass of land. Ireland is completely surrounded by water, and we call it an island. It is much smaller than Australia.

Look at the map of Europe again. How many islands can you find? Only the largest islands are shown on the map. There are many small islands as well.

A **peninsula** is a piece of land almost surrounded by water. In

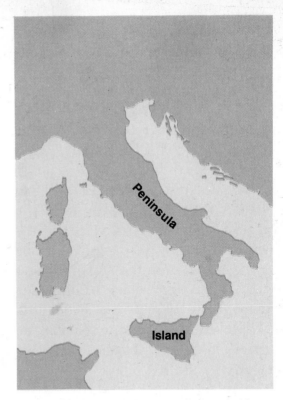

Italy is a peninsula. It is almost surrounded by water. Sicily is an island. It is completely surrounded by water.

fact, the word *peninsula* means "almost island." In the United States, Florida is a peninsula. In Europe, the main part of Italy is a peninsula. It is shaped like a boot. Spain and Portugal are on a peninsula. So are Norway and Sweden. Find these peninsulas on the map of Europe.

Do you know the difference between an ocean and a **sea?** *The* sea means the same thing as the ocean. But *a* sea is smaller than an ocean. A sea can be part of an ocean. The North Sea is part of the Atlantic Ocean. The Barents

Sea is part of the Arctic Ocean. Or, a sea may be surrounded by land. Look at the map of Europe. Find the Mediterranean (MED uh tuh RAY nee un) Sea. Did you know that *Mediterranean* means "middle of the dry land"? How many other seas can you find?

The Caspian (KAS pee un) Sea is like a huge salt lake. It is the largest inland body of water in the world. The lowest part of Europe is the surface of the Caspian Sea. It is 28 meters (92 feet) below sea level! How can a sea be below "sea level"? An inland sea can be lower than the level of Earth's oceans.

Oceans, seas, and rivers have been very important to Europe. For centuries, people from Europe sailed out to explore the world. They traded with faraway lands. They used ships to carry people and goods. Their waterways were like our highways. The best "road" from one place to another might be the sea or river.

Sometimes, a river forms a natural boundary between nations. The Rhine River separates France and West Germany. Find the Rhine River and the Danube (DAN yoob) River on your map. Then look farther east and find the Volga River.

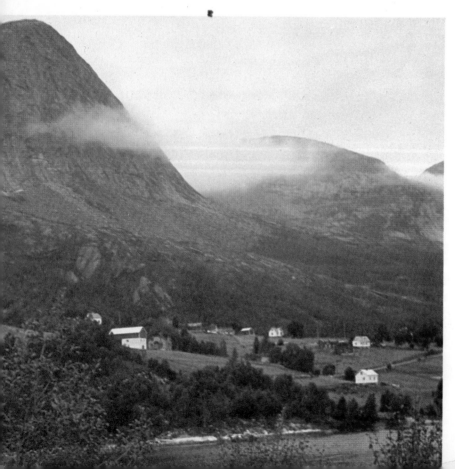

Norway is part of the northern highlands region of Europe. There are many mountains and high hills along Norway's coast.

Highlands and Lowlands

Europe is a small continent. It is not quite as large as our country, the United States. It is less than half the size of our continent, North America. Australia is the only continent smaller than Europe. But Europe has many different kinds of land. We will learn about four regions of Europe.

In the north of Europe are the northern highlands. These highlands stretch from Iceland through Norway, Sweden, and Finland.

South of the northern highlands is the European (YOOR uh PEE un) plain. This plain goes from one side of the continent to the other. It stretches from the west coast of France to the Ural Mountains. The land of the plain is flat or gently rolling. Much of the soil is fertile. In fact, the plain is fine for farming and for factories. Many people live close together on the European plain.

Farther south are the central European uplands. This region is central because it is near the middle of Europe. It is called the **uplands** because of its hills and plateaus. Portugal and Spain are in this uplands area.

Finally, there is the Alpine (AL pyn) region. This region was named for its most famous mountains, the Alps. It includes steep

People from all over the world visit the Swiss Alps. They hike in summer and ski in winter.

mountains, high hills, and fertile river valleys. Look at the physical map on pages 232 and 233. Find the mountain groups that make up the Alpine system. They go across the continent, from west to east.

The Pyrenees (PIR uh neez) Mountains are a natural boundary between France and Spain. The Alps form a semicircle around the peninsula that Italy is on. The parts of the Alps in Switzerland are called the Swiss Alps. The parts in Italy are called the Italian Alps.

Now find Greece. It is on the peninsula east of Italy. This is called the Balkan Peninsula. The Balkan Mountains are here. The Balkans stretch from the Mediterranean Sea east to the Black Sea.

North of the Balkans are the Carpathians (kahr PAY thee unz). They form a smaller semicircle than the Alps. East of the Balkans are the Caucasus (KAW kuh sus) Mountains. They are between the Black Sea and the Caspian Sea. The Caucasus Mountains separate Europe from southwest Asia. The highest mountain in Europe, Mount Elbrus (EL broos), is in the Caucasus. All these mountain chains are part of the Alpine mountain system.

EUROPE — CLIMATES

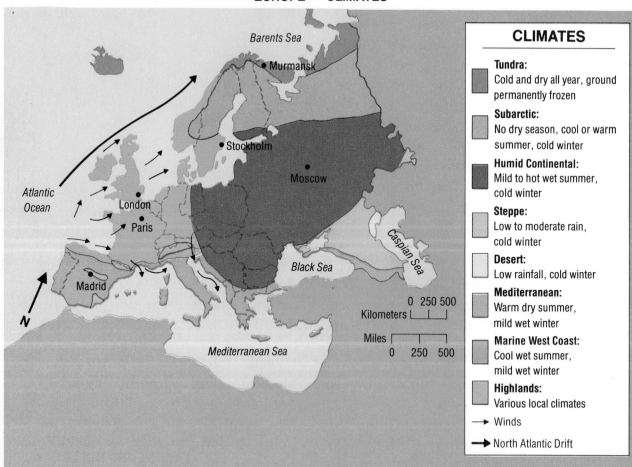

CLIMATES

Tundra:
Cold and dry all year, ground permanently frozen

Subarctic:
No dry season, cool or warm summer, cold winter

Humid Continental:
Mild to hot wet summer, cold winter

Steppe:
Low to moderate rain, cold winter

Desert:
Low rainfall, cold winter

Mediterranean:
Warm dry summer, mild wet winter

Marine West Coast:
Cool wet summer, mild wet winter

Highlands:
Various local climates

→ Winds

→ North Atlantic Drift

The North Alantic Drift is a current of warm ocean water. Winds blow off
this warm water. They keep the climate of western Europe mild.

Europe's Climates

Europe stretches all the way from the Mediterranean Sea to the Arctic Ocean. Southwest Europe has a warm, dry, Mediterranean climate. This climate is named for the warm Mediterranean Sea. Northeast Europe has subarctic and tundra climates. Here, it is usually cool or very cold. The climate is also cool in the high mountains of Europe. But in most parts of Europe, the climate is mild. Look at the climate map of Europe on the facing page. You can see that western Europe has mild, wet winters.

This seems odd. It is not what you would expect. If you look at a globe, you will see why. Southern Europe is at the same latitude as the northern United States. Rome, Italy, is as far north as Boston, Massachusetts. That means Great Britain is as far north as Labrador in Canada.

Even Norway has a fairly mild climate. Why isn't Europe colder?

Western Europe owes its mild climate to the North Atlantic Drift. This is a current of warm ocean water. It starts at the Gulf of Mexico as the Gulf Stream. The Gulf Stream flows northeast. It joins with a cold current from Labrador and warms it. Then, the combined current flows across the North Atlantic Ocean. Winds blow off this warm ocean water. These winds keep the climate in western Europe mild.

The warm Atlantic winds do not reach eastern Europe. There, the weather changes more from season to season. Winters in eastern Europe can be bitter cold. Rivers ice over. Snow stays on the ground until spring. In the Soviet Union, winters are colder and summers are hotter than in western Europe.

As you can see, much of Europe is a good place to live. It has a lot of flat land and fertile soil. Europe has mild, pleasant climates. It has many rivers and seas. Unlike Africa, it has many good seaports. Europe may be a small continent in size. But many of Earth's people live there.

REVIEW

WATCH YOUR WORDS

1. A small body of land surrounded by water is a(n)____.
   peninsula   sea   island

2. Part of an ocean may be called a ____.
   river   sea   lake

3. The meaning of the word ____ is "almost island."
   Mediterranean   peninsula   mainland

4. By "the Continent," English writers mean the____of Europe.
   mainland   islands   country

5. Hills and plateaus are____.
   lowlands   mountains   uplands

CHECK YOUR FACTS

6. How many continents does Earth have? How does Europe rank in size?

7. How did the Mediterranean Sea get its name?

8. Why are oceans, seas, and rivers important to Europe?

9. Name four land regions in Europe.

10. What gives western Europe a mild climate? Explain.

THINK ABOUT IT

11. How is an inland sea like an island? How is it different?

12. How is a continent like an island? How is it different?

Lesson 2: Resources of Europe

FIND THE WORDS

deposit   developed   market

There are many resources on the continent of Europe. But the people do not have some important resources that they need. Europe has large areas of fertile soil. So Europeans farm much of their continent.

Many European farmers raise a lot of food on their land. They know and use modern ways of farming. They use fertilizer and modern farm machinery. They also grow many different kinds of foods. Some parts of Europe are good for special crops. In France and Italy, farmers grow grapes. Olives grow on trees in Spain, Greece, and southern Italy. Many European nations grow potatoes, sugar beets, and grains. Many farmers also raise cattle for milk and cheese. Fish are an important resource, since Europe has many bodies of water.

Even so, most European nations cannot produce enough food to feed their people. These nations have to buy food from other countries. Great Britain has to import half its food. France is different. French farmers produce more food

Great Britain is an island nation. The British catch many fish off their shores.

than the French people need. Thus, France can export food to other nations.

In several parts of Europe, there are large coal deposits. A mass of a mineral found in the ground is called a **deposit.**

Coal is important in Great Britain, France, East and West Germany, and Poland. There are iron mines near the coal deposits in France and in East and West Germany. This is very useful. Both

NONLIVING RESOURCES OF EUROPE

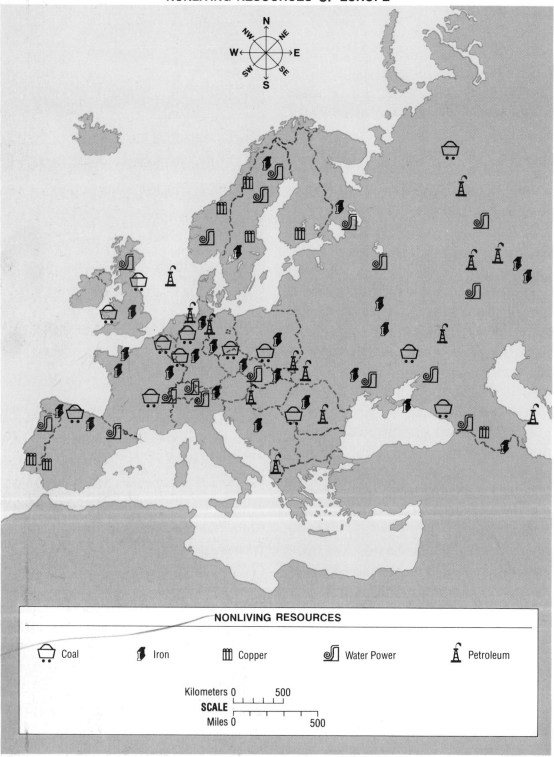

NONLIVING RESOURCES

⛏ Coal   🪨 Iron   ⛏ Copper   〰 Water Power   ⛽ Petroleum

SCALE

Kilometers 0 — 500

Miles 0 — 500

coal and iron are needed to make steel. So steel is made in this region. Farther east is the Soviet Union. It is very rich in coal and iron ore. Thus, a lot of steel is made there, too. Iron ore is also found in Sweden and northern Spain. Look at the resource map of Europe. Notice the areas where coal and iron ore are found.

Many European nations burn coal to make electricity. In Norway, Sweden, and the Alps, water power runs electric power plants. Petroleum, or fuel oil, is another source of energy. Petroleum has been found beneath the North Sea. It is found in the Soviet Union. But most European nations have little or no petroleum. They have to import it.

Like North America, Europe is a highly developed continent. A **developed** region is one that has many factories. The people of a developed region make good use of their natural resources. Many more people live in cities than in the country. More people work in factories, offices, stores, and repair shops than on farms.

Here is one way to tell how developed a nation or region is. Find out how many people work on farms. The fewer farm workers there are, the more developed the region is. Suppose only 10 or 20 workers out of every 100 work on farms. Such a region is developed.

Top: Fine grapes are grown in Italy. *Bottom:* Many people in West Germany work in factories.

The nations of Europe have many factories. European people use modern ways to manufacture goods. But Europeans have to import many raw materials for their factories. Europeans do not grow cotton. They don't raise enough sheep for the wool they need. So they have to import cotton and wool to manufacture cloth and clothes. They have to import metals like aluminum to build and run modern factories.

For centuries, a few European nations ruled most of the land on Earth. Europeans needed many raw materials for their factories.

Remember the nations of Europe that had colonies in Africa and South America? Those continents had raw materials that Europeans needed.

Europeans also wanted markets for the goods they made. A **market** is a place where goods can be sold. The people who buy the goods are also called the market. Colonies were ready-made markets for manufactured goods.

European nations have lost their colonies. But Europe is still one of the most developed regions on Earth. And Europeans still use resources from all over the world.

REVIEW

WATCH YOUR WORDS

1. Most of the nations of Europe ___ petroleum.

   export   deposit   import

2. European nations got ___ from their colonies.

   finished goods   raw materials   factories

3. People who buy goods are called the ___.

   market   colonies   Europeans

4. A ___ region has many jobs in its cities.

   tundra   farming   developed

5. A mass of a mineral in the earth is a ___.

   bank   deposit   crop

CHECK YOUR FACTS

6. Name four foods that Europe's farmers grow.

7. Name four things that Europeans import.

8. Why is it good if coal and iron ore are found near each other?

9. How can you tell if a region is developed?

10. How were colonies useful to Europe? Name two ways.

THINK ABOUT IT

Europe imports food, raw materials, and petroleum. It exports finished goods. Suppose war broke out and stopped this trade. What do you think would happen?

Lesson 3: People of Europe

FIND THE WORDS

Indo-European   literate   rival
free trade   tariff

Europe is the second-smallest continent. It covers only 7 percent of Earth. But Europe has over 15 percent of the world's people. These facts tell you that Europe is crowded.

More than 700 million people live in Europe today. That is a lot of people for so little space. Look at the population map of Europe below. The map shows you that the people of Europe are not spread evenly over the continent. Great Britain, the European plain, and northern Italy have the most people. These areas have the most factories, too. People like to live in places with good land and a comfortable climate. They also live where they can get good jobs. The far north of Europe and the high mountains have the fewest people.

People build factories where they can get power to run machines. Coal, gas, and petroleum

POPULATION AND INDUSTRY IN EUROPE

SCALE
Kilometers 0 — 500
Miles 0 — 500

KEY

National Borders	Industrial Areas

PEOPLE

Per Square Kilometer	Per Square Mile
under 10	under 25
10 to 50	25 to 125
50 to 100	125 to 250
over 100	over 250

can be burned to supply this power. The forces of moving wind and water can supply power, too. So can energy from the sun and nuclear (NOO klee ur) energy. All these forms of energy can be changed into electricity. The electricity makes the machines work.

Then workers are needed to run the machines. Raw materials are needed to make finished goods. Transportation is needed to move workers and goods around. Level lands tend to have good sources of power. They tend to have good transportation. They often have useful raw materials. So level lands are good places for factories and people.

Europeans: Alike and Different

Europe has 27 major nations. Each nation has at least one large culture group. Some nations have several culture groups within their borders. And sometimes, members of one culture group live in different nations. Each culture group has its own language, history, customs, and beliefs. From this, you might think Europeans are very different from one another. But Europeans also have many things in common.

Most Europeans are White. The people of northern Europe tend to have light skin and blond hair. In southern Europe, many people

have slightly darker skin and dark hair. However, nations like Spain, Italy, and Greece have blond people, too. Recently, people from other continents have been moving to Europe. Nations like Great Britain and France now have some Black and Asian peoples.

Most Europeans are Christians. Many people in southern Europe are Catholics. Many in northern Europe are Protestants. Jewish people also live in many nations of Europe. The Jewish people have been very important in European history. Some Muslims, too, have

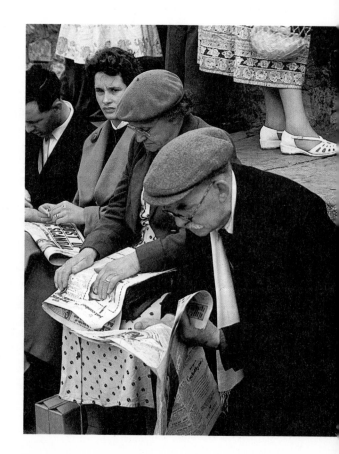

moved to Europe from the Middle East. As you can see, in Europe, many people are religious.

Still, in some parts of Europe, people are not allowed to worship freely. They are taught not to believe in God. This is especially true in the Communist countries of eastern Europe.

The people of Europe speak about 50 different languages. Yet almost all these languages belong to the same family. Most are **Indo-European** languages. Languages in this family are spoken all the way from India to western

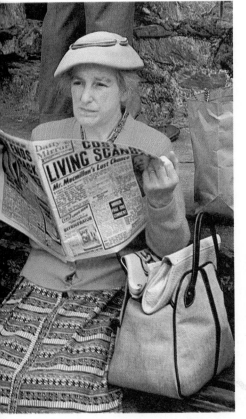

Many different peoples are Europeans. Each culture group in Europe has its own language, history, and customs.

247

Europe. English and German are Indo-European languages. So are French, Spanish, and Italian. So are Greek and Russian. And there are many more.

Most Europeans are **literate.** That means they can read and write. Most have good schools. Most get good health care. Most also have good food and get enough to eat. This means that most Europeans can expect to live at least 70 years. In some parts of the world, people live only 40 years or so.

Rivals and Partners

For hundreds of years, some Europeans were rivals. A **rival** competes with another person or group for something they both want. *Rivals* used to be people who got their water from the same *rivus*, or stream. Great Britain, France, Germany, and Spain have often been rivals. They were rivals for land, power, and wealth. Sometimes, they fought wars with one another.

Since World War II, many European peoples have been trying

MAIN LANGUAGES OF EUROPE

KEY
- - - National Borders

Kilometers 0   1000
SCALE
Miles 0   500

Icelandic
Finnish
Norwegian
Swedish
Russian
English
Danish
Dutch
Polish
German
French
German
Hungarian
Romanian
Bulgarian
Turkish
Portuguese
Spanish
Albanian
Italian
Greek

N NE E SE S SW W NW

to work together. Many nations of western Europe are now partners in the Common Market. They work together to help Europe's businesses grow. These nations practice free trade with one another. **Free trade** means that there are no taxes on imports. A tax on imported goods is called a **tariff** (TAIR if). Governments often put tariffs on goods from other countries. That way, the imports won't be cheaper to buy than goods made in their own country. The Communist nations of eastern Europe do not belong to the Common Market. They have their own trading group. This group is called COMECON.

Today, many Europeans are planning their futures together. People from western Europe no longer rule the world. But Europeans still have descendants all over the Earth. They have carried their languages to every continent. They have spread their culture and beliefs all over their planet. They have changed the world with their discoveries and inventions. They may be crowded together in a small space. But they have been among the most creative people in history.

REVIEW

WATCH YOUR WORDS

1. People who can read and write are ___.
   literate   illiterate   Indo-European

2. English, French, and Spanish are ___ languages.
   Alpine   Mediterranean
   Indo-European

3. Groups that compete against each other for the same goal are ___.
   partners   rivals   nations

4. ___ raise the price of imported goods.
   Common Market countries
   Europeans   Tariffs

5. Member nations have ___ within the Common Market.
   tariffs   free trade   rivals

CHECK YOUR FACTS

6. Where in Europe do most people live?

7. Why are level lands good places for factories? Give three reasons.

8. Name three ways in which Europeans are alike. Then name three ways in which they are different.

9. Why do most Europeans live for a long time?

10. Western Europe and eastern Europe have different trading groups. What are these two groups called?

THINK ABOUT IT

11. Do you think free trade is always a good thing? Why, or why not?

12. In Europe, people who speak different languages live close together. What problems could this cause? What is good about it?

Lesson 4: Nations of Europe

There are 27 nations in Europe. There are also 6 **ministates,** or tiny nations. Two nations of Europe have most of their land in Asia. These two nations are Turkey and the Soviet Union, or U.S.S.R.

The largest and smallest nations on Earth are in Europe. The Soviet Union is the world's largest nation. It is more than twice as large as the United States. Vatican City is the world's smallest nation. This ministate is in Italy. It lies within the city of Rome.

Nations as we know them have existed in Europe only a few hundred years. Look at the map of Europe's nations. This map shows the political boundaries of today. These boundaries have changed many times in Europe's history. The names of some of Europe's nations have changed, too. We still say "Russia" when we mean the Union of Soviet Socialist Republics. We still speak of "Germany," although that nation has been split in two. We still say "England" for the United Kingdom of Great Britain and Northern Ireland. The new names are longer.

Empires of the Past

The nations of Europe have fought many wars and battles over land. Through history, the map of Europe has changed many times. Once, much of western Europe was part of the Roman Empire. First, the city of Rome conquered the rest of Italy. Soon, the Romans ruled all the lands around the Mediterranean Sea. At last, Rome spread its empire over three continents. The Roman Empire stretched from the Caucasus Mountains to the Atlantic Ocean. It went south to the Sahara and north to the North Sea.

The Romans built roads all over their empire. These roads linked different parts of Europe together. People said that "all roads lead to Rome." The Romans carried a great culture to the lands they conquered. They spread their laws and their language, Latin. The French, Spanish, Italian, and Portuguese languages all come from Latin. After Rome became Christian, the Romans also spread the Christian religion.

The Roman Empire lasted hundreds of years before it fell. Over the centuries, other empires and kingdoms joined parts of Europe together. Later, wars split these empires apart.

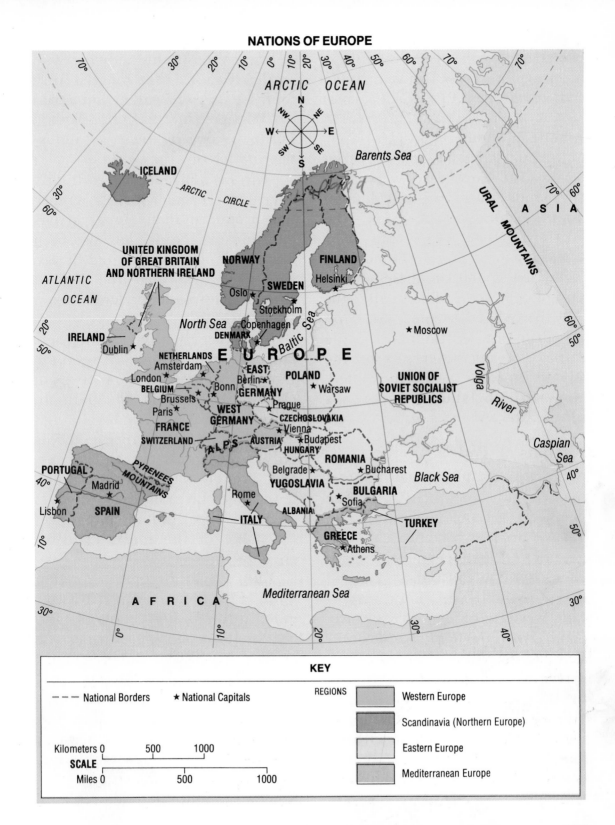

NATIONS OF EUROPE

ARCTIC OCEAN

Barents Sea

ICELAND

ARCTIC CIRCLE

URAL MOUNTAINS

ASIA

ATLANTIC OCEAN

UNITED KINGDOM OF GREAT BRITAIN AND NORTHERN IRELAND

NORWAY

FINLAND
Helsinki ★

SWEDEN
Oslo ★
Stockholm ★

North Sea

Copenhagen ★

DENMARK

Baltic Sea

★ Moscow

IRELAND
Dublin ★

NETHERLANDS
Amsterdam ★

EUROPE

London ★

BELGIUM
Brussels ★
Bonn ★

EAST
Berlin ★
GERMANY

POLAND
★ Warsaw

UNION OF SOVIET SOCIALIST REPUBLICS

Volga River

Paris ★

WEST GERMANY
Prague ★

CZECHOSLOVAKIA

FRANCE

SWITZERLAND

Vienna ★

ALPS

AUSTRIA

★ Budapest

HUNGARY

Caspian Sea

PORTUGAL

PYRENEES MOUNTAINS

Belgrade ★

ROMANIA
★ Bucharest

Black Sea

Madrid ★

YUGOSLAVIA

Rome ★

BULGARIA
Sofia ★

Lisbon ★

SPAIN

ALBANIA

ITALY

TURKEY

GREECE
★ Athens

AFRICA

Mediterranean Sea

KEY

– – – National Borders ★ National Capitals

REGIONS

Western Europe

Scandinavia (Northern Europe)

Eastern Europe

Mediterranean Europe

SCALE

Kilometers 0   500   1000

Miles 0   500   1000

Many nations built empires overseas. Europeans have always been explorers. In the year 1000, Leif Ericson (LEEF AIR ik sun) sailed from Norway to North America. About 500 years later, Columbus sailed to America from Spain. The Europeans were finding lands they had not known about before. They called the Western Hemisphere *the New World.* Spain, Portugal, France, the Netherlands, and Great Britain set up colonies there. Eventually, the tiny British Isles ruled lands on six different continents. People said, "The sun never sets on the British Empire!" As Earth rotated, some British lands were always turning toward the sun.

Nations of Today

Europeans no longer control most of the lands on Earth. The people in the colonies wanted to govern their own countries. Most colonies gained their independence. Yet the nations of Europe are still important. Four important western nations are France, Italy, West Germany, and Great Britain. We will study them.

France is a fortunate nation in many ways. The soil is fertile. The climate is mild and varied. The farmers grow more than enough food to feed the people. France also has iron and coal. Industries use minerals like these to make goods. An **industry** (IN dus tree) is a branch of manufacturing and trade. Nations that manufacture many goods are called **industrial** (in DUS tree ul) nations. Today, France is one of the great industrial nations of the world.

The French people are highly educated. Through history, France has produced many great artists and thinkers. France has also been a good friend to the United States. The French helped the United States win independence from Great Britain.

The French have taken their language and culture all over the Earth. People speak French from Canada to Algeria to Vietnam. Once, France ruled many foreign colonies. Today, France controls only a few lands outside Europe. But French paintings, perfume, food, and fashions are famous. Paris is the capital of France. It is one of the most beautiful cities in the world.

Italy did not become one nation until 1870. Before then, it was divided into smaller countries. The city of Rome no longer rules the western world. But Rome is still a great city. It is the capital of Italy. Visitors to Rome can see ruins from the time of the Roman Empire. They can also visit Vatican City. It is the home of the pope. The pope is the head of the Roman Catholic Church.

EIGHT EUROPEAN NATIONS

Nations with the most land	Area		Number of people
	square miles	square kilometers	
FRANCE	211,207	547,026	53 million
SPAIN	194,884	504,750	37 million
SWEDEN	173,648	449,750	8 million
FINLAND	130,119	337,009	5 million
NORWAY	125,181	324,219	4 million
Nations with the most people	Area		Number of people
	square miles	square kilometers	
WEST GERMANY	95,742	247,973	61 million
ITALY	116,303	301,225	57 million
GREAT BRITAIN	94,226	244,044	56 million
FRANCE	211,207	547,026	53 million
SPAIN	194,884	504,750	37 million

Italy does not have many natural resources. The nation has to import many materials to run its factories. Also, Italy has many mountains. These highlands cannot be farmed. So Italy imports some of its food. Even so, Italy is an important modern nation. Its factories make large amounts of steel and many cars. The art and music of Italy are world-famous.

Italy has had many changes in government. No one group has been strong enough to rule alone. So several groups have had to join to run the government. Often, the groups have trouble getting along.

West Germany has recovered from defeat in World War II. Today, it is the leading nation of western Europe. It has more people and factories than any other western European nation. Only three nations in the world produce more goods than West Germany. They are the United States, the Soviet Union, and Japan.

West Germany also has many of the resources needed to run its factories. It has plenty of coal and iron. It also has very modern equipment. After World War II, much of the nation was rebuilt. Thus, many factories are new.

Paris is the capital of France. The Eiffel (EYE ful) Tower is its most famous landmark.

Vatican City in Rome is the world's smallest nation. It is ruled by the pope. St. Peter's Church, shown here, is the largest Christian church in the world.

Germany was divided into two separate nations after World War II. Today, West Germany is part of western Europe. It has a democratic government. East Germany is part of eastern Europe. It has a Communist (KOM yuh nist) government. In a **Communist** country, the government owns and runs all the businesses.

Berlin used to be Germany's capital city. Today, the capital of West Germany is Bonn. Berlin is split in two. West Berlin is like an island in the middle of East Germany. The Soviet Union controls East Berlin. West Berlin is controlled by the United States, Great Britain, and France. The United States, Great Britain, France, and the Soviet Union were allies in World War II. An **ally** is someone who works with you, not against you. Today, the United States and the Soviet Union are not allies. In fact, in 1961, the Communists built a wall in Berlin.

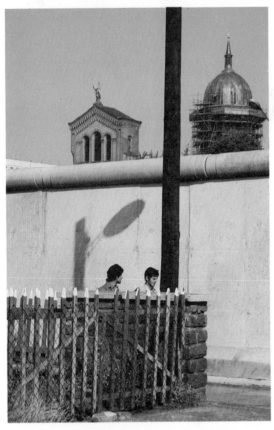

The Berlin Wall divides the Communist part of Berlin from the free part.

West Germany has more factories than any other nation in western Europe.

This wall keeps people from leaving East Germany.

Great Britain has good harbors and a mild climate. It is located on islands off the west coast of Europe. Its full name is the United Kingdom of Great Britain and Northern Ireland. London is the capital of Great Britain.

The British have always been a nation of traders. British ships once sailed all over the world. Those ships brought back raw materials for British factories. The factories made clothes, machines, and other products. Those products were then shipped to other countries for sale. Raw materials came from the British colonies.

Since World War II, Great Britain has had bad times. The British Empire no longer exists. The former colonies now trade with other countries besides Great Britain. Also, many British factories are old. They are not as good as new factories in other countries.

The British people have always solved their problems in the past. Today, the British are trying to make factories more modern. This will help the workers to produce more goods. Great Britain no longer has great wealth. But Great Britain still has a lot of influence. Today, it is the leader of the Commonwealth of Nations. This is a group of former British colonies.

FUN FACTS

Today, most cars have engines that run on gasoline. But many early cars ran on steam. In 1770, a French inventor made a steam tractor. Then, in the early 1800s, English inventors made horseless carriages that ran on steam. Hot coals were burned to make the steam. These coals often fell out on the road. Sometimes, they set the fields on fire. Steam cars also poured smoke into the air. And they made a lot of noise. To control them, the British government passed a law in 1865. The law set speed limits. Steam carriages could go only 6 kilometers (4 miles) per hour in the country. They could go only 3 kilometers (2 miles) per hour in town. The law also said that someone had to walk in front of each steam carriage to warn people. This person had to wave a red flag! As long as Britain had this law, it did not have many steam cars.

REVIEW

WATCH YOUR WORDS

1. West Germany and France are ___ nations.
   Asian   industrial   Communist

2. East Germany is a(n) ___ nation.
   Communist   Catholic   island

3. Vatican City is a ___.
   colony   capital   ministate

4. The United States and the Soviet Union were once ___.
   ministates   allies   kingdoms

5. West Germany and France have many ___.
   islands   ministates   industries

CHECK YOUR FACTS

6. Name the capitals of Great Britain, France, Italy, and West Germany.

7. Why was the Roman Empire important to Europe?

8. Which western European nation has the most factories?

9. Why did it hurt Great Britain to lose the British Empire?

USE YOUR CHART

10. Which nation in the chart has the most land?

11. Which nation in the chart has the most people?

12. What two nations are in both parts of the chart?

13. List three large nations that have few people.

14. List two small nations that have many people.

THINK ABOUT IT

15. What facts about Europe would you put in the *Guinness Book of World Records*?

16. Suppose you could live in Great Britain, France, Italy, or West Germany. Which would you choose? Would you know the language?

CHAPTER REVIEW

WATCH YOUR WORDS

1. Great Britain and Ireland are____.
   peninsulas   islands   continents
2. Most of Italy is a(n)____.
   island   ministate   peninsula
3. France is part of the____of Europe.
   mainland   nation   island
4. The Mediterranean is a(n)____.
   ocean   lake   sea
5. ____compete with one another.
   Rivals   Allies   Colonies
6. ____are on the same side.
   Rivals   Allies   Colonies
7. A tax on imports is____.
   free trade   a tariff   a deposit
8. No tax on imports is____.
   a deposit   a tariff   free trade
9. Which two words describe nations with many factories?
   illiterate   industrial   developed
10. Which two words are opposites?
    literate   industrial   illiterate

CHECK YOUR FACTS

11. What is the natural boundary between Europe and Asia?
12. Name four land regions of Europe.
13. What are the famous mountains in Switzerland called?
14. What is the North Atlantic Drift? How does it affect Europe's climate?
15. Name three raw materials that Europeans import.
16. Why are there many people and factories on the European plain?
17. Name three ways in which most Europeans are alike.
18. What are the world's largest and smallest nations?

19. Which nation of western Europe has the most people and factories?
20. Why aren't British factories as good as those in West Germany?

TRUE OR FALSE

21. Europe is larger than North America.
22. The Caspian Sea is the lowest part of Europe.
23. Most European nations grow all the food they need.
24. France exports food to other nations.
25. Europe's political boundaries have changed many times.

CLOSE THE MAP GAP

26. Draw or trace an outline map of Europe. Color the peninsulas red and the islands green.
27. Label two oceans and five seas. Give their names.
28. Label the Alps, the Pyrenees, the Caucasus, and the Ural Mountains. Color these mountains brown.
29. Label Great Britain, France, West Germany, Italy, and the Soviet Union.
30. Mark a triangle in areas where both coal and iron ore are found.

THINK ABOUT IT

31. Europe has many nations and languages. How is traveling across Europe different from traveling across the United States?
32. Europe has many mountains, islands, and peninsulas. Suppose the whole continent was a large, square plain. Would Europeans be any different? Why, or why not?
33. Why did people say "The sun never sets on the British Empire"?

2 LIVING IN A COLD LAND

Lesson 1: A Nation on Two Continents

FIND THE WORDS
taiga   steppes   time zone

The Soviet Union is the largest nation on Earth. It spreads across two continents, Europe and Asia. It goes from the Black Sea and the Baltic Sea to the Pacific Ocean. Its full name is the Union of Soviet Socialist Republics. Maps often use just the initials, U.S.S.R. Many people also use the old name, Russia.

Land and Climate of the Soviet Union

Three-fourths of the Soviet Union is in Asia. But most of the people in the Soviet Union live in

Europe. The European part of the nation is west of the Ural Mountains. Much of this land is on the European plain. It is flat or gently rolling land, with some low hills. Here is where most Soviet farms and factories are found.

The Asian part of the nation is east of the Ural Mountains. Here is a huge area called Siberia. This area is very rich in natural resources. The Soviet government has tried to get people to settle there. But not many people want to move to Siberia. The climate there is cold much of the year.

The Soviet Union has five main climate areas. In the far north is the tundra. This is a very cold area north of the Arctic Circle.

Trees do not grow on the tundra. The ground is frozen much of the year. Polar bears, seals, and reindeer live on the tundra. Here, there is much ice and snow.

South of the tundra is the **taiga** (TY guh). There are great forests in the taiga. Winters are long and cold. Yet it is not too cold for trees to grow. Wolves, bears, and elk live in the taiga. There are big cities in this region, too. Find Leningrad and Moscow on the climate map below.

South of the great forests of the taiga are grasslands. The grasslands in the Soviet Union are called the **steppes** (STEPS). A *steppe* is a grassy plain. Here, winters are not as long and cold as they are in

CLIMATES OF THE SOVIET UNION

CLIMATES

Tundra: cold and dry all year, ground frozen

Taiga: no dry season, cool to warm summer, cold winter

Steppe: low to moderate rain, cold winter

Desert: low rainfall, cold winter

Highlands: rainfall varies, cool summer, cold winter

KEY
• Cities
--- National Borders

SCALE
Kilometers 0   600
Miles 0   600

the tundra and taiga. Summers are often dry. Sometimes, there are droughts on the steppes.

In the far south of the Soviet Union are deserts. Here, very little rain falls. But people have brought water from other places to irrigate parts of the land. Many people now work on irrigated farms in the deserts.

On the southern border of the Soviet Union are mountains. The highest mountains have snow on top all year round.

The Soviet Union is rich in natural resources. It has forests and farmlands. It has petroleum, coal, iron ore, and many other minerals. But these resources are scattered across the nation. Getting the resources to the people who use them is a problem. To solve this problem, the Soviet Union has built some of the longest railroads in the world.

There are great forests in the taiga.

Traveling in Time and Space

You have looked at the climates of the Soviet Union from north to south. Here is another good way to see how large the Soviet Union is. Suppose you went all the way across this huge nation, from west to east. You would go about 10,940 kilometers (6800 miles). And you would pass through 11 time zones!

One way to measure space is to think about time. People have divided Earth into time zones. Each **time zone** stands for 1 hour. There are 24 time zones on Earth. This is because Earth rotates on its axis once every 24 hours. Each time zone is 15 degrees wide in degrees of longitude.

Look at the map of the Soviet Union on page 261. Find the cities of Leningrad and Vladivostok (VLAD uh vos TOK). You can see that these cities are far apart. It is 2 P.M. in Leningrad. It is not long after lunch. The sun is still high in the sky. Many hours of daylight are left. At the same moment, it is 9 P.M. in Vladivostok. It is dark. People have already had dinner. Children are getting ready for bed.

Suppose you travel from west to east. The time gets 1 hour later when you enter a new time zone. Suppose you travel from east to west. Then, the time gets 1 hour earlier when you enter a new time zone.

WHERE WE ARE IN TIME AND PLACE

TIME ZONES IN THE SOVIET UNION

| NOON | 1 PM | 2 PM | 3 PM | 4 PM | 5 PM | 6 PM | 7 PM | 8 PM | 9 PM | 10 PM | 11 PM | MID-NIGHT |

Kilometers 0 1000 3000

Miles 0 1000 3000

Now suppose you are catching a train in Leningrad. You plan to go by train all the way to Vladivostok. That way, you can see quite a lot of the Soviet Union. Use the transportation map below to trace your route.

Leningrad is a port on the Baltic Sea. The Baltic Sea is part of the Atlantic Ocean. Vladivostok is a port on the Pacific Ocean. In what direction will you travel from Leningrad to Vladivostok?

Leningrad is a very beautiful city. From Leningrad, you will go to Moscow (MOS kow). Moscow is the capital of the Soviet Union. It is also the largest city. After another day and night on the train, you will cross the Ural Mountains. Now you are in Asia! Next, you will arrive in the city of Chelyabinsk (chel YAH binsk). There, you will board the Trans-Siberian Railway to cross Siberia. This is the longest railroad in the world.

SOVIET UNION: TRANSPORTATION

Leningrad was once called St. Petersburg. It has many beautiful canals.

Near Chelyabinsk, a farmer carries hay in a wagon.

It will take you across much of Asia.

Now you will ride over hundreds of miles of steppes. Remember, steppes are grasslands. Then you will come to Novosibirsk (NOH voh si BIRSK). This is the largest city in Siberia. It has long, cold winters. Your next stop is Irkutsk (ir KOOTSK). Sometimes, the temperature there drops to 50 degrees below zero! Near Irkutsk is Lake Baikal (by KAWL). It is the deepest lake in the world.

Finally, you will reach Vladivostok. This city is the Soviet Union's window on the Pacific Ocean. It is west of Japan. From Vladivostok, ships sail to all parts of the world.

You have now traveled nearly 10,000 kilometers (6000 miles). You will have to set your watch ahead 7 hours. But it has taken you much longer than that to travel over this great distance. Your train did not move as quickly as Earth turns!

Lake Baikal is the deepest lake in the world.

REVIEW

WATCH YOUR WORDS

1. Grasslands in the Soviet Union are called the____.
   savanna   taiga   steppes

2. Great forests grow in the____.
   steppes   taiga   tundra

3. Polar bears live on the____.
   tundra   taiga   steppes

4. Farms in the desert are____.
   grassy   very cold   irrigated

5. You have to change your watch when you travel across____.
   boundaries   time zones   mountains

CHECK YOUR FACTS

Look at the Maps

6. In what climate area is Odessa? Kiev? Tiksi?

7. When it is 3 P.M. in Gorki, what time is it in Irkutsk?

8. Name the island nation to the east of Vladivostok.

Look at the Lesson

9. What are two other names for the Soviet Union?

10. Name three mineral resources found in the Soviet Union.

THINK ABOUT IT

11. Why do you think most Soviet people prefer Europe to Siberia?

12. The Soviet Union crosses 11 time zones. The United States crosses 7. What does this tell you?

Lesson 2: The Land of the Midnight Sun

FIND THE WORDS

twilight   midnight sun
headland
fjord   lichen   moss

In the far north of Europe is an area called Lapland. It is not a country. It stretches across four different nations. Lapland covers the northern parts of Norway, Sweden, and Finland. It also includes a peninsula of the Soviet Union. Most of Lapland is north of the Arctic Circle. People who live there are almost "on top of the world."

Remember, Earth is tilted on its axis. The sun is never directly overhead at the North Pole. The sun's rays hit Earth at a slant north of the Arctic Circle. That makes far northern regions cold. Winters are long and cold in Lapland. Summers are short and cool. The weather there is never warm.

LAPLAND

265

This boat is going through a fjord in Norway.

Most parts of the United States have mid-latitude climates. In much of the United States, winter lasts about 3 months. But Lapland lies in the high-latitude climate zone. Winters in Lapland are nearly 9 months long!

Do you know what **twilight** is? It is the time after sunset and before dark. Twilight means "half light." The light is very faint at twilight. Lapland sometimes has twilight instead of night or day. It also has months of total darkness. For 2 months in the winter, people in Lapland never see the sun rise! The North Cape of Norway is the part of Lapland closest to the North Pole. At the North Cape in winter, there is only twilight at noon.

In the summer, the opposite is true. There are two months when the sun is always in the sky. It is light all day and all night. You can even see the sun at midnight! This part of Earth is called "the land of the **midnight sun.**" Look at the picture of the midnight sun on page 20.

In the west, Lapland is part of Europe's northern highlands. Norway is famous for its headlands and fjords. A **headland** is a high point of land that juts out into the water. A **fjord** (FYORD) is a long, narrow inlet with high cliffs on either side. Lapland also has many lakes and rivers. There are many fish to be caught in Lapland. Also, lakes are often used in place of roads.

Few trees grow in Lapland north of the Arctic Circle. Those that do are small and stunted because of the cold. In northeast Lapland is the tundra region. Most of the ground is covered by **lichen** (LY ken) and **moss.** Mosses and lichen are plants that cover the ground like a thick, soft rug. They are the reindeer's favorite foods!

South of the Arctic Circle is a subarctic climate zone. Here are great forests full of pine, fir, spruce, and birch trees. In the Soviet Union, do you remember the name of the forest zone?

The Lapps have to dress warmly. They live in a cold land.

The Lapps of Lapland

The people of Lapland are known as Lapps. They were given that name by the Swedish. *Lapp* means "nomad." These people call themselves the Samme, or Samelats. The Lapps look more like the Chinese than like other Europeans. Also, most Lapps are no more than 5 feet in height. The Lapps are not related to other groups of Europeans. Their ancestors probably came from central Asia thousands of years ago.

For hundreds of years, many Lapps were nomads, or wanderers. They hunted and fished for food. They trapped animals for furs. What was more important, they kept large herds of reindeer. The reindeer supplied them with most of the things they needed to live. They had reindeer meat, milk, and cheese to eat. They used reindeer skins to make tents, shoes, coats, and blankets. They used reindeer bones and antlers to make pots, bowls, knives, and other tools. They used other parts of the reindeer to make rope. They threw away very little of the reindeer they killed.

The Lapps were free to move their herds from place to place looking for food. In the winter, the herds went north. There, they would feed on the mosses and lichen. The Lapps lived near their herds in tents. When the Lapps moved on, they loaded their belongings on wooden sleighs. The sleighs were pulled by reindeer! In the summer, the herds went south to the forests. There, the young reindeer were born.

For centuries, the Lapps' way of life was much the same. The reindeer provided most of the things the Lapps needed to live. For other things, like medicines, the Lapps traded with people who lived farther south.

Lapland and Change

Today, Lapland is divided among four nations—Norway, Sweden, Finland, and the Soviet Union. Lapland also has some valuable resources, especially iron ore and trees. Each of these facts has helped change the way Lapps live.

The nations where the Lapps live now require Lapp children to go to school. School begins when

Some Lapps are still nomads. They live in tents and travel with their reindeer herds. Others work in forests, in mines, or on farms.

These Lapp children are enjoying a picnic.

FUN FACTS

Dasher, Dancer, Prancer, Vixen, Comet, Cupid, Donner, Blitzen. Those eight reindeer—sometimes led by *Rudolph*—pull Santa's sleigh. They are make-believe reindeer. Real reindeer don't fly over the rooftops. But they do live near the North Pole. And, when they travel, they cover a lot of ground.

The reindeer of Europe and Asia are small, but strong. A reindeer can pull a sled weighing twice as much as the reindeer does. Even pulling that weight, it can go 64 kilometers (40 miles) a day. To find food, reindeer travel hundreds of miles. Their hooves allow them to get a good grip on the ice. Reindeer don't slip and slide around. Here is another interesting fact about reindeer. Female reindeer are the only female deer in the world that have antlers.

The Lapps have tamed their reindeer. But the reindeer native to North America have always been wild. They are called caribou. They don't pull sleds for anyone—even Santa Claus!

the children are about 7. Some of the children go to school for 4 years. Others go for 5 to 8 years if they pass an exam. Still others, if they pass another exam, can go to college. But many Lapp children do not live near schools. They may live too far from school to travel back and forth each day. So they have to live at boarding schools.

At the schools, the children study geography, history, reading, and math. They live, sleep, and eat at school, too. The Lapp children go home only on holidays or in the summer. Sometimes, when young people finish school, they no longer want to tend the herds. Some might get jobs in the mines. Others might work in the forests.

The forests in southern Lapland are very valuable. The trees are cut for lumber and for wood pulp. The lumber is used to build houses and other things made of wood. The pulp is used to make paper. In these forests, the Lapps can always find jobs. They live in wooden homes near their work.

There are large iron mines in Lapland also. The iron ore is taken from the ground and sent farther south. There, it is made into many different products. The Lapps can get jobs in the mines. When they do, they no longer tend herds of reindeer.

The governments that control Lapland no longer let the Lapps roam over all the land. This, too, is changing the Lapps' way of life. Some Lapps have settled along the rivers. There, they built wooden homes and started small farms. Many of these people still have herds of reindeer. But each year, fewer and fewer Lapps live as they did in the past.

REVIEW

WATCH YOUR WORDS

1. Near the North Pole on summer nights, you can see the____.
   savanna   rain forests
   midnight sun

2. Reindeer like to eat____and____.
   fish   mosses   cheese   lichen

3. A narrow inlet between steep cliffs is a____.
   fjord   headland   peninsula

4. A point of land that juts into the sea is a(n)____.
   fjord   island   headland

5. ____is after sunset but before dark.
   Sunrise   Twilight   Night

CHECK YOUR FACTS

6. Lapland is now part of what four nations?

7. Why are winters in Lapland long and cold?

8. Name five ways the Lapps used their reindeer.

9. Why do Lapp children go to boarding school?

10. Name two resources of Lapland. How are they used?

THINK ABOUT IT

11. Vadso and Vardo are ports on the Arctic Ocean. Even in winter, they are ice-free. Can you guess why?

12. Suppose that for 2 months every winter, you never saw the sun. How would your life be different?

CHAPTER REVIEW

WATCH YOUR WORDS

Match the word with the clue.

1. taiga   **A.** grassy plains
2. fjord   **B.** cliff jutting into the sea
3. headland   **C.** cold region with no trees
4. steppes   **E.** narrow inlet between cliffs
5. tundra   **F.** region of subarctic forests

CHECK YOUR FACTS

6. What is the largest nation on Earth?
7. Name four climate areas of the Soviet Union.
8. How many time zones are there on Earth?
9. How are Leningrad and Vladivostok alike? How are they different?
10. Where is Lapland? Who governs it?
11. What is the midnight sun?
12. Name some of the many things Lapps get from their reindeer.

TRUE OR FALSE

13. The climate is comfortable in Siberia.
14. North of the tundra is the taiga.
15. The Soviet Union has many natural resources.
16. Moscow is the capital of the Soviet Union.
17. Lapland is a nation.
18. Winters in Lapland are almost 9 months long.
19. In winter, Lapps can see the midnight sun.
20. Lapps work on farms, in forests, and in mines.

FIND THE TIME LINE

21. List these events in the right order. Start with the one that came first.

    1 Governments said Lapp children had to go to school.
    2 The ancestors of the Lapps came to Lapland to live.
    3 Young Lapps finished school, and some found new jobs.
    4 Lapp families moved around Lapland with their reindeer herds.

USE YOUR MAPS

Look at the map of the Soviet Union on page 261. Use this map to answer these questions.

22. Give the right direction (northeast, northwest, southeast, or southwest):

    Leningrad is ___ of Vladivostok. Novosibirsk is ___ of Tashkent. Tashkent is ___ of Irkutsk. Vladivostok is ___ of Leningrad.

23. When it is 4 P.M. in Gorki, what time is it in Leningrad?

THINK ABOUT IT

24. Suppose Earth was not tilted on its axis. What would happen to "the land of the midnight sun"?
25. Suppose Earth had 12 time zones instead of 24. How wide would each time zone be?
26. Suppose you go west until you enter a new time zone. Will the time be earlier or later there?
27. Explain why the Lapps' way of life is changing.
28. How are the Lapps of Europe like the Mossi of Africa? How are they like the nomads of Africa?

UNIT REVIEW

WATCH YOUR WORDS

Use the words below to fill in the blanks. Use each term only once.

allies	market
free trade	peninsulas
industrial	rivals
islands	seas
mainland	tariffs

Not all of Europe is attached to the ___ . Some parts are ___ , surrounded by water. Europe also has many ___ , with water on three sides. Other parts of Europe have coasts on inland ___ .

Europe is a land of many nations. Some nations of western Europe used to be ___ . They competed with one another for power and land. Now, many of these nations are ___ . They work together to reach their goals. They are trading partners. In the Common Market, they practice ___ . That means they don't put ___ , or import taxes, on one another's goods.

Europe has many highly developed, ___ nations. These nations have many factories. They manufacture many goods. The people who buy goods are the ___ .

CHECK YOUR FACTS

1. Name three nations of Europe that are on peninsulas.

2. Name one nation of Europe that is on islands.

3. Name three of Europe's seas.

4. Where is the European plain?

5. Name three groups of mountains in the Alpine system.

6. What mountains separate Europe from Asia?

7. Why is western Europe's climate mild?

8. What are two ways Europeans use coal?

9. List five languages that Europeans speak.

10. Why did the boundaries of Europe's nations change?

11. How is manufacturing different in Great Britain and West Germany?

12. What is a time zone?

13. Why are railroads important to the Soviet Union?

14. What are the seasons like in Lapland?

15. Name three kinds of work people do in Lapland.

PUT IT ALL TOGETHER

16. Draw or trace an outline map of Europe. Put these places on the map and label them:
    a. Great Britain, France, West Germany, Italy, and the Soviet Union
    b. the capitals of those five nations
    c. the Atlantic Ocean, Arctic Ocean, and Arctic Circle
    d. the Mediterranean Sea, Black Sea, and Caspian Sea
    e. the Pyrenees, Alps, Caucasus, and Ural Mountains
    f. Norway, Sweden, Finland, and Lapland

CLOSE THE MAP GAP

From Hawaii to Maine, the United States crosses 7 time zones. This map shows 4. Use it to answer the questions below.

17. When it is noon in New York City, what time is it in San Francisco?

18. When it is 8 P.M. in San Francisco, what time is it in Chicago?

19. When it is 10 A.M. in Salt Lake City, what time is it in New York?

20. When the sun rises in New York, is it dark or light in San Francisco?

21. Why does the United States have different time zones?

THINK ABOUT IT

22. Why do more people live in Europe than in South America?

23. What things make Europe a more developed continent than Africa?

TRY SOMETHING NEW

24. Make a map of an imaginary island nation in the Northern Hemisphere. Include a key, a scale, and a compass rose.
  a. *Put these things on your map:* northern forests, eastern mountains, a southern desert, a fertile plain, two rivers, three highways, a railroad, deposits of iron ore and coal
  b. *Answer these questions. Then show the answers on the map.*
    (1) Where would you put your capital city?
    (2) Where would you build a sawmill to cut wood?
    (3) Where would you put a steel mill?
    (4) Where would most of the people live?
    (5) Where would most farms and factories be found?

ASIA

Kilometers 0   500   1000
SCALE
Miles 0   500

EUROPE

UNION   OF   SOVIET   SOC

Mediterranean Sea

Black Sea

TURKEY
Plateau of
Asia Minor

CAUCASUS MOUNTAINS

URAL MOUNTAINS

Ob River

S I

CYPRUS
LEBANON
Damascus
ISRAEL
EGYPT
JORDAN

SYRIA

Baghdad

Euphrates
River

Tigris
River

IRAQ

Tehran

IRAN

Caspian Sea

Aral Sea

AFRICA

KUWAIT

Persian Gulf

AFGHANISTAN

HIMALAYAS

Indus River

Lahore

P
O

SAUDI
ARABIA

QATAR

UNITED ARAB
EMIRATES

PAKISTAN
Karachi

Delhi

NEPAL

Red Sea

YEMEN

P.D.R. OF
YEMEN

OMAN

Ganges River

INDIA

Mt.
Evere

PHYSICAL MAP OF ASIA

ELEVATION	
Meters	Feet
over 4,000	over 13,100
2,000 to 4,000	6,600 to 13,100
1,000 to 2,000	3,300 to 6,600
200 to 1,000	660 to 3,300
sea level to 200	sea level to 660
below sea level	below sea level

Bombay

DECCAN
PLATEAU

BA

Arabian Sea

Madras

KEY

--- National Borders   • Cities

MALDIVES

SRI
LANKA

Bay o

EQUATOR

INDIAN   OCEAN

Bering Sea

OCEAN

80°
160°
170°
70°
60°
50°
40°

150°
140°
130°
120°
110°

ARCTIC CIRCLE

Lena River

180°

ERIA

REPUBLICS

Lake
Baikal

Amur River

170°

30°

JAPAN

MONGOLIA

NORTH
KOREA

Sea of
Japan

Tokyo

20°

GOBI
DESERT

Peking

Seoul

Osaka

Tientsin

Hwang Ho

SOUTH
KOREA

PACIFIC OCEAN

A

CHINA

Yangtze

Shanghai

160°

TAIWAN

HONG KONG (U.K.)

150°

10°

BURMA
LAOS
Hanoi
PHILIPPINES

INDOCHINA
Mekong River
Manila

Rangoon
THAILAND
VIETNAM
South China
Sea

0°

Bangkok

Ho Chi Minh City

CAMBODIA

EQUATOR

MALAY
PENINSULA
BRUNEI

MALAYSIA

PAPUA
NEW GUINEA

SINGAPORE

140°

INDONESIA

110°
120°
130°

Jakarta

CHAPTER 1 ASIA AND ITS PEOPLE

Lesson 1: Land and Climate

Asia has "the most" of many things. It is the largest continent on Earth. That means it has more land than any of the other six continents. It has Earth's highest mountains and lowest sea. It has the world's largest and highest plateau. Asia is also the continent with the most people. It has the nation with the most people, China. Three-fourths of the Soviet Union, the largest nation on Earth, is in Asia.

Look at Asia on a globe. Some of the islands of Asia are south of the equator. Some of the mainland is north of the Arctic Circle. So Asia covers a lot of the Northern Hemisphere. Measure Asia from south to north. It goes to 78° north latitude.

Asia also goes across most of the Eastern Hemisphere. It covers 170° of longitude. Asia crosses 11 of Earth's 24 time zones. You can see that Asia is huge!

Now look at the map of Asia on pages 274 and 275. The Arctic Ocean is to the north. To the west are the Mediterranean Sea and the Red Sea. The Indian Ocean is to the south. The Pacific Ocean is to the east. Northeast Asia almost touches North America.

Like Europe, Asia has many peninsulas and islands. One peninsula is in the west, between the Mediterranean Sea and the Black Sea. It is called Asia Minor. The Asian part of Turkey is there.

Three large peninsulas are in the south. The peninsula in the southwest is called Arabia. It is between the Red Sea and the Persian (PUR zhun) Gulf. Arabia is the largest peninsula on Earth. Much of this peninsula is desert land.

Find the peninsula in the middle. The southern part of India is on this peninsula. Notice the mountains in the northern part of India. These mountains are like a wall. They cut India off from the rest of Asia. This makes India seem like a separate part of the continent. So India is called a **subcontinent.**

The peninsula in the southeast is called Indochina (IN doh CHY nuh). Indochina was named for India and China. It is east of India and south of China. Indochina even has a small peninsula of its own! This is called the Malay (MAY lay) Peninsula. It stretches south almost to the equator.

Asia has another peninsula in the east. See if you can find it on the map. North Korea (kuh REE uh) and South Korea are there.

Mountains and deserts cross the center of Asia. The deserts stretch all the way from Arabia to China. Find the Gobi (GOH bee) Desert on the map. This desert is a huge area of rough, dry land.

The Arabian Desert is very hot and dry.

The Gobi Desert is in east-central Asia.

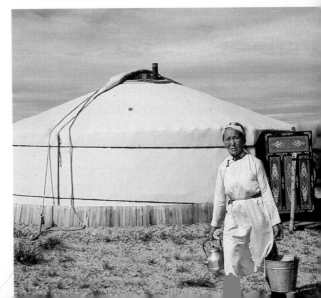

FUN FACTS

Earth's largest continent:	Asia has three-tenths of the land on Earth.
Earth's highest mountain:	Mount Everest is 8850 meters (29,028 feet) above sea level. Suppose you could put Pikes Peak in Colorado on top of Mount Rainier (ray NIR) in Washington. Mount Everest would still be higher!
Earth's lowest sea:	The Dead Sea is 400 meters (1312 feet) below sea level. This is the lowest point on the surface of the Earth.
Earth's largest peninsula:	Arabia
Earth's largest and highest plateau:	The plateau of Tibet is 4878 meters (16,000 feet) above sea level. It covers 200,000 square kilometers (77,000 square miles) of Earth's land.
The most people:	Almost 6 out of every 10 people on Earth live in Asia.
The nation with the most people:	China.

Mountains cut across Asia in many different directions. They separate northern Asia from southern Asia. On the map, you can trace these mountains with your finger. Follow them from the Black Sea northeast across the continent. Asia has more than 75 mountains that are higher than 6098 meters (20,000 feet).

India's mountains are called the Himalayas (HIM uh LAY uhz). They are the highest mountain system on Earth. The highest mountain in the world is in the Himalayas. It is Mount Everest (EV ur ist). Mount Everest is on the border between Nepal and China. It is a towering 8850 meters (29,028 feet) high.

Besides mountains, Asia has many high plateaus. Find Tibet in western China. The plateau of Tibet is called "the roof of the world." This plateau is the largest area of high land on Earth.

A continent as huge as Asia has many climates. You studied the climates of northern Asia when you studied the Soviet Union. Southwest Asia does not get much rain. People have to irrigate the dry land to grow crops.

South Asia and southeast Asia have a **monsoon climate.** In such a climate, there is a cool season, a hot season, and a rainy season. The islands of southeast Asia have tropical climates. Lowlands there are hot and wet all year.

Most of east Asia lies in the mid-latitude climate zone. In many ways, east Asia's climates are like those of the United States.

Mount Everest is the highest mountain in the world.

REVIEW

CHECK YOUR FACTS

1. Name five features in which Asia is first in the world.

2. Asia (does/does not) stretch from south of the equator past the Arctic Circle.

3. Name three peninsulas of Asia.

4. Name two desert areas in Asia.

5. What is the highest mountain system on Earth? What is the highest mountain?

6. What is the largest area of high land on Earth?

THINK ABOUT IT

What feature makes southern India a peninsula? What feature makes India a subcontinent?

Lesson 2: Resources of Asia

FIND THE WORDS

spice   OPEC

For many long years, Europeans searched for an ocean route to Asia. The Portuguese sailed all the way around Africa to reach India. Columbus thought he could reach China and Japan by sailing west. When he discovered America, he thought he had found the East Indies. India and the East Indies were famous for their spices.

Meanwhile, India had been trading with its neighbors for hundreds of years. India lay in the middle of important ocean trade routes. The first great empire in India was founded 1800 years before Columbus set sail.

Many different spices grow in Asia. One group of islands in Indonesia was even called the Spice Islands. A **spice** is part of a plant that tastes hot, sharp, or sweet. Spices are used to flavor and season food. Europeans wanted Asian spices such as black pepper, ginger, nutmeg, and cloves. Spices made food seem better to eat. Also, people long ago did not have ice all year to keep food fresh. Spices covered the bad taste of food that had spoiled.

Europeans also prized Asian tea, cotton, and silk. Tea and cotton come from plants. Silk is made by moths, called silkworms, that spin cocoons of silk. Silk was China's secret for about 3000 years. Everyone who saw and touched it wanted this soft, smooth cloth. Silk, cotton, and tea are still important to Asia. But now, Asia's petroleum is the resource other continents want most. The peninsula of Arabia has more petroleum than any other place on Earth! Today, petroleum is used to heat homes, to run engines, and to make electricity.

To most Asians, fertile soil is their continent's most important resource. Much of the land in Asia is very rugged or dry. But large areas of rich soil are found in Asia's river valleys. Enough rain usually falls there to grow good crops. These crops provide food for millions of people. Some rivers also have large, fertile deltas at their mouths. Much rice grows there. Rice is Asia's most important food crop. Wheat is also very important. Farmers in northern India and China grow wheat.

Look at the two resource charts on page 282. Each chart shows 10 of Asia's nations. It shows some major resources they have. They have other resources, too.

Much rice is grown on the fertile delta land of southern Vietnam. This is the coastal plain, as seen from an airplane.

First, look at the chart of living resources. Where would you find cotton, wheat, and rice? Did you know that most of the world's tea and rubber grow in Asia? Wood is cut from the forests. Fishing is important on peninsulas and islands.

Now look at the chart of non-living resources. You can see that many nations in southwest Asia have petroleum. Saudi Arabia, Iran, and Indonesia have a lot of petroleum. They export it, or sell it to other nations. Have you ever heard of **OPEC** (OH pek)? It is the Organization of Petroleum Exporting Countries. Half the OPEC countries are in southwest Asia,

around the Persian Gulf. Indonesia also belongs to OPEC.

On a continent as huge as Asia, many of Earth's resources are found. Asia has many more nations and resources than the ones shown on the charts. But Asia's resources are not distributed evenly across the continent. Also, not all resources are fully used. India is rich in natural resources. But many of these resources have not been developed. Indonesia has great mineral wealth. But it has little industry. It has fertile soil. But people in Indonesia do not grow enough food for their own needs. Nations are poor when

ASIA — NONLIVING RESOURCES: MINERAL WEALTH

	Petroleum	Coal	Iron ore	Tin	Copper	Salt
SAUDI ARABIA	✓					
TURKEY	✓	✓	✓		✓	
IRAN	✓	✓	✓		✓	✓
INDIA		✓	✓		✓	✓
MALAYSIA	✓		✓	✓	✓	
THAILAND	✓		✓	✓		✓
VIETNAM		✓	✓	✓		
INDONESIA	✓	✓	✓	✓	✓	✓
CHINA	✓	✓	✓	✓	✓	✓
JAPAN		✓				

ASIA—LIVING RESOURCES: SUGAR AND SPICE . . . AND RICE!

	Rice	Wheat	Corn	Sugar sugar cane	Sugar sugar beets	Spice (pepper)	Tea	Cotton	Silk	Wood	Rubber
SAUDI ARABIA	✓	✓	✓								
TURKEY	✓	✓	✓		✓			✓			
IRAN	✓	✓	✓		✓		✓	✓	✓		
INDIA	✓	✓	✓	✓		✓	✓	✓	✓	✓	✓
MALAYSIA	✓					✓	✓			✓	✓
THAILAND	✓		✓	✓				✓		✓	✓
VIETNAM	✓		✓	✓			✓			✓	✓
INDONESIA	✓		✓	✓		✓	✓			✓	✓
CHINA	✓	✓	✓	✓	✓		✓	✓	✓		
JAPAN	✓	✓			✓		✓		✓	✓	

Saudi Arabia is one of the OPEC countries. It exports petroleum.

their people do not have the money, machines, and knowledge to use their resources.

Japan has very few natural resources. But Japan has much more industry than India and Indonesia. There are many more scientists and engineers in Japan. Even without a wealth of resources, Japan is a rich land.

REVIEW

WATCH YOUR WORDS

1. Black pepper is a____.
mineral   sugar   spice

2. The OPEC nations____petroleum.
import   export   lack

3. Rice and cotton are____.
living resources
nonliving resources   foods

4. Coal and copper are____.
living resources
nonliving resources   fuels

5. Wood and silkworms are____.
living resources
nonliving resources   plants

CHECK YOUR FACTS
Look at the Charts

6. What is Asia's leading food crop?

7. What Asian nations have both cotton and silk?

8. Find a nation that has coal, iron ore, and tin.

9. Find a nation that has both pepper and salt.

10. Name five Asian nations that have petroleum.

THINK ABOUT IT

Why do you think petroleum is worth more today than it was in the past?

Lesson 3: People of Asia

FIND THE WORDS

B.C.	A.D.	Orient	Occident
		dialect	

Over half the people in the world live on the continent of Asia. So it is not surprising that there are many different groups of Asians. Look at the pictures of people in this unit. You can see what a wide variety of people Asia has.

All the world's major religions started in Asia. The Jewish, Christian, and Muslim religions began in southwest Asia. Look at the map of Israel and western Jordan on page 285. Find the area between the Jordan River and the Mediterranean Sea. This was the Promised Land in the Bible. Find the city of Jerusalem (juh ROO suh lum). Jerusalem is a holy city to Jews, Christians, and Muslims.

The calendar we use today starts with the birth of Jesus Christ. Christ was born in Bethlehem. The years before Christ was born we write as B.C. (before Christ). The years after Christ's birth we write as A.D. [anno Domini (AN oh DOM un NY), "in the year of the Lord"]. For dates A.D., we count forward from the birth of Christ. For dates B.C., we count

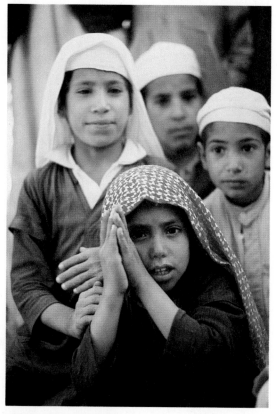

These school children live in Saudi Arabia. They are Asians.

back. When no letters are used with a date, it is A.D. The year 1000 means 1000 A.D.

The prophet Muhammad lived from 570 to 632 A.D. He lived to be 62. The religious teacher Buddha (BOO duh) lived from 563 to 483 B.C. He lived to be 80. Buddha lived more than 1000 years before Muhammad. He lived 500 years before Christ. Muhammad lived 600 years after Christ. Do you see how A.D. and B.C. are used?

WHERE WE ARE IN TIME AND PLACE

CRADLE OF RELIGIONS

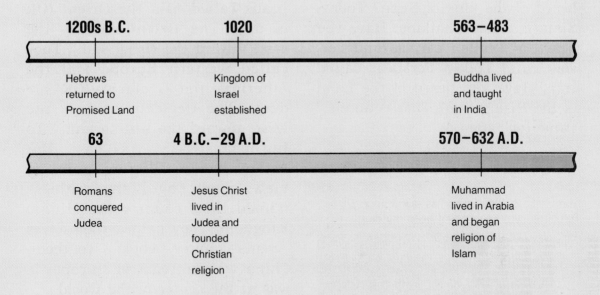

1200s B.C.	1020	563–483
Hebrews returned to Promised Land	Kingdom of Israel established	Buddha lived and taught in India

63	4 B.C.–29 A.D.	570–632 A.D.
Romans conquered Judea	Jesus Christ lived in Judea and founded Christian religion	Muhammad lived in Arabia and began religion of Islam

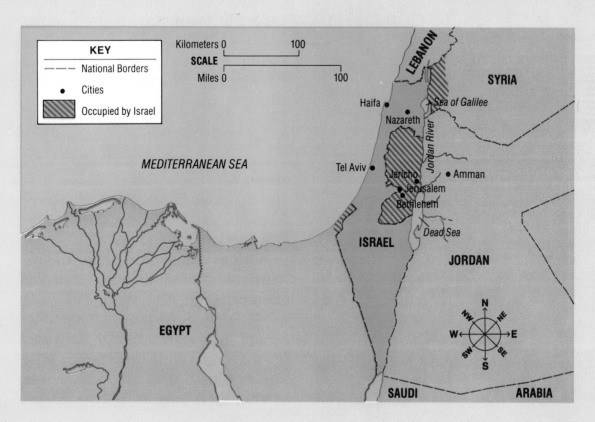

KEY
National Borders
• Cities
Occupied by Israel

Kilometers 0 ___ 100
SCALE
Miles 0 ___ 100

LEBANON
SYRIA
Haifa
Sea of Galilee
Nazareth
Jordan River
MEDITERRANEAN SEA
Tel Aviv
Jericho
Amman
Jerusalem
Bethlehem
ISRAEL
Dead Sea
JORDAN
EGYPT
N
NW NE
W E
SW SE
S
SAUDI ARABIA

Asian Cultures

Asia had many rich kingdoms and empires in the past. Have you heard of the king of Siam? Today, Siam is called Thailand. Have you heard of Persian carpets and Persian cats? Today, Persia is called Iran. Have you heard of the Land of the Rising Sun? That is another name for Japan.

The Great Wall of China has stood since 220 B.C. For how many years has it been standing?

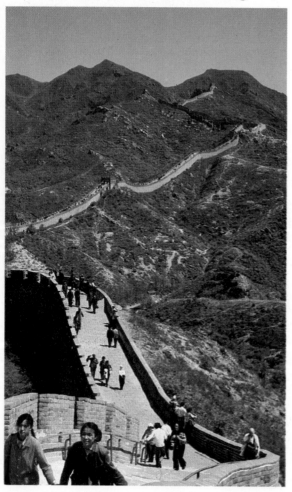

China

One of the oldest Asian cultures is that of China. Long ago, Europeans called Asia the Orient (OR ee unt). The **Orient** means "the east, toward the rising sun." They called western Europe and the Americas the Occident (OK suh dunt). The **Occident** means "the west, toward the setting sun." To Europeans, Asia was east. But Asians had a different point of view. Long ago, the Chinese named their country the Middle Kingdom. They named themselves "center-country people." To them, China was not east of Europe. It was at the center of the world.

The Chinese of long ago were expert at many arts. Some painted birds, flowers, horses, and other outdoor scenes. Others made fine vases or wove glossy silk cloth. Chinese craft workers made fine plates, cups, and bowls. People from Europe called these dishes "china." It was the Chinese who invented gunpowder. They used it to make firecrackers explode. They also made printing possible by inventing paper and type!

China was protected by mountains on the south and west. On the north, the Chinese built a wall to keep invaders out. They finished this wall around 220 B.C. The Great Wall of China still stands today. It is 2400 kilometers (1500 miles) long.

Today, the Chinese no longer call their land the Middle Kingdom. Now they call it "the Central Glorious People's United Country." In English, it is called the People's Republic of China. China has had a Communist government since 1949. Today, many people work in factories. But most of the people work together on large farms. There, they grow the nation's food.

People in China work very hard. They try to grow larger crops each year. But often, this is not possible. When drought and floods strike China, the government imports food. The government also provides schools and health care. Many Chinese people are learning to speak English now.

Still, Communist Party leaders make important decisions for the Chinese people. The government tells people where to live and what jobs to do. People are not free to choose for themselves.

Asians Today

Today, there are hundreds of different culture groups in Asia. Each of these groups has its own history, language, customs, and beliefs. Sometimes, many different culture groups live in one nation. In India alone, people speak more than 1500 languages and dialects! A **dialect** (DY uh LEKT) is a different form of a language spoken in a special way.

The Chinese try to grow larger crops each year. Here, farm workers walk through an irrigation ditch. They have come to see a successful farm.

You can see that Asians are very different from one another. Still, many Asians have much in common. About 80 out of every 100 of them are poor. Most are farm families who grow the food they eat. Many get less food than they need each day. Most Asians outside of China and Japan can expect to live only 50 years.

Asia has some of the world's largest cities. Even so, most Asians live in small villages. Life does not change quickly in Asian villages. In some places, people have farmed the same way for hundreds of years.

Most Asians live in small villages. Life there changes very slowly. This Asian village is near the Himalayas.

REVIEW

WATCH YOUR WORDS

1. Europeans called Asia the____.
Occident   Orient   Continent

2. Europeans called America the____.
Continent   Orient   Occident

3. A different way of speaking a language is a____.
culture   dialect   belief

4. Buddha was born in 563____.
A.D.   A.M.   B.C.

5. Muhammad was born in 570____.
A.D.   B.C.   P.M.

CHECK YOUR FACTS

6. List three religions that began in southwest Asia.

7. What are Siam, Persia, and the Middle Kingdom called today?

8. List two things that the Chinese invented.

9. What did the Chinese build to protect China on the north?

10. Do more Asians live in cities or in villages?

THINK ABOUT IT

Do you think your country is the middle of the world? Why, or why not?

Lesson 4: Nations of Asia

FIND THE WORDS

income   calorie

Look at the political map of Asia on page 291. You can easily see that there are many nations in Asia. Leaving out the Soviet Union, there are 40 Asian nations. Some, like China and India, are huge. Others are very small. The nation of Singapore is a city.

Now look at the chart on page 290. It gives you some facts about nine nations of Asia. The first five are the nations with the most people. The last four are nations that are interesting for some other reason. The chart also includes the United States in the middle. That way, you can compare the United States with these Asian nations.

The first three columns tell you how large each nation is. They tell you its size and how many people it has. Of the eight nations on Earth with the most people, six are in Asia. One of these is the Soviet Union. The other five are in the chart. The two not in Asia are the United States and Brazil.

The last three columns also give you some important facts. But you have to know how to read the figures. Column four tells you how many people in every 100 are farmers. Usually, the more farmers a nation has, the less developed it is. With fewer farmers, more people work in offices, factories, or stores. These people make goods or provide services for others. Look at the chart again. Find two highly developed nations in Asia.

Column five tells you the average income per person each year. This is what each person would get if all the nation's income were divided evenly. **Income** usually means money earned or received. In the chart, income also includes what people produce for their own use. Food can be income in this sense.

You can see that some nations have very low incomes. In nations with low incomes, most people are usually farmers. Notice the very high income in Saudi Arabia. Saudi Arabia used to be a poor nation. Now it sells petroleum to other nations. This has made Saudi Arabia very rich. The nation has built new highways, schools, and office buildings. It has also helped other Arab nations. Now, Saudi Arabia plans to build many new factories. It does not want to depend on petroleum alone.

The last column in the chart is very important. It tells how much food value each person gets on the

NINE ASIAN NATIONS

Nation	Area square miles	Area square kilometers	Number of people	Farmers per 100 people	Income per person per year	Daily food (in calories)
CHINA	3,691,502	9,561,000	933 million	70	$ 440	2170
INDIA	1,261,810	3,268,090	638 million	70	$ 200	2070
INDONESIA	735,000	1,903,650	145 million	66	$ 300	1790
JAPAN	142,811	369,881	115 million	19	$ 8,500	3280
BANGLADESH	55,126	142,776	85 million	85	$ 106	1840
UNITED STATES	3,615,191	9,363,353	227 million	4	$11,280	3330
ISRAEL	7,992	20,700	4 million	10	$ 4,330	2960
SAUDI ARABIA	829,995	2,149,690	8 million	65	$13,750	2270
TAIWAN	13,885	35,961	18 million	42	$ 2,200	2620
TURKEY	301,380	780,574	43 million	67	$ 1,200	3250

FUN FACTS ... about Japan

Japan is a very beautiful nation. It is covered with hills and mountains. It has many forests and lakes. The highest mountain in Japan is Mount Fuji (FOO jee). It is 3776 meters (12,388 feet) above sea level.

The climate of Japan is much like the climate of the United States. In southern Japan, the summers are long and hot. The winters are mild and not cold. This is the kind of climate found in the southern United States. In northern Japan, the winters are cold and snowy. The summers are warm. This is the kind of climate found in the state of Maine. All of Japan gets enough rain to grow crops. This means that Japan has no deserts.

Japan's chief crop is rice. Two unusual farm products are mulberry trees and bamboo plants. The leaves of the mulberry tree are the favorite food of silkworms. The silkworms spin balls of silk threads, called cocoons. Factories make these threads into beautiful silk cloth and clothing. The bamboo plant is used in many ways. People eat the sprouts. They make baskets and furniture from the thick, hollow stems.

Fish are also an important resource to the Japanese. Find Japan on the map. Why do the Japanese eat fish?

average each day. Every day, your body burns up energy. Food gives you that energy. A **calorie** is a unit of heat. It is used to measure the energy that food gives you. You need that food energy to stay healthy. On the average, 10-year-olds need about 2400 calories a day. Young men need about 2900 calories. Young women need about 2100 calories.

Now look at the chart. The average person in the United States takes in 3330 calories per day.

Many people may eat too much in the United States. They take in more calories than their bodies can burn. But in some Asian nations, people do not get enough food. Find two such nations in the chart. India is better off than Indonesia and Bangladesh. But one Indian in every four does not get enough calories to stay healthy.

Japan

Except for the Soviet Union, the most developed nation in Asia is Japan. This is true even though Japan does not have many natural resources. The Japanese people work well together. Since World War II, they have had good leaders and a democratic government. In industry, Japan ranks third in the world. Only the United States

These children go to school in Tokyo, Japan.

and the Soviet Union have more industry than Japan. They are giant nations. Japan covers only 369,881 square kilometers (142,811 square miles). It is smaller than the state of California. But Japan has five times as many people as California. Japan is one of the world's most crowded nations.

Japanese cars, TV sets, cameras, and other goods are sold all over the world. More Japanese goods are sold in the United States than in any other country. Yet the Japanese have to import most raw materials used in their factories. They buy large amounts of iron, coal, and petroleum from other nations. Japanese farmers are experts at growing large crops. But Japan does not have enough farmland. It is an island nation. It has fertile plains. But most of Japan is covered by mountains. There is not much level land. So the Japanese import some of their food. They buy wheat, vegetables, and fruit from the United States.

Developing Nations

The nations of Taiwan, Singapore, and Israel are developing very fast. So are some of the OPEC nations, such as Saudi Arabia, Iraq, and Kuwait (koo WAYT). These OPEC nations are not fully developed. Still, they provide a better living for their people than most Asian nations do.

China and India

South of the Soviet Union, China and India are the largest nations in Asia. In fact, China is the third-largest nation in the world. It has by far the most people of any nation. One out of every four persons on Earth is Chinese! Now, China has close to a billion people.

China has rich natural resources. It has petroleum, coal, iron ore, and many other minerals. These minerals are all needed for industry. China now has more than 15 cities with over a million people. It is in these cities that China's factories are found. Still, most Chinese live and work on farms.

Only 40 years ago, India was a colony of Great Britain. Then, British India included what is now India, Pakistan, and Bangladesh. In 1947, British India became independent. It was divided into two nations. This division separated two different religious groups, Muslims and Hindus (HIN dooz). The part where Hindus lived became India. The two parts where Muslims lived became West and East Pakistan. In 1971, East Pakistan became a separate nation, Bangladesh.

Today, India has more people than any other nation except China. It is often called the world's largest democracy. That is

Tokyo (TOH kee OH) is the capital of Japan. Great numbers of people live in Tokyo. Japan is one of the world's top industrial nations.

because it has a government that is freely elected.

Indonesia

Indonesia is a little smaller than Saudi Arabia. But it has almost 20 times as many people. Indonesia is made up of thousands of islands. These islands stretch for over 5000 kilometers (3000 miles) along the equator. Some islands, such as Java and Bali, have many people. Others, such as Sumatra (soo MAH truh), have fewer people. Today, Indonesia is a poor

293

nation. But it has many natural resources. Find it in the resource charts on page 282. Indonesia has a lot of fertile soil. It has petroleum, coal, iron ore, tin, and other minerals. So it will probably develop more in the future.

The Future

Most of the nations of Asia face the same problems. The number of Asians is growing every day. These people need food and jobs. All over Asia, people are working hard to improve their lives. Experts are teaching farmers better ways to grow food. Governments are working to provide more schools and better health care. Governments want businesses to build more factories. With more industry, resources can be better used. More Asians will have good jobs. Asian nations will have more valuable products to sell. They can earn more money from exports. Then they can use some of the money to import extra food. That way, poor Asian nations could become as well off as Japan!

REVIEW

WATCH YOUR WORDS

1. Money that people earn or receive is their____.
   expense budget income
2. People measure food energy in____.
   pounds calories fat

CHECK YOUR FACTS

Look at the Chart

3. What Asian nation is almost three times as large as India?
4. What Asian nation in the chart seems to be the poorest? Which three Asian nations seem to be the richest? (*Hint:* Look at the income column.)
5. What rich Asian nation has an unusually large number of farmers?

6. What four Asian nations have the most food for their people?

Look at the Lesson

7. After the Soviet Union, what is the most developed nation in Asia?
8. Which Asian nation has the most people? How many people does it have?
9. What three nations of today were part of India until 1947?
10. How are Asians working to improve their lives? Name three ways.

THINK ABOUT IT

Why are nations with many farmers less developed than nations with many city workers?

CHAPTER REVIEW

WATCH YOUR WORDS

1. The ___ means "the east."
   Occident   Orient   OPEC

2. India is called a(n) ___ of Asia.
   island   continent
   subcontinent

3. Regions that have a ___ have three seasons.
   monsoon climate   desert   tundra

4. Long ago, Europeans wanted Asia's ___.
   dialects   petroleum   spices

5. The letters ___ mean "before Christ's birth."
   A.D.   B.C.   D.C.

6. The letters ___ mean "after Christ's birth."
   A.D.   A.B.   B.C.

7. The ___ means "the west."
   pole   Orient   Occident

8. The money a person earns or is given is ___.
   expense   savings   income

9. In India, people speak in many different ___.
   nations   dialects   calories

10. The average American gets over 3000 ___ per day.
    calories   spices   minutes

CHECK YOUR FACTS

11. What is the largest continent on Earth?

12. What nation of Earth has the most people?

13. What are Asia Minor, Arabia, and Indochina?

14. What do the letters of OPEC stand for?

15. Name three great religions that began in Asia.

16. What is East Pakistan called today?

USE YOUR CHARTS

Use the chart on page 290 to answer questions 17–19.

17. What three Asian nations are richest in income?

18. In which two Asian nations do people get the most food?

19. In which two Asian nations do people get the least food?

Use the charts on page 282 to answer questions 20–21.

20. Write *Saudi Arabia, Indonesia,* and *Japan* across the top of a piece of paper. Under each nation, list its living resources from the chart. Then list its nonliving resources.

21. Look at your answers to questions 17–19. Are the nations with the most natural resources the richest nations?

THINK ABOUT IT

22. Which would you rather visit: the Himalaya Mountains or the desert of Arabia? Why?

23. Which nation would you rather visit: Japan or China? Why?

24. Look at the resource charts. Which poor Asian nation would you choose to develop? Why?

TRY SOMETHING NEW

25. Read more about one of the religions that began in Asia. Use a library book or an encyclopedia. Then write a one-page report.

CHAPTER 2

LIVING IN A MONSOON CLIMATE

Lesson 1: India Today

FIND THE WORDS

monsoon   monsoon season
credit   irrigation
irrigation canal   competition

India is one of the largest nations in Asia. It has about three times as many people as the United States. But it has only one-third as much land. Would you guess that India is crowded? If so, you would be right. India is a very crowded country. There are over 638 million people there. And the population keeps growing. Only China has more people than India does.

The Himalaya Mountains stretch across northern India. Three great rivers begin in the mountains. They are the Indus (IN duss), the Ganges (GAN jeez), and the Brahmaputra (BRAH muh POO truh). The Indus River flows through Pakistan. The Ganges and Brahmaputra flow through India and Bangladesh. All three rivers pass through lowlands on the way to the Indian Ocean. Many people live in the river valleys.

Seasons in India

People in India divide the year into three seasons instead of four. They do this because they live in a monsoon climate. A **monsoon** is a wind that changes direction when the season changes. One season lasts from October to March. In India, these months are the coolest season of the year. But India's weather is still mostly warm, even then. Dry winds blow across India from the north and east. Almost no rain falls.

India's next season lasts from March through May. During these months, the weather turns hotter. The land becomes very dry. Most plants dry up at this time.

India's third season is the rainy season. It is called the **monsoon season.** In India, the monsoon season begins in June. Wet winds blow across India from the south and west. They are called the summer monsoons. These winds bring heavy rains. The rains continue off and on from June through September. During the rainy season, farmers in India plant their crops.

Growing Food

India has thousands of small villages. Most of the people live in these villages. In fact, three out of every four Indians live in the countryside. They are farmers who grow the food they eat. More than half of these farmers are poor.

FUN FACTS

All parts of India do not get the same amount of rain. The heaviest rains fall in the east. Cherrapunji (CHEHR uh POON jee) is north of the nation of Bangladesh. Every year, Cherrapunji gets about 500 inches of rain. One year, from 1860 to 1861, over 1000 inches of rain fell there!

The picture at the right shows a city on the Ganges River during the monsoon season. Like Cherrapunji, this city is in northeast India. The streets are flooded. But the traffic keeps right on going.

Most farm families own or rent their farms. But many large families have very small pieces of land. And some families have no land at all. They work in exchange for food when there is work to be had.

The government of India has been working to help farmers grow more food. First, the government wants farmers to use new rice and wheat seeds. These "miracle seeds" grow much more grain than regular seeds do. Farmers who use the new seeds can grow three or four crops a year. They can grow only one or two crops with regular seeds. But the rice from the new seeds does not taste as good. Also, the new seeds need fertilizers to grow well. Remember, a fertilizer adds special minerals to the soil. These minerals help crops to grow. Fertilizers are very expensive, though. Poor farmers need credit in order to buy them. Someone with **credit** can buy goods without money by promising to pay later. To provide farmers with credit, local areas in India need banks.

Second, the government is building many canals for irrigation. **Irrigation** means irrigating, or bringing water to dry land. An **irrigation canal** is a ditch or pipe made by people. Water can flow through such a canal from one place to another. With irrigation,

Indira Gandhi is head of India's government. The government wants farmers to grow more food.

farmers can grow crops on dry lands. That means more of India's land can be used for farming.

Industry in India

India is one of the world's top 10 industrial nations. It is rich in natural resources. It has a lot of iron ore and coal. It manufactures steel, chemicals, machines, and consumer goods. It exports cotton cloth and tea. It has even sent a satellite into space. But India's businesses face many problems.

One problem is that India's businesses spend most of their money on machines. They do not provide enough jobs for India's people. Another problem is that

India has a long, rich history. This building is the Taj Mahal (TAHZH muh HAHL). It is built of white marble set with jewels.

the government has tried to control the businesses. This has slowed down business growth. A third problem is that India does not import or export many goods. Nations that import and export goods compete with other nations for business. Suppose two businesses in different nations are trying to get the same customer. Each business tries to do better than the other. Each tries to offer a better product or charge a lower price. This is **competition.**

There are other problems, too. India does not have enough electric power for its farms, factories, and mines. It does not have good transportation to move people and

People in India dug this irrigation canal. It carries water to fields where "miracle" rice seeds are grown.

goods. Trains are slow. Ships have to wait in port for weeks to be unloaded. Trucks travel on narrow, crowded highways. Many villages have no roads. People in the countryside use animals to pull carts and plows.

Also, millions of Indians have no work at all. Millions more cannot find full-time jobs. Many people who have no land and no jobs leave their villages. They crowd into cities. There, they hope to find a way to make a living. But not many do. Most do not have enough education to get city jobs. Now, with three harvests a year, there is more work for them on the farms.

Progress in India is not easy. Change is often slow. India is a very old land. People have lived there for thousands of years. Life in the villages has stayed much the same. Now, village people are being asked to give up familiar customs. It is hard for many people to change to new ways.

REVIEW

WATCH YOUR WORDS

1. A customer with ____ can buy now and pay later.
   competition   culture   credit

2. When businesses have ____ , they often try to do better.
   no competition   competition machines

3. A(n) ____ brings water to dry land.
   irrigation canal   fertilizer miracle seed

4. A(n) ____ adds special minerals to soil.
   miracle seed   fertilizer irrigation canal

5. India's rains come in the ____.
   winter   fall   monsoon season

CHECK YOUR FACTS

Look at the Map (See page 291.)

6. What is the capital of India?

7. What large nation is west of India?

8. What large nation is to the north of India?

9. What small nation is almost surrounded by India?

10. What ocean is south of India?

Look at the Lesson

11. India has (more/fewer) people than the United States.

12. What is a monsoon?

13. How many seasons are there in India's monsoon climate?

14. How can India's farmers grow more food? Name two ways.

15. List two problems that India's businesses face.

THINK ABOUT IT

Why does competition often make people work harder?

Lesson 2: Life in a Village of India

FIND THE WORDS

extended family   landlord
seedbed   water buffalo   paddy

Each year, more people move to India's cities. Each year, more factories are built there. As you know, most Indians do not live in cities or work in factories. Most live in small villages and work on farms. Village life in India has not changed much for hundreds of years.

In the villages, most people live in extended families. An **extended family** is made up of grandparents, parents, and children. They all live together. Sometimes, the family also includes aunts, uncles, and cousins. All family members work for the good of the family.

In the villages of India, parents arrange their children's marriages. The young people do not choose whom they will marry. Each has to marry a suitable person of her or his own social class. When a young Indian woman marries, she leaves home. She goes to live with her husband's family. When a young Indian man marries, he stays at home. He brings his wife to live in his parents' house. The oldest mother in each house is the most respected family member.

In the villages, the houses are small. They may have only two or three rooms. Sometimes, a newly married couple will add on a room for themselves. Village homes are furnished very simply. People have cots for sleeping. They have pots, pans, and bowls for cooking and eating. Most homes have mats to cover the dirt floor. Most also have a place to store food. Family members spend most of their time outside.

Most village homes do not have electric power or running water.

This Indian woman has a mark on her forehead. It shows she belongs to a high social class.

Sometimes, a village has only one well. All the people get water for cooking and drinking from that same well. Sometimes, villagers also get drinking water from a nearby stream. But they might use the same stream for washing clothes. They might also use it for getting rid of wastes. Village people who do this are not healthy. Dirty water makes people sick. It carries disease.

In the villages, houses are built close together. That way, they do not take up too much land. Land is too valuable to be wasted. It has to be used for planting crops.

Just outside the villages are the fields. There, the crops are grown. Most families have to work in the fields. Some families own their own land. Many other families rent land from landlords. A **land-lord** is a person who owns land and rents it to others. In the villages of India, the rent is not money. It is part of the crop the farmers grow. Other people neither own land nor rent it. They work by the day when they can find work to do.

Village people often help each other in many ways. Some may weave cloth. Others may make

In India, some farmers still use old ways of farming. Here, a camel turns a waterwheel. The water is used for irrigation.

pots and dishes. Still others may make tools or build things of wood. Village people trade their work and goods among themselves. That way, they get the things they need.

Growing Rice

This is the way many village people grow rice in India. First, they prepare a seedbed. A **seedbed** is a small piece of land with good soil. There, rice seeds can start to grow. Next, the people must get the rice fields ready. This is hard work. The ground must be broken up with a plow. That way, the soil below the surface is brought to the top. The rice will be planted in this loose, rich soil. Most villagers in India use a water buffalo to pull the plow. A **water buffalo** is a large, strong animal with wide horns.

Now the people have to wait for the winds to change. Soon the monsoon season will start. They watch for the first clouds to appear. At last, the rains begin! Then the women take the young rice plants out of the seedbed. They plant the rice in the flooded fields. Rice fields have to be kept under water.

In the months that follow, the rice crop grows. The weather stays hot and wet. The rice plants get heavy with seeds of grain. The people must keep the fields free of

Above: In many Asian villages, farmers use strong animals to pull their plows. This farmer is plowing rice paddies.
Below: Monsoon rains have flooded this paddy. Now Indian women can move young rice plants from the seedbed. They replant the rice in the fields. Soon, rice grains will grow.

weeds. They must also keep rats from eating the grain. You may have heard a rice field called a rice **paddy.** When rice seed is growing, it has a brown hull on it. A hull is an outer covering. The rice with the hull is also called paddy.

303

Around the end of August, the winds begin to shift again. The weather changes. Now there is less rain. The people can harvest and dry the rice. They tie the stalks into bundles. They will eat the grains of rice as food. They will burn the stalks as fuel. They may also use some stalks to repair their roofs. They put aside some of the rice grains, too. Those grains will be seed for next year's crop.

New Ways to Farm

The government of India is trying to help village people grow better crops. You read about these efforts earlier. In many villages, the government has given the farmers new rice seeds. These new seeds yield more grain. Experts have also shown the people how to use fertilizer. But often, the farmers have no money to buy fertilizer. They have no extra rice to sell. They need their whole crop to use as food. If they had credit, they could use the new methods to grow more rice.

All over south Asia, governments are trying to turn more land into farmland. The main way to do this is to irrigate dry land. In a monsoon climate, water can be stored during the rainy season. Then, during the dry season, it can be used to wet the land. This is one kind of irrigation. Another kind is bringing water to lands that are dry all year. In the next lesson, you will learn about an irrigation project in India.

REVIEW

WATCH YOUR WORDS

1. Rice seeds are first planted in a ____.
   field   stream   seedbed
2. Indian farmers often use ____ to pull their plows.
   electric power   water buffaloes   paddies
3. Village people in India live in ____.
   extended families   large houses   fields

CHECK YOUR FACTS

4. Name four relatives who may belong to an extended family.

5. How do Indian farmers who rent land pay their landlords?
6. Where do village people get their water? Why do some people get sick?
7. List five steps in growing rice.
8. When do the farmers plant rice in the fields?
9. Name two kinds of irrigation.

THINK ABOUT IT

Do most people in the United States live in extended families? Why, or why not?

Lesson 3: An Irrigation Project in India

FIND THE WORDS

feeder canal

There is an area of dry land in northwestern India. It is known as the Great Indian Desert. This desert also stretches into eastern Pakistan. Find it on the map of India on page 306. The Great Indian Desert is a land of sand dunes, bushes, and grasses. There are no trees. Little rain falls in the desert, even during the monsoon season. But much of the land in the desert is fertile. It simply needs water for plants to grow.

Parts of this desert have been irrigated for hundreds of years. Canals from the Indus River bring water to large areas. In the late 1800s, the British added to this irrigation system. They built new dams to hold water back. They also built new canals to send the water across the land.

Part of the Great Indian Desert lies in Rajasthan (RAH juh STAHN). Rajasthan is the second-largest state in India. In 1948, the government of the state decided to build a big irrigation project. The state got the help of the national government of India. The plan was to create 10,000 square kilometers (about 4000 square miles) of new farmland. That is an area a little smaller than our state of Connecticut. The land would be sold to farmers who had no land. The state would lend poor farmers money to buy the farms.

There were three rules for the people who bought farms. First, they could own no other land.

Irrigation canals like this one in India can bring water to the desert.

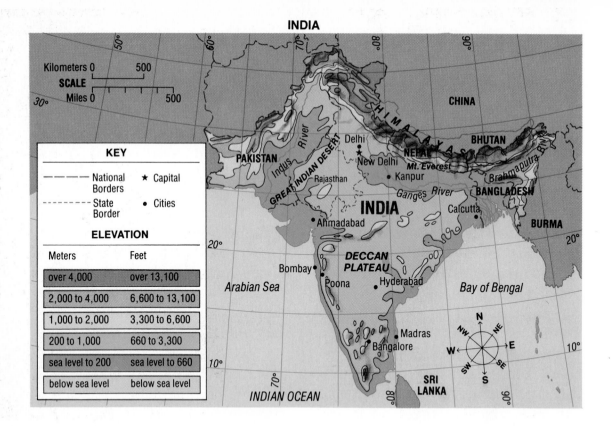

INDIA

KEY

—————— National Borders   ★ Capital

- - - - - - State Border   • Cities

ELEVATION

Meters	Feet
over 4,000	over 13,100
2,000 to 4,000	6,600 to 13,100
1,000 to 2,000	3,300 to 6,600
200 to 1,000	660 to 3,300
sea level to 200	sea level to 660
below sea level	below sea level

Second, they had to know how to farm. Third, they had to have been born in Rajasthan. Thousands of people got farms in this way. Years later, between 1974 and 1980, the irrigation system was improved. More canals were built. The people lined the canals with tiles. That way, the water flowed more freely. More desert land was made into farms. Here is a story about one family that was helped by this project.

Sita (SEE tah) and Ranjit (RUN jeet) both grew up in Rajasthan. Both had several sisters and brothers. Both lived on farms and

helped their parents with the work. When Sita and Ranjit were old enough, their parents arranged for them to marry. Sita left her parents and went to live in Ranjit's parents' house. After a while, the family built on an extra room for Sita and Ranjit. They had already added a room for Ranjit's brother Janak (JAN uk) and Rima (REE mah), his wife.

As time passed, Ranjit and Sita saw that life was getting harder for the family. The family fields didn't get any larger. But these fields had to feed more and more people each' year. Sita and Ranjit

Sita and Rima get water from a well in their village.

had three children. Janak and Rima had four. And now the youngest brother, Pandit (PUN deet), was going to get married. Ranjit's two sisters had married and moved away. But with all the new families, the farm could not produce enough food for everyone.

Then Ranjit and Sita heard of the Rajasthan Canal project. They both knew that life would be better if they had their own land. So Ranjit made the long trip to apply for a loan to buy a farm. He had to make several trips before he was successful. Finally, he was told that he could get a loan. He was told where to find the farm that he could buy.

When Sita and Ranjit left home with their children, they were afraid. They did not know what the future would hold.

At last, they arrived at their farm. There, they saw there was much work to be done. Water had to be brought to their fields. To do this, they had to help build small canals, called **feeder canals.** These feeder canals were connected to the large canals. The large canals brought the water from the Indus River. Ranjit and Sita also had to build a house for themselves in the village. They saw that many other families were also starting new farms. All the farm families had the same work to do.

Ranjit and Sita did not have to wait for the monsoon season to plant their crops. They only waited until the weather was warm. Now, they could control the amount of water that flowed to their fields.

Several years passed by. Life became better for Sita and Ranjit and their children. They grew more than enough food for themselves. They had food left over to sell. With the money they earned, they made payments on their loan. They bought sheep to supply them with wool. They also bought things for their home.

Then Sita and Ranjit asked Rima and Janak to come and join them. The farm could support the two families. Two families were also needed to do all the work. Now, both families live on the irrigated farm.

All over India, the government is building irrigation projects. The government leaders want India to raise more food. They want to make India a modern nation. They want to help the people help themselves. To do this, they must make changes where the people live. And most people in India live on farms.

REVIEW

CHECK YOUR FACTS

1. Where is the Great Indian Desert?
2. From what great river does the water come to irrigate this desert?
3. What were the three rules for people who bought new farms?
4. In what state of India do Sita and Ranjit live?
5. How did Sita and Ranjit bring water from the large canals to their fields?

THINK ABOUT IT

What things did the government of India do to help Sita and Ranjit? What things did they do to help themselves?

CHAPTER REVIEW

WATCH YOUR WORDS

1. Farmers in India plant their crops during the ___.
   cool season   dry season
   monsoon season

2. With ___ , people can grow food in the desert.
   paddies   irrigation   seedbeds

3. Farmers with ___ do not have to wait for rain.
   landlords   competition
   irrigation canals

4. A rice field is called a ___.
   paddy   feeder canal   monsoon

5. Often, rival businesses try to get the same customers. This is ___.
   credit   competition   income

6. Poor farmers need ___ to buy land and fertilizer.
   credit   competition   landlords

7. A(n) ___ owns land and rents it out to others.
   extended family   paddy   landlord

8. Sita, Rima, Ranjit, and Janak belong to a(n) ___.
   dialect   extended family   landlord

9. A ___ is a wind that changes direction with the season.
   paddy   dialect   monsoon

10. ___ bring water to family fields.
    OPECs   Feeder canals   Paddies

CHECK YOUR FACTS

11. Which nation has more people, India or the United States?

12. Name two rivers that start in the Himalaya Mountains.

13. When is the monsoon season in India? Describe the weather.

14. How are India's new rice and wheat seeds better than regular seeds?

15. What is an irrigation canal?

16. How can India turn more land into farmland?

TRY SOMETHING NEW

17. Pretend that you live in a monsoon climate. You have no farm machines or irrigation canals. How will you grow rice? List each step in order.

USE YOUR MAPS

Look at the map of India on page 306. Use it to answer these questions.

18. Give the right direction (north, south, east, or west):
    India is ___ of Pakistan. Pakistan is ___ of Bangladesh. The Himalaya Mountains are ___ of Delhi.

19. Give the right direction (northeast, northwest, southeast, or southwest):
    The Great Indian Desert is in the ___ of India. Calcutta is ___ of Delhi. Madras is ___ of Calcutta. Bombay is ___ of Madras.

20. What is the capital of India?

THINK ABOUT IT

21. What things are helping India's farmers grow more food?

22. What things tell you that India is not a fully developed nation?

23. Suppose India had twice as many people 100 years from now. What might happen?

24. How is India's climate different from the climate where you live?

25. Why is good transportation important to businesses?

UNIT REVIEW

WATCH YOUR WORDS

Use the words below to fill in the blanks. Use each term only once.

A.D.   monsoons   paddy
B.C.   monsoon season   peninsulas
extended family Occident   seedbed
feeder canals   OPEC   spices
irrigation canals Orient   subcontinent

Asia is the largest continent on Earth. It has ____ such as Asia Minor, Indochina, and Arabia. It even has a(n) ____ , India. Europeans called Asia the ____ , which means "the east." They called western Europe and the Americas the ____ , which means "the west." In the past, Europeans wanted Asia's ____ to flavor their food. Today, many industrial nations buy Asia's petroleum. Some Asian nations that export petroleum belong to ____.

Many religions started in Asia. Our calendar begins with the birth of Jesus Christ. Buddha lived before Christ. He was born around 563 ____ . Muhammad lived after Christ. He was born around 570 ____ .

Most people in India are farmers. In the past, they had to wait for the ____ to plant crops. During that time of year, winds called ____ bring heavy rains. Now, many ____ have been built in India. They bring water to dry lands. Small ____ bring water from the large canals to family fields. To grow rice, farmers first plant seeds in a(n) ____ . Later, they move the rice plants to a field called a rice ____ . Everyone in the ____ helps with the work.

CHECK YOUR FACTS

1. Which continent of Earth has the most people?

2. Which nation of Earth has the most people?

3. What is the highest mountain in the world? What mountains form the highest mountain system?

4. What is the lowest sea in the world?

5. What is Earth's largest and highest plateau?

6. What peninsula of Asia has the most petroleum?

7. Name two of Asia's most important food crops.

8. What are these countries called today: Siam, Persia, the Land of the Rising Sun, the Middle Kingdom?

9. Where did the Chinese build the Great Wall of China? Why did they build it there?

10. Which is the most developed nation: China, Israel, or Japan?

TRUE OR FALSE

11. India has more people than China.

12. Most of India's people live in cities.

13. Most of India's people work on farms.

14. India is one of the world's top 10 industrial nations.

15. India has good transportation.

THINK ABOUT IT

16. Which Asian nation would you most like to visit? Why?

CLOSE THE MAP GAP

17. Draw or trace an outline map of Asia. Color the peninsulas red and the islands green.

18. Label the Mediterranean Sea, the Red Sea, the Caspian Sea, and the Persian Gulf. Then label the Indian Ocean, the Pacific Ocean, and the Arctic Ocean.

19. Put the Indus, the Ganges, and the Brahmaputra rivers on the map.

20. Label the Himalaya Mountains and the Gobi Desert.

21. Label Turkey, Saudi Arabia, India, Indonesia, Japan, and China.

FIND THE TIME LINE

22. List these events in the right order. Start with the one that happens first. End with the one that happens last.

___The rice is harvested.
_2_Rice seeds are planted in a seedbed.
___The rice fields are flooded.
___The rice plants get heavy with grain.
___Seeds are saved for the next rice crop.
___Rice fields are plowed.
___Rice plants are planted in the fields.
_1_The monsoon rains begin.

USE YOUR CHARTS

23. Look at the chart of nine Asian nations on page 290.
a. Which one of these nations has the most income per person?
b. Which two of these nations have the most daily food?

24. Look at the resource charts on page 282.
a. What nation has 10 of the living resources?
b. What nation has the fewest living resources?
c. Which two nations have all six minerals shown?
d. Which two nations have only one major mineral?

GET CHART SMART

25. Copy the chart below on a separate sheet of paper. Then fill in the blanks. Get the missing facts from the charts on pages 282 and 290.

Nations	Living resources	Nonliving resources	Number of people	Income per person
CHINA	8		933 million	
INDIA		4	million	$200
INDONESIA	7		145 million	
JAPAN		1	million	$8,500
SAUDI ARABIA	3		8 million	

26. Answer these questions based on your chart.
a. Which nation in this chart has the fewest people?
b. Which nation has the most income per person?
c. Which nation is second in income per person?
d. Which three nations have the most resources?

GLOSSARY

A.D. *anno Domini* (AN oh DOM un NY), "in the year of the Lord," used with dates after the birth of Jesus Christ (284)

ally (AL EYE) a person or nation that works with you, not against you (254)

altiplano (AHL tee PLAH noh) the Spanish word for a plateau (149)

Antarctic (ant AHRK tik) the climate area closest to the South Pole (55)

Antarctic Circle the line of latitude that is about 66° south of the equator (55)

Arctic (AHRK tik) the climate area closest to the North Pole (55)

Arctic Circle the line of latitude that is about 66° north of the equator (55)

artifact (AHR tuh FAKT) any object that people make (65)

axis (AK sis) an imaginary line through the center of Earth, from pole to pole, around which Earth turns (18)

bay a part of the ocean that is partly surrounded by land (99)

B.C. "before Christ," used with dates before the birth of Jesus Christ (284)

boundary a line that divides one place from another (26)

breadbasket a region where a lot of grain is grown (121)

canal a waterway that people build across land. A ship canal connects one body of water with another. An irrigation canal brings water to dry land. (74, 298, 307)

canyon a deep, narrow valley with steep sides (127)

capital a city where the government of a state or nation meets (97)

capitol a building where a group of representatives meets to make laws (97)

cardinal directions the four most important directions: north, south, east, and west (32)

centimeter (SEN tuh MEE tur) a unit of measurement equal to 1/100 of a meter or 2/5 of an inch (31)

climate the average weather a place has over a period of time (51)

coast land next to an ocean (74)

colony an area of land ruled by a foreign country (97)

commercial farming farming in which crops are grown to be sold (207)

compass a map drawing of arrows that point north, south, east, and west (32)

Congress in the United States, the group of representatives that meets to make laws for the nation (97)

conservation (KON sur VAY shun) the wise use of natural resources such as water, forests, soil, and fuels (84)

continent one of the seven large masses of land on Earth (21)

credit the ability to buy goods without money by promising to pay later (298)

culture a people's way of living, including their behavior, beliefs, language, and artifacts (65)

customary (KUSS tuh MEHR ee) **system** the system of measurement that measures in inches, feet, and miles (31)

delta an area of rich soil at the mouth of a river (112)

desert a very dry place where few plants can grow (62)

developed having more factories and businesses than farms (243)

drought (DROWT) a long period of time with little or no rain (222)

elevation (EL uh VAY shun) the height of land above sea level (41)

empire a group of lands or nations under one government (158)

equator (i KWAY tur) an imaginary line around the middle of the Earth (23)

export (EK sport) a product that one country sells to another (156)

federal district a special area where the capital of a nation is located (98)

fertile soil soil which contains the minerals that plants need (58)

finished goods products that have been manufactured or made ready for use (208)

free trade trade between nations in which there are no taxes on imports (249)

geyser (GY zur) a hot spring that shoots water and steam into the air (127)

globe a round model of Earth (21)

governor the chief leader of a state (97)

grid a pattern of squares on a map (35)

gulf part of an ocean with land curving part way around it (74)

hacienda (HAH see EN duh) the Spanish word for a ranch or plantation (174)

harbor a protected place on a coast where ships can anchor (105)

headland a high point of land that juts out into a body of water (266)

hemisphere (HEM uh SFIR) one of four half circles that Earth can be divided into: the Northern, Southern, Eastern, or Western Hemisphere (23)

herding keeping animals together while they find grass to eat (202)

high-latitude climate a cool or cold climate found near the North Pole or the South Pole (54)

import (IM port) a product that one country buys from another (156)

industrial (in DUS tree ul) manufacturing many goods (252)

industry (IN dus tree) a branch of manufacturing and trade (252)

intermediate (IN tur MEE dee it)

directions northeast, northwest, southeast, and southwest (34)

irrigate to bring water to (dry land), as by using pipes or canals (128, 298)

island a piece of land completely surrounded by water (235)

isthmus (ISS muss) a narrow strip of land that connects two larger masses of land (74)

key a list explaining the symbols and colors used on a map (26)

kilometer (KIL uh MEE tur *or* ki LOM uh tur) a unit of measurement equal to 1000 meters or 3/5 of a mile (31)

lake a large body of water surrounded by land (77)

landforms the shapes of land on Earth. Mountains, hills, plains, and plateaus are landforms. (46)

lines of latitude (LAT uh TOOD) the lines on a map or globe that run east and west. They measure distance north and south of the equator. (37)

lines of longitude (LON juh TOOD) the lines on a map or globe that run north and south. They measure distance east and west of the prime meridian. (37)

living resources plants, animals, birds, and fish (57)

mainland the chief land mass of a continent (235)

map a flat drawing of Earth or a part of Earth (25)

market a place where goods can be sold (244)

meridian (muh RID ee un) a line of longitude (39)

meter a unit of measurement equal to 3.28 feet (41)

metric system the system of measurement that measures in centimeters, meters, and kilometers (31)

mid-latitude climate a climate area in which the weather changes from season to season (51)

midnight sun the sun seen at midnight during the summer in the Arctic and Antarctic (266)

monsoon a wind that changes direction when the season changes (297)

monsoon climate a climate with three seasons: the cool season, the hot season, and the rainy season (278)

mountain the highest form of land on Earth (46)

mountain range a group or row of mountains (46)

mouth the place where a river flows into the ocean (194)

nation a land where people live under one government (26)

natural boundary a natural dividing line between places, such as a river (27)

natural gas a mixture of gases found in the ground, used as a fuel (105)

natural resources anything found on Earth that people can use (57)

nonliving resources land, water, and minerals (58)

North Pole the place that is farthest north on Earth (18)

oasis a place in a desert where there is water (62)

Occident (OK suh dunt) **1** the west **2** western Europe and the Americas (286)

ocean one of the four very large bodies of salt water on Earth (21)

Orient (OR ee unt) **1** the east **2** Asia (286)

parallel (PAR uh LEL) a line of latitude (38)

peninsula (puh NIN suh luh) a piece of land almost surrounded by water (90, 235)

petroleum (puh TROH lee um) a thick, dark liquid found in the ground and used as a fuel; oil (81)

physical map a map that shows the height or shape of land (44)

plain a big, open area of flat land (47)

plantation a large farm where crops are grown (174)

plateau (pla TOH) an area of high, flat land (47)

political boundary a line that divides one city, state, or nation from another (27)

political map a map that shows political boundaries (44)

population the number of people who live in a place (60)

port a town on the water where ships can load and unload goods (107)

prairie a large area of flat or rolling grassland with few trees (76)

prime meridian (PRYM muh RID ee un) the imaginary line at which longitude starts. It passes through Greenwich, England. (39).

profit the extra money left from a sale after expenses are paid (226)

province a part of Canada that is like a state in the United States (86)

ranch a large farm where animals are raised (174)

raw material a product found in nature that can be improved by manufacturing (208)

rival a person who competes with someone else for the same thing (248)

savanna (suh VAN uh) a tropical grassland (54)

scale a diagram that shows what a map distance equals in real distance (29)

sea level the surface of the ocean. (41)

season a part of the year in which the weather in a place is much the same (18)

seaway a water route to and from the ocean (88)

sierra (see EHR uh) a range of steep, jagged mountains (75)

source the place where a river starts (193)

South Pole the place that is farthest south on Earth (18)

state one of the 50 parts that make up the United States. Each state has its own land, people, and government. (97)

steppes (STEPS) grassy plains (259)

subarctic (sub AHRK tik) just south of the Arctic Circle (55)

subcontinent part of a continent that seems separate from the rest. The mountains that cut India off from the rest of Asia make India a subcontinent. (277)

subsistence farming farming in which people grow the food they need to live (202)

symbol a picture on a map that stands for a real thing (26)

taiga (TY guh) a subarctic climate area where there are great forests (259)

tariff (TAIR if) a tax on imported goods (249)

territory a part of a country that has not yet become a state or a province (86, 98)

time zone one of 24 areas on Earth within which all places have the same clock time (260)

tropical climate a warm or hot climate found near the equator (51)

tropical rain forest a lowland area near the equator where heavy rains make thick forests grow (54)

tundra (TUN druh) the climate area just south of the Arctic, where the ground is frozen most of the year (55)

valley the low, flat land between hills or mountains (47)

volcano an opening in the earth through which hot melted rock, ashes, smoke, and gases can shoot (134)

314

INDEX

CREDITS

Maps by Continental Cartography (except pp. 17, 19, 151, 195, 216, 261, 262, 273). Charts by Function Thru Form Inc. **20:** Russ Kinne. **21:** Bob Capece/McGraw-Hill.
24: Loren McIntyre/Woodfin Camp. **29:** Bettmann Archive.
38: (L) EPA. (R) Paolo Koch/Photo Researchers. **42:** U.S. Travel Service. **46:** M. Serralier/Photo Researchers. **49:** (T) Peter Menzel/Stock Boston; (B) Peter Arnold, Inc. **50:** Michael Collier/Stock, Boston. **54:** (B) Carl Purcell. **55:** (L) Victor Englebert; (R) S.J. Kraseman/Photo Researchers. **58:** (T) Jacques Jangoux/Peter Arnold, Inc.; (M) Dan McCoy/Rainbow. **61:** Bernard Wolff/Photo Researchers. **62:** Dan McCoy/Rainbow. **64:** George Holton/Photo Researchers. **65:** Kal Muller/Woodfin Camp. **66:** Marc and Evelyne Bernheim/Woodfin Camp. **70–71:** McGraw-Hill. **72:** Jim Goodwin/Photo Researchers. **74:** Baron Wolman/Woodfin Camp. **76:** Sigmund Samuel/Canadiana Gallery. **77:** Paolo Koch/Photo Researchers. **81:** Porterfield-Chickering/Photo Researchers. **84:** Kent and Donna Dannen/Photo Researchers. **89:** Erich Hartmann/Magnum. **90:** Russ Kinne/Photo Researchers. **91:** Porterfield-Chickering/Photo Researchers. **92:** Marc Bernheim/Woodfin Camp. **93:** George Holton/Photo Researchers. **96:** Paolo Koch/Woodfin Camp. **102:** William Strode/Woodfin Camp. **105:** Hank Morgan/Rainbow. **107:** Leif Skoogfors/Woodfin Camp. **113:** Jim Anderson/Woodfin Camp. **114:** Farrell Grehan/Photo Researchers. **115:** Southern Living/Photo Researchers. **119:** Granger Collection. **122:** Jim Anderson/Woodfin Camp. **123:** David Barnes/Photo